CW01622024

SAG

THE FAL...

Rlan, thank you for being a part of the journey. Hope you enjoy the read.

Sage

ROACH

THE FALLIBLLE

Published by ROACH

The Falliblle is a registered title under ROACH, an independent publishing entity committed to bold storytelling at the intersection of technology, philosophy, and culture.

Cover and interior illustrations by Attila Vaszka & Justyna Kaźmierska

Edited by Félicité Mbenga

Designed in the United Kingdom. Typeset in Portugal.

For rights inquiries, collaborations, or media, contact:

ROACH

hello@sageabiola.com

www.sageabiola.com

First Edition, 2025

ISBN: 978-1-0369-2562-8

N
W
E
S
Nemes
(Neh-mez)
Jiwa
The Fal
Silany
(Sih-lah-nee)
Nexus-10
(formerly Arambisch)

For we may admire the minds of scientists, but it is the hearts of artists that we fall in love with - not for what they know, but for what they make us feel.

—Sage Abiola

For you. For me. For us.

CONTENTS

THE NEMERIAN
MANIFESTO · 88 LAWS

CHAPTER 1
Children of Silany

Georgia Wise tossed The Manifesto—an amalgamation of philosophical laws distilled into eighty-eight unquestionable truths—in the staffroom bin. Nemerian state propaganda was her husband's thing—not hers. Phillip Wise was obsessed with it all. Always had been.

"*It's nonsense girl, what are they sellin' us now?*" her father would often grumble. The century-long parade of tired Nemerian efforts to erase the Old World—another tedious lie among hundreds, since their seizure of power, was, as always, guaranteed to sour his mood. The Bear Man, they used to call him. To Georgia, he was simply Papa. *God, if he were here now.* She smiled and the warmth of his memory wrapped itself around her—until she remembered she was here in the present, not with him in the past.

A chill spread through her hands. The Manifesto had felt like ice-cold metal. Just the way the Nemerians liked it. *What was wrong with these people?* It reminded her of holding Phillip's hand. Maybe if she could hold onto his hand—onto him—long enough, he would warm up and they could be together, properly, the way she'd always wanted. Not cold and contrived like their marriage, forever hidden in the shadow of The Manifesto, with its rules to make people perfect. "You're naturally perfect, girl, moles and all," the Bear Man used to say. He was around when the oppression began—when they started building the wall and patrolling the borders of Silanese minds and lands. In just a few years, Nemerian propaganda had infiltrated their lives, promoting the philosophy of Ascension—a state of perfection that demanded separation even from self. 'Purity, and total control'. Segregation followed soon after, and with it, the quiet desecration of community, identity and, eventually, humanity. He died soon after, his heart broken not only by what he lost, but by what he foresaw: a future where his daughter would grow up behind unmarked walls, taught to fear difference, and deprived of the freedoms he had once taken for granted. His death was not sudden. It was a slow unravelling of hopelessness triggered by the weight of isolation, unreachable dreams, and a life made smaller by forces beyond his control. It marked the first sorrow of a generation betrayed—a sorrow too vast for one lifetime.

Downstairs, the Red Sea Café was mostly empty. The lunchtime rush was over. Just a few pairs of Silanese pensioners remained, nursing glasses of wine, or brandy, or picking at slabs of cake. One of the patrons took the corner table that overlooked the whole café. He could monitor the bar easily from there and it made Georgia's stomach churn.

Her friend June, Red Sea's other waitress, passed her in the aisle. Georgia elbowed her, not gently at all, unsettling the glasses on her tray.

"Careful!"

"You OK?" Georgia asked her as she rearranged the tray and washed her hands. June's face was ashen. She looked unwell. Come to think of it, she'd been tetchy all shift.

"Am I ever?"

"Why didn't you tell me he was here?"

"You were upstairs."

"Can you serve him?"

"No, he only orders from you."

"OK. I've got it from here." Georgia whipped out a pad and pencil from her apron pocket and sidled over to the awaiting patron, setting her face into an inscrutable no-means-no mask in readiness for whatever may come. Georgia was like June's older sister, so she was okay to deal with this guy: Mok, or Blok, or Tok, or whatever he was called, this squat, hairy hillock of an Etronium miner, in his grime-streaked overalls and dirty fingernails. He'd been at the Café every afternoon for three weeks. He wasn't there for the fish soup or the spicy sausage. He was there to get warm in his pants, and Georgia had hips that could turn a man's thoughts slow and heavy. No matter what she wore, she wore it like a woman. Phillip could never see the allure, yet it was the only thing the tattooed miners went there for. That and the ale. At times it made her hate the world, but they tipped during winter, so Georgia gritted her teeth and endured the leery stares, clinging pitifully to whatever dignity she had left. In her former years, she'd play the game, offering a wink here and there, but not these days. These days, she gave only what was required. Nothing more, nothing less.

"What do you want to order?" Georgia spun a pencil as she spoke and saw that something was different about him today. He didn't seem to want to look her in the eyes. With his head cocked to one side, he removed a folded sheet of paper from his breast pocket.

"Oh, put it away," she said brusquely. "I don't need another poem. The last one was gauche." *Gauche.* She liked the word *gauche.* She'd learnt it from Lilliana only recently, at the Salon.

"Miss Georgia Wise..." he said.

"Mrs," she interrupted. She shouldn't mind these guys. They kept things moving in Silany, Nemes, and the cosmos. They just got on with it.

Kept drilling. Kept mining. And something somewhere in her didn't have an issue with that. The woman's body had been a source of admiration and inspiration since the beginning of time. Lilliana would often say it was a woman's duty to develop her own value system and self-esteem. Only then would a man respect her.

"If you would only let me take you out one time, you would see the real me and how we are wasting our one chance of happiness...'

"Meatballs and a brown beer?"

"Listen..."

"I am just a waitress, I can be nothing else, I am already married to one man who thinks I can become his ideal woman. I can't handle two of you creatures."

She wrote down his order and turned. She let him watch her walk. As soon as she handed over the order at the chef's hatch, June was en route.

"Poor old lovestruck soul."

"Poor him?" Georgia raised her eyebrows. "What about us?" And then she dropped them. "You wanna do something tonight?"

"Maybe. I need to talk to someone."

"So do I."

"Ballet?"

"Too tired. Salon?"

"Too noisy."

"C'mon. We'll find a quiet corner. Maybe Lilliana can tell us how to deal with heartsick miners, or re-ignite our souls with a new philosophy, a fresh take on the Old World, on the latest on Nemes or something."

June's eyebrow raised, "We don't belong at those Salons."

"Lilliana says we do. Or *Lillianaaa*. I never know her name."

"Okay, but if this turns into another seven hours of listening to Ascension drivel like the last time, I'm not going again."

Georgia winced. "Agreed. But I need to check. Don't know if it's Salon or party tonight. By the way, what do you need to talk about?"

June sucked her lip and looked away. "Nothing. It's silly."

Later that evening, Georgia and June found themselves easing their way through a swaying crowd gathered around a drone-hop quartet called LexLexington playing on the corner dais. They were looking for Lilliana but keeping one eye on the room and its walls. The place was grand. It was taller, more angled and—with more intense chiaroscuro, shadow and vibrance than the two women were used to, it was hard not to admire. Maybe if they met Lilliana in the café it would be different, but this was not a working-class Silanese diner. This was where women came to talk high-level, high concept, develop themselves, evolve. *Yeah, evolve their big heads. Shrink their small hearts.* That's what the women of the Salon decided. They talked about it all on the way in and how they'd get snagged by people who wanted to get the inside skim on how the "lower" orders of Silany thought. And that's exactly what happened. Last time Georgia was there she'd worked out that she and June were the only Salonistas who stood up all day and worked with their hands. What a contrast to the miners. There were no tattoos in this room. The rest had servants and husbands who worked, in some way, for Nemes, either in service sectors, Etronium stocks, or smuggling demerit goods over the wall. But it was all rumour; baseless words driven by ego and woven into stories. Now that Georgia was there, she wished she was at home holding a book and tucked into her chair by the window, watching the rain. Story books, that's all she read, and that's all they were to her, these stories about these women's men. If they were true, they wouldn't go on about them all the time. Or maybe that was just Georgia's way of justifying why she never talked out loud about Phillip.

When Phillip came along, he changed everything, convincing her of small things at first and then moving onto bigger issues, such as her faults. He was able to point them all out one by one. Her father's faults included. Man's faults. They made sense to her, but at the same time they confused her. She liked the imperfections, and despite all the propaganda pasted on glass posters and beam ads across the clouds—what she saw them selling as perfection and God-like excellence—what they had termed *Ascension*—she saw as just a manufactured lie. Nemes wasn't perfect, it was just well packaged in Silany. It wasn't progress and it wasn't prosperity. It was paid advertising, and she didn't understand what they were selling. Whatever it was, Phillip bought it all. In fact, according to him, he was born with it all—with half of his genes showing Potential—or Nemerian Potential as it was known 10 years back. He was half perfect, known locally as a "One-Half". In contrast, Georgia was all Silanese. Like her father, she was all heart. Phillip described the Silanese once as "warm hearts, warm hands, cold brains."

Georgia: *I've got a mind of my own, thank you very much.*

Phillip: *Is any mind truly its own? We're simply echoes of the thoughts that came before us. Illusions who cast no shadows.*

It was hard not to get drawn into the bickering, but after a while she learnt how to avoid it. Then came the silent war. While he continued reading, studying, disappearing into his library, working on himself—always on himself—he forgot to live, and in his devotion to Ascension, he forgot her. She wore her loneliness like a heavy cloak, and in her isolation she found comfort in the fading memory of her father's voice insisting that her imperfections made her perfect. Yet, her husband's refusal to accept any flaws only widened the chasm between them.

She had been imperfect when she'd agreed to marry him. She'd been imperfect that night six weeks ago when she was with him in their bed for one of their once-in-a-blue-mooners. He had come in from a Friends of

Ascent meet, drunk. She felt sorry for him. Sympathy—the thing we all want once in a while but should never ask for. It was her blind spot. And he knew that, so she was his whenever he needed it, a lame fuck. It was awful. She hadn't yet told him she was worried there might be a consequence of that night.

In the cloak room, the Perco Sisters grabbed hold of her and June and talked about the double agenda of the supposedly persecuted Ed-El minority—a new cult encouraged by the Nemerians to speed up and encourage Ascension through performing grotesque rituals, according to Marcia Perco. They talked for what seemed like hours. Georgia wasn't really listening—her gaze settled on the coat handle in the centre of the cloak room, where it caught light and glimmered gold. Once the sisters finished talking, they walked on. Marjorie Cadge cornered them in the powder room where she extolled the virtues of the new Helen H pamphlet about how to Ascend *in half the time it usually took!* Utter bullshit. It's all in their heads, Georgia kept repeating. When Pete Kite took them to one side, he wanted to know what each of them thought of the collection of texts he called the *Silanese Equator*, a treatise that outlined why the Silanese were doomed, why they were beaten, and why it was a waste for the best of the Silanese to languish in dirt and darkness and despair when they could prosper in Nemes. Technology is prosperity! "That's not what prosperity is, you moron," Georgia heard a voice tell her. "That's what marketing is." She just didn't want to join in. Instead, she allowed her agreeable self to enjoy them all. They were, after all, her people too.

"Just think, we could be drinking hot tea with the other Salonistas—making our ears bleed," she told June, who still hadn't told her all she needed to. When June didn't respond Georgia glanced at her with concern. She looked like she was struggling to swallow; the drawing of each breath a painful battle. She was unblinking, adrift in a sea of her own suffering.

Her eyes, slightly gazed, told Georgia she wasn't really present. She was just a warm body in the room.

Around the room, the so-called arty elite hung around in clusters discussing the new vogue of novels that had become a new genre: "peasant-punk"; whether Jacquerie Headkick was as epoch-defining as Marsov's previous opus *BrainDrainBlues;* whether Milo Quartz Ford's *Up and Eight* was inspired by the new sexual position the "young folk"; the dream that one day Arambisch would be encircled by glass mountains; whether Nemerian yoga was a religion or a philosophy; whether Ascension was a consensual hallucination that propagated the Nemerian elite's superiority and abetted the Silanese's inferiority; whether any one of the night's guests had received an anonymous tip from the Resistors, seeking to break down the perceived Omnipresence of Nemes; or even whether Nemes had become so advanced that as the end of The Manifesto suggested "There Was No State". Some even whispered of Arambisch, the old name for the Silanese capitol, and its lost works and monuments. It was official though, Arambisch was now Nexus-10.

They eventually found Lilliana in her dimly lit library. She had sunk into the worn, padded purple sofa, her greying blonde hair piled messily atop her head. Her scarlet ballgown had pooled at her feet and an empty champagne glass rested in her lap, the rim of which glinted like a diamond caught by a ray of light. Sitting beside her were Celia, Abigail, and Maria, ladies of a certain age married to men of a certain type, and like Lilliana, they held governess positions at esteemed schools, much like the one where Phillip taught, if you could call it that. In reality, he levied Nemerian propaganda, grooming unsuspecting minds into evolved 'alpha versions' of who they ought to be—cold, empty and stripped of their humanity. The debate was normally the same: could those of the Silanese race, but who had some Nemerian genes—Potential—*develop* and become more Nemerian and less

Silanese? The answer, given over a decade back, was a definitive "yes," so the new question was a derivative of the science—a science which, back then, existed more as an idea than an accepted discipline. Can the purebred Silanese convert at all? For Georgia, there was a third, and far more important question that was seldom asked. *Why are they teaching these things to our children?*

"Oh, I wish I had set myself to tilt at it when I was young," Lilliana said. "But as I did not, I have always, as you know, tried to make the best of things here, on our side of the Fal." It was the name they gave to the wall that divided the states. *Who names a wall? The Nemerians.* It was just another way to highlight their superiority in this place. But that was up for debate. More likely, the Silanese let it happen. Their silence, their compliance, their assent: it was their nature. Again, this was open to debate. Though not according to some, like the ones who had read The Manifesto.

"How long is our side going to last?" Celia asked. "They have ascended dozens of our best today. We can't run a state if our elite are plucked and the lower classes multiply unchecked."

"And dumber," Maria said. "We'll end up not as a nation but a jungle."

"Georgia," Lilliana shouted when she spotted Georgia loitering in the doorway. "Didn't see you there. How are you, my love? Have you all met Georgia?"

Her eyes looked as innocent as those of a child and yet she was a lion. That was the power Lilliana had. She was mother to them all, security guard and advocate wrapped into a brave sophistication that didn't even care if the Faj came to take her away to—wherever they took people to. The Faj were the secret police, Nemerian special ops, sworn to protect Nemes and serve Silany. She also didn't care if she was taken by The Wolves for speaking what she called Woman's Truth. The Wolves were AI systems connected to Pano's Watch, the Panopticon that would pick up on the scent of a crime and then send in these wolves—cyborg wolves. They were advertised as real wolves to keep the Silanese in line, which you couldn't do with *these* women. The more advanced the surveillance became, the more the threat of death grew, and the more these women had to talk about. They were okay with death—it was one of the many things they talked about. Three years ago, they had offered a sacrifice to the moon of Capricorn. It was a symbolic ritual that marked the start of a new epoch: the end of the fear of death. After it, they were free to talk about everything. Especially their husbands. This was the nature of the Salon; it was all about high-level conversation, the occasional witchy rituals, and a mildly snobbish Lilliana. She was notably more modest than most of her peers—not as full of herself as the rest of them. She was pleasant—interested, respectful, but that was the extent of it. They'd met at Phillip's behest. He'd somehow thought Lilliana might offer some insight into his thinking, his desire to Ascend. But all they had ever talked about had been Georgia's dancing; how over time ballet had become more than a workout; it was a way of being for her. And she didn't need to always re-orient her ideas to accommodate the maxims of the intellectuals striving to escape their base Silanese condition. Just because her husband had been told he had Nemerian Potential, he didn't have final say on everything. And Lilliana found this oh so fascinating. No one from her own caste thought, she'd said, as *fiercely* as this. Georgia must come to the Salon. Georgia must learn things that they couldn't talk about here, at this "party." The real salons had a different vibe. Parties like this were just where the girls would recruit women like Georgia into the fold.

Georgia felt the need to talk to Lilliana now. She would like to get the woman on her own to talk about how she could possibly have Phillip's child when they were at such loggerheads. However, she knew Lilliana was one to be respected, not trusted.

"Excuse me." Celia was into women. Everyone knew she hated men because her husband slept with Lilliana. In her vengeance, she sought retribution by ruining young, happily married girls, some said, while wearing a seahorse mask. "Is your friend all right?"

Georgia looked around. She couldn't see June.

"Oh, she's probably gone to the ladies."

"Right," said a nonchalant Celia while quietly stepping away.

*

Georgia found June slumped on the tiled floor in the cloakroom, crying her eyes out.

"June, what's the matter? What on earth has happened?"

"Artie's left me."

"Oh, you poor thing." Georgia pitied her in that moment, reminded of how pathetic she could be around Phillip.

"He's been selected."

A pause.

"To Ascend?"

'Yes. He's become one of *them* those snotty bitches were going on about."

June and Artie had been engaged for four years. The obstacle preventing them from getting married was the same obstacle preventing Phillip and Georgia from having children. Like Phillip, Artie had been told he had Potential. *Nemerian Potential by Nathan Bogod* was the book Artie'd been celebrating up until spring. Nathan Bogod was a Count and the son of a famous shipping merchant. A banker, his opus was the final contribution to the people of Silany before he died at 103 years old. In it, he joins the genetic sciences with the work of an old-world mystic. Too spooky for most but the main frame was easy to swallow: some Silanese folk were born with

Nemerian genes. Those folk can develop. Other folk can't. And everyone's been tested. Now the Count's dead and his picture is everywhere, and there is a statue of him the size of the Manhattan building, with his monocle and his stick. Those who were tested and came back *N* for positive, then had a knock on the door—a visit from out of Nemes. It was their time. Like winning the lottery, everything would change for them suddenly. People like Artie. It was only a matter of time before they were selected to Ascend. But rumour had it different. Word on the street was that even a full Silanese could one day Ascend from their base Silanese condition and upgrade genetically. It was just a rumour but it was catching on quickly. + Manifesting Potential was no longer a right reserved for the one-fourth and up alone. In today's post-Bogod world, the Silanese born, could also upgrade, if they dedicated their lives to The Manifesto. This is why Phillip kept shoving that stupid book in Georgia's bag.

Georgia stood up and leaned against the wall, looking out of a south-facing window to give herself something to do while she pondered what to say. In a way, every woman wanted this for their husband, but didn't. And it was the same for the men, for the women were tested too. Not all of them though. Women like Lilliana knew the system. She was not a creature of statute. She was not a legalist or conformist, blindly following the herd. She was sovereign. Nobody knew how she did it, but casting her mind back to something her Papa said to her, once, Georgia suspected it had something to do with being free.

Directly opposite, the view was three-quarters blocked by an old moss-covered stone wall with weeds creeping out of the cracks. To the west of the wall, small brick buildings were perched upon small brick buildings, precariously balanced on concrete pillars and roofed in by green corrugated iron. This was one of Nexus-1o's many favela regions. At twilight, there was a strange beauty to its higgledy-piggledy human chaos. Somewhere over there, though, was the Fal, and its most outstanding architectural feature, Pano's Watch, the great tower that monitored Silany.

"All that potential we had together wasted," June cried. "Trashed for a higher purpose—*Himself*."

Not wanting to be disloyal to Phillip, Georgia didn't say a thing. Phillip's pursuit of what The Manifesto called *Wisdom* was similar in spirit, if not in action, to Artie's absolute submission to Nemerian ideals.

"The Nemerians," June spat out, "just want to cherry-pick the best of us. If they can keep most of us ignorant, they somehow get us desiring what they have."

"You want what they have?" Georgia asked. Arms crossing, brow rising.

"I want to go wherever Artie goes. Besides, evolution of the mind and body doesn't sound so bad. Perfect..." and the word fell out of an almost closed mouth "...harmony?" Her eyes lifted to meet Georgia. "Who wouldn't want that?"

"You've changed your tune!" Georgia tried to pick her up.

"I've got to Ascend, Georgia." She pleaded. "I've got to go with him."

"But you wouldn't be June anymore, girl. Is Artie really worth the sacrifice of who you are? And what is perfect order and harmony, anyway?" Georgia had managed to stand her up again. "Aren't we all a bit wonky? Isn't that what makes us beautiful?" she surmised.

"I don't care to be wonky!" June's gaze was haunting. She clearly wasn't herself. "This..." she fluttered her hand up across her torso and swiped across her face. "This is *too much* pain." Tears shone in her eyes and a sob, deep and guttural, ripped from her throat. "They...They live in a clean world, where absolutely anything is possible," she sputtered. "I could live peacefully with my Artie."

A clean and perfect world? Georgia had heard variations of this from Phillip over the years. It was a web of lies. The road to perfection, paved with deception. The Manifesto could do that though—provide the people of Silany with false hope. Yet, Georgia would on occasion ask herself this: what is wrong with falsely hoping? But she'd shake it off again. The image of her father, and her mother too. "Remember girl, nothin' wrong with being what you are. Ya mother and I—we love ya just the way you are. You gotta love yourself too. Then you can love everything else—warts and all—and hope for the right things. Even the unloved can hope. But if they don't love themselves first, they're lost." Papa was right, that was the right kind of hope, not this superficial version with promises, promises, promises. If it were real, it wouldn't promise. It would just *be*. Georgia came back to the moment—the distant memory of her parents fading quickly. June was hurting.

"June, listen to me" Georgia said, digging her fingers into June's shoulders and giving her a gentle shake. "Stuff the clean lines. Don't read their stupid brochures. Artie didn't want to take you with him? Fine. You can live here with me. Whole and free...You can still have it all. You know, the joy of friendship, the thrill of love, of art and truth, of *family*. I know it's scary here, the Pano's Watch, the Fal, the Faj, and the Wolves—but they feed us lies, June. To hell with them! To hell with the Nemerian fundamentalists!" There was an edge to Georgia's voice. She knew the peace June's little heart yearned for and the ache brought on by its absence. But Georgia resolved that it was more important to set her friend straight. She needed to make sure June's feet were firmly planted on the ground, and not hopping around to the beat of Viktor K. Mankz's *Concerto X-0413.*

"And you've got all that with Phillip? All those children that you don't have?"

Georgia inhaled sharply. This conversation wasn't about her but—"June let's get away from this lot and go to Vish-Tap for an espressotini. There's something I need to tell you."

Having crossed the road outside the August mansion, Georgia waited in front of a blacked-out window that indicated it was the home of a Resistor. While the Ascenders—ever devoted to the preservation of the Nemerian state—strived to climb the sanctioned ranks of power, the Resistors were their antithesis—working tirelessly to dismantle the state entirely. They conducted their business undercover to avoid the all-seeing eye of Pano's Watch. Georgia felt safe waiting here. Resistors were noble and righteous even if sometimes their methods were questionable. She never mentioned the comfort she found in them to Phillip, but at times it made her wonder if she had been one in a past life.

Georgia often thought of life, death and the afterlife. From what she recalled, she had even talked to her mother about it. The idea that the soul leaves the body and travels on may have been her way of detaching from life and preserving herself from the pain and eventuality of death. Either way, apart from both her parents who died peacefully in their sleep, Georgia had never had to face or deal with death. There was homeless Ted, the guy she used to give a coin to on a Friday, but that didn't really count.

It was dark now and gauzy rain fell, covering the asphalt with a glittery sheen. The air smelled of wet metal and fresh earth, with a hint of electricity, whatever that smells like. Georgia hadn't dressed for rain. She hugged her thin cardigan tighter to her chest, its scratchy material already clinging to her skin.

Georgia had somehow managed to lose June, who'd said she needed to go to the ladies to fix her panda eyes and would meet Georgia outside.

Georgia shuddered as a passing car sent a wave of dirty puddle water crashing over, driving her back into the disguised front of the house. As it pulled away, she noticed it was a Skimatik, a driverless goods transporter ubiquitous in Nemes but only occasionally seen in Silany. Georgia had never seen one slow down, ever, but about 300 yards away she heard a sickening thud, and it stopped abruptly. Shortly after, a grinding sound could be heard and then the wild cry of something beastly. Maybe it had hit a fox—A real AI Wolf even.

A Silanese old banger, a station wagon from the dark ages trailing black diesel fumes, whizzed past but jerked to a stop before it ran into the back of the Skimatik. The impatient driver honked his horn. In response, the Skimatik shunted rightwards into the other lane before driving off. From where Georgia stood, in the space where the Skimatik had been, there was something remaining in the road—a dark, red heap. The fox? Her heart raced when the driver of the station wagon got out of his car and hurried towards it. There was something frantic about his steps that she didn't like. As though time was slowing down.

She ran forward to see what the driver was looking at and immediately dropped to her knees.

"Sheesh," the man said. "Them smart trucks are stupid enough not to brake and savvy enough to hightail it when they hit someone."

Georgia said nothing and simply stared. It was her. It was her friend—June. The rain cascaded down her friend's now still body. Each drop danced on her skin, tracing delicate pathways across her face, and mingling with the tears which now stained her cheeks. Dull eyes wide open, June was a portrait of reluctant surrender. Her gaze fixed on the sky as if searching for answers even now amidst a swirl of thoughts.

Georgia was frozen. She might have spoken, she wasn't sure. Her ears were ringing. Lifting up June's head onto her lap, her throat suddenly felt as if two hands were squeezing it tight. She rocked June's head so gently believing she could chivvy her awake without alarming her.

"Nemerian piece of shit," the man muttered.

"Can you call someone?"

"I've called someone."

"You idiot."

"Pardon, lady?"

Georgia said nothing.

"You know her? You think she...?"

Georgia slid her palm over June's eyes and waited, for what she did not know. Sometime later, red and amber lights flashed about her, and firm hands helped her up, sirens and voices talking all around.

After hours at some semi-derelict police processing unit out in Flex 4, the statements she'd made, the insinuations she'd flapped away, particularly the idea that June had committed suicide as some sort of anti-Nemerian protest like Och Kann had. Och self-immolated fifteen years ago. Now in the half-dark of the breaking morn, Georgia wandered the beloved, narrow streets of her city. She passed an Old-World stone sign, set low to the ground. On it was inscribed the original name of the capital—Arambisch. Most of the lettering was worn and all that could be read was the sloping left hand bar of the A, the ascender of the *b* and a curving squiggle indicating the *s*. Arambisch, Arambisch—oh for Arambisch! It was incredible that the state of Nemes, which had long-since taken over and renamed the city of Arambisch, Nexus-10, had not completely destroyed this piece of evidence from the Old World. They'd replace everything with Nemes if they could. If not for the Silanese's resistance, they probably would have by now. Arambisch—Georgia always took it as a symbol of freedom. Something would course through her veins every time she walked by it. Dignity, or something that made her feel confident and light. But not today. Today she was numb and there was a strange, almost metallic taste in her mouth. She hadn't told Phillip where she was. In fact, she'd turned down the opportunity for a policewoman to pay him a visit and have him come and collect her.

It was yet early, and none of the shops were open yet, other than a few fruit stalls just setting up for the day. Plastered next to the stalls was a line of motivational posters, instructing the population to "Live by Necessity, Not Want."

She stopped outside a favourite shop of hers. This old place, they sold the kinds of gifts she'd like to get for people: artwork, candles, small bowls made from clay. It was the only shop she knew of that sold handmade cards. *Wish,* it was called. They sold nothing made from Etronium. She even had a coffee there once with the owner, the old man with the funny eye. She'd doubt he'd remember; the man had been there for decades. He didn't even wave at people these days. Not long ago, they came for his wife and off she went. Nobody knew why. Some whispered that she had Ascended. The old man was mute after that. She peered through the window at a green wooden cuckoo clock. Next to her, against the outside wall, was a huge pile of refuse—old clothing, used bottles, tins. It would be sorted through and collected by the Rag-X, refuse collectors that some thought of as more like a militia who ensured nothing would go to waste. That was the theory at least. A faded neon poster hung above the pile: "If it ain't lean, it ain't green."

Georgia could now see the old man at the back of the store. There was still an hour to go before he would open. Georgia pressed her hand against the glass window. It wasn't quite a wave, rather a small gesture that meant something all the same. Places like these old stores sold real things. She thought of Papa, this place, Silany and realised she wasn't ready to let go of it. The old man had turned, with half of him remaining in the shadows. He used to move about with an old tape machine in the back there playing lonely piano tunes by men with names like Frank, Johnson and Ray. Maybe he was wondering who the freak outside was, leaning against his shop window with an open mouth looking so forlorn like many of the Silanese. Though he'd seen everything on his road—Atlantic Drive was used to the creatures and crawlers of Arambisch—looting, break-ins, stores like this were well weathered—they were something you could hold, grab onto and feel.

Georgia pulled her hand away and turned to face the bazaar, an open cobbled strip that stopped just past her feet. Then there were the new parts, the parts which were developed, "upgraded" as they called them, and lit by a system that was plugged into Nemes. It was all Etronium. *Plastic fantastic*, Georgia called it, shining angled buildings and ugly structures that weren't architectural at all. They were anti-life as far as Georgia was concerned, square blocks that did not fit in and were not welcome here. Twenty per cent of the state now consisted of this rubbish, a highly efficient order driven by machines mostly. Offices rarely needed people for them to function. The plan was to get to fifty per cent Etronium friendly by the next decade. Though whose plan it was remained unclear.

A train track was built across the top of the shops, but these used to be old shops selling real things: meat, veg, fish and cheese with mould you could eat. As a younger woman, she would sit on the bench under the silver birch at the end of Atlantic Drive where it splits before the park starts and watch the old trains come in. She exhaled, looking left and right. There was no bakery anymore, no paper shop and the vets had hung up a sign which read "Not a Chance," yet the offices were all lit and producing, with no people inside them. Real things were void of the living. She held onto her heart and searched the sky for its blue. Silany had changed, Nemes and its lies eeped in through its cracks, breaking the hearts of its people, men like *Papa*, and women like Georgia. But not everyone thought so. Some people, like those with Potential in them, strived to uphold the Nemerian values and its way of life, so they didn't see it like Georgia did.

She turned the corner onto Trinity Road and approached a building. The house was a two-storey, flint-walled with a corrugated iron roof, indistinguishable from the rest of the buildings on the street. Taking a deep breath, she turned the handle of the heavy door and stepped into the hall of her home.

She pulled off her shoes and stepped in stockinged feet to the lounge. She dropped the album *Figure of Eight* onto the turntable and swung the needle across to the well-worn track *Dawn Chorus and the Dreams of Underlings* by The Prisms, Silany's best known jump-jazz orchestra. She watched the spinning record as the music flowed, the beauty of the composition washing over her in cascades until her eyes closed. June had loved this music too, and they had danced pirouettes and arabesques to it for whole afternoons. Phillip didn't like it, but then again, he didn't warm to any music, or at least it rarely took him away from his philosophical considerations when she tried to make him listen. She knew she was being theatrical, reappearing like this after a lost night and playing The Prisms at full volume, but it would draw him away from his philosophising. That had been the style of their marriage all along: she had a passion for living and he did not.

*

Twelve years before, Georgia had met Phillip at a party. She noticed him across the room while he was looking disdainfully over everyone else there. He wasn't tall but his face was pleasant enough. She was surprised to find his attention on her when there were more beautiful women in the room his own age. As he approached her, he had the air of someone mooching around an art gallery because it was raining. She held herself upright and smoothed her hands along her hips. *Thirty is the new twenty.* She recognised his suit as a bespoke outfit from Nate Jonz, the most upmarket tailor in the New World. At least here was a man who knew how to take care of himself and, by extension, who would able to look after her. Looking back, Georgia felt she should have been wary because the first comment he had made was about his mother. Growing up against a backdrop of war stories, the New World, Nemes and the future, it's likely that Phillip represented it all. More likely, she wanted him to be what she had been promised subliminally, through the radio, on the tv, and up the wall of every shop, like Wish and the old bakery—the dream of Nemes: Progress, evolution, something *better*. So, when Phillip had walked on over, clean and well groomed, academic and forward moving, she softened her resolve. She didn't understand why or know how to resist.

"My mother was Ruth Wise, the concert pianist. Your poise reminds me of her."

"She wasn't from around here then?"

"My father was. She was Nemerian. But she died."

"I'm sorry to hear that."

"I've always been sorry. I was brought up here as a result but I'm not from here, I've always known it. When you know, you just know."

—*You too can live with us*–

Later that evening, she allowed him to see her in her negligee and explore her body. She didn't understand why. As it turns out, she didn't actually like him. She just thought she did.

That first night, he had seen her as a simple, unsullied girl he could raise up, and encourage to become what she had the potential to be. One year into their courtship he'd all but confirmed this when he told her that he saw her as his "project."

*

The music stopped so abruptly it sounded like the record had been ripped from the turntable. She stopped swaying and opened her eyes. Phillip was standing in the doorway in yesterday's shirt, a tumbler held loosely in one hand. His hair was perfect, and his beard precisely trimmed to a sheer curve.

"Georgia," he began. "I've not slept all night. I have to teach this morning."

She wondered if he had sat up all night with his whiskey, fretting that something had happened to her. He was a good talker, but more truthfully, he was a coward who needed to feel important, who needed to save someone who wasn't actually drowning. She didn't like him back then, and that first night should have been the last time she saw his mask of a face. Maybe it was decades of mind control, or perhaps it was the infiltration of Nemerian propaganda into Silanese institutions, markets, and culture—whatever it was, it made her want him. In the end, she had turned out to be Silanese to the core. She had bought what he was selling. Just as the Silanese had been duped into compliance by the Nemerians, their lust for ambition and self-betterment rendering them putty before Nemes.

"I've been at a police station," Georgia said, her voice hoarse.

Phillip frowned. "Tell me exactly what happened."

"June."

"Yes, June, what about June?"

"She was...knocked down...by one of those…lorries. She didn't stand a chance..."

"What lorries?"

There was a long pause and Georgia's hand moved to her face. She exhaled and suddenly it hit her. June was dead. Georgia closed her eyes.

"The lorries that come over from Nemes," she whispered, as though saying it quietly would make it less true.

"I very much doubt that. They are such intuitive machines. Absolutely safe. Made with the highest attention to detail, able to pre-empt any road-based situation and offset..."

She watched his mouth move. She always imagined he was presenting something to a child when he spoke to her. He was always preaching. He just wasn't very convincing.

"Ask me if I am *OK*, Phillip."

"What? Why do you need me to do that? Are you not OK?"

She stepped away from him. "June. She died."

Phillip furrowed his brows once more in a feeble attempt to convey empathy. "What a...shame."

A shame. That was it? He had a way of bringing her into a bickering row as if he derived pleasure from her distress. She just wanted him to hold her.

"I blame Artie, you know he—"

"It's not about blame. It's called grief," Phillip said ponderously. "I remember hearing of when my mother, Ruth, passed. It was hard...but then existence *is* hard."

She nodded. Why? she didn't know.

"Did you read The Manifesto?"

"Phillip, June is dead because Artie believed all that rubbish and abandoned her for it." Georgia felt her chest rising, her confidence now assured.

Blinking hard, Phillip turned his grey eyes to her as if seeing her for the first time.

"I thought you said she was hit by a truck?"

"I think she may have jumped," she said with a whisper.

"Well, that wasn't very fair on Artie. It's *her* fault he left her. She should have been a more compatible companion," he said, a sourness in his voice.

"Phillip, Artie Ascended."

"What? Artie?!" Phillip's face contorted. "They Ascended *Artie*? Why him? That little shit has nothing on me—he's a *painter* for crying out loud. A bottom-feeder—!"

"He's a state engineer," Georgia pointed out, coolly.

"What does a man have to do to be recognised around here! How long must he suffer the embarrassment of being passed over?" Phillip curled his lip in a way that made Georgia flinch. He knew as well as she did that the selection process was unknown at worst, and random at best. Why or how people were chosen was a total mystery. No doubt the Nemerians revelled in that fact. "That little punk, Artie. *That's* the standard now? Hmm, I ought to…to contact someone and...and complain. Perhaps if enough of us complain, he could be reverted and replaced with a much stronger man such as myself." He slumped in a chair suddenly fatigued. His arms stretched out wide and he loosened his grip on the glass. It crashed to the floor and shattered, the dregs of his drink trickling towards Georgia's stockinged feet. Against the dark wood, the spilt liquor could have passed for blood. June's blood.

Georgia's stomach roiled. The Ascension had taken her friend. *Soon it could take Phillip*. "I'll see to it," she said. "Then I've got to get ready for work. We're short staffed today." Georgia was exhausted. Even her words came out slowly. Phillip though, was full of energy, hate mostly, but it was enough to charge him up for the day, the charge ever increasing as she walked away from him. She moved toward the bathroom without thinking. The day and what had happened to June, what her husband was, all came up out of her as a giant roar of soup and meat.

The vomit in the toilet somehow felt good to see; it was the closest depiction of the day she'd had and that made her feel good again.

*

That afternoon, she lay back on a raised platform while a female doctor smeared gel over her abdomen then rolled the ultrasound wand over it. In Silany, there were no specialised jobs, so doctors tripled as midwives, nurses, and sonographers. And as the black and white image swam up on the screen with the pulsing sound of two tiny heartbeats, there was no mistaking the fact that Georgia was pregnant with twins.

"Mrs. Wise, congratulations."

"Children..." She was struggling to get the words out. A flush of colour to the cheeks. It felt too late for children. I *should be in my thirties and Phillip forty-four.* It was all back to front. Then the breathing returned. Her hand loosened its grip on the bedpost. "Children...of Silany."

CHAPTER 2
The Rules

"Rusty is here." The pressure of Phillip's hand on Georgia's shoulder lifted as he left her and the twins to go and make his great speech. The long-awaited guest of honour from "the other side" had arrived—it was time. The room was crammed with Friends of Ascent activists, mostly teachers from Phillip's school, their partners, and colleagues of their partners who had naturally fallen in with the gang. An arrogant clan of aspiring academics, most of them wearing glasses, moustaches and expensive suits. A double-dose of fatherhood had boosted Phillip's self-importance. He strutted across the room like a crowing silky bantam. Georgia tried not to laugh and sat on her own instead while her babies fed. The guests gathered in groups around the room, ignoring her once they'd had a coo, apart from Lilliana, who was at least willing to cuddle a crying baby and give Georgia a break. It was more than she sometimes got from Phillip.

A thin, angular, pale-faced Rusty Barnfather stood in the middle of the room and downed a tumbler of whisky in one go celebrating his arrival from Nemes. He looked around, his presence enough to diminish everyone else's. Phillip lifted his glass and gave it a tinkle with a fork. It was his time.

"Ladies. Gentlemen. As you'll all be aware, we're gathered here to celebrate the birth of my twin boys. I'm a very proud man. These two boys—Richard and Norman—are going to be men in no time." His voice lowered. "I've not been able to be a man." Obviously searching for sympathy, yet feeling obliged to entertain, he blundered awkwardly on. "I've taught for many years now, and I've given my life to the improvement of young minds." At this, his head fell, his voice became a near-whisper, and a hand began to clench. "But I've always wanted more." It was a mock display of humility—likely rehearsed before a mirror, one might surmise. "Let me tell you that my boys will be successful, yes! They will become established as men in Silany, and they will develop." His chest began to rise and his arms opened to welcome the attention. "I want them to be what they came here to be. In years to come they will Ascend! Men...*raise a glass to that*."

Murmurs of approval rose from the guests and they lifted their glasses one by one. Georgia's hand shook as she lifted her own. She had expected a tone-down speech, something less flashy, meant just, for the boys. Not some puff to impress Rusty Barnfather.

"Let me tell you a story."

Oh God, Georgia thought. Here comes a parable of guiltless greed.

"A man goes into a bar and the bartender refuses to serve him." He began to pace slightly. "What do you think he should do?—Wait! I'm not asking you to answer the question." A few nervous laughs. It was awful and as his wife, it couldn't have been more painful to watch. "All that man has to do is jump over the counter and take the drink for himself. Take it. If it belongs to him in his mind then he *can* take it...If he is unwilling to take, he has limited his rights. He is harming others and himself by not demonstrating the fullness of his capabilities, ergo, himself. Being less of himself, he is doing his society a great disservice."

Lilliana sat forward in her own seat. And next to her, Georgia swallowed hard, tasting something sour in her mouth. *All I want is for these boys to be kind, considerate, natural and law-abiding. But that will never be enough for him. There's no point in discussing it with him.*

"Finally," Phillip declared. "One more thing. Come forward please, Rusty."

Lumbering out of his seat, Rusty stepped up. Phillip flung one arm around his shoulder and slapped the other hand across his chest. Beside Rusty's towering frame, Phillip looked like a twig. Georgia suppressed her simper.

"This, my friends, is Rusty Barnfather. He's the best of all men and the source of my inspiration. A Silanese man who has Ascended. Now a Nemerian, he has made a fortune in cybernetics. Without going into details, he's stuck with me through thick and thin. He doesn't know it yet, but he's about to have the pleasure of becoming godfather to my two boys."

For just a second, Georgia allowed her practised composure to slip. *He might have asked her opinion first.*

"I'm speechless." Rusty looked bored already.

Everyone in the room began to clap. Phillip gave Rusty one of his manly pats on the shoulder and sent him back to his chair. Rusty sat and spread his legs, demonstrating that he didn't care for this place. Georgia noticed the expression they both carried—Phillip's four-drinks-in-and-deserves-four-more beam. *God. He's trying too hard.*

He hadn't even properly introduced her to Rusty, the nonchalant devil, let alone discussed with her why he'd be the ideal guardian for her children. Yes, she'd heard all about him, his achievements, but she'd heard many stories over the years, few of which had been true.

At her breast, Richard coughed and sicked up milk over the skirt of her dress. Lilliana must have noticed. Bobbing up fairy-godmother-like beside her, Lilliana held out her arms for Richard. "Here, let me take him." She began patting his back against her shoulder.

"I'm so sorry," Georgia said.

Lilliana smiled. "You have nothing to apologise for. That's what we mothers do—help each other out."

Georgia appreciated Lilliana's kindness, but she couldn't help but wonder what she may have to pay for it in future. "Come to the kitchen with me," Georgia said. "I need to get a cloth."

"I'll get one for you."

"No, not here. Not in front of these people. C'mon."

In the kitchen, Georgia lay Norman down in a basket and started to dab at her dress with a wet muslin cloth. Lilliana rocked Richard from side to side.

"Good," Georgia said. "In here, where Rusty can't get at him!"

"He seems a fine man," Lilliana said, faintly amused.

"All this talk of Nemes already when, look at them, they're babies. I'm worried he'll put too much pressure on them."

"It is their future."

"I know. And I suppose it's good to have some ambition. Still, it scares me, you know?"

She threw the cloth into the sink. The burble of the party in the other room amplified as though it was inside her own head. Her temples squeezed tight around her mind. She glanced over at Lilliana, expecting her to respond. Lilliana said nothing and cocked her head instead. Lilliana's Godson, Joshua, had graduated from the University of Nemes two years ago and was now working in the banking sector out of the FDS, the Financial District of Silany in downtown Little Jiwa. Unlike many Ascenders, Joshua had managed to maintain his contact with his Silanese family by staying this side of the Fal. Only a few who Ascended, entered Nemes and, like Rusty, journeyed back here from time to time, but most never returned. Some, like Joshua's friend Matthew, even signed a contract stating how they would not return. Families were obliged to honour the contract by framing it and placing it on a wall in their home. There were other Nemerian Services designed to inspire the Silanese to *grow, evolve, develop*, all detailed in The Manifesto's handbook: Protocols of Nemes.

"I was just thinking about your Joshua," Georgia said. "He's turned out nicely, hasn't he? Maybe I should let my two make up their own minds when they're older."

"Ah, Joshua, that makes me feel so old," Lilliana lamented.

Georgia offered a sympathetic smile. "You don't look a day over 50."

"Makeup, dear. It helps with the wrinkles."

Instinctively, Georgia's hands went to her face and the crow's feet around her eyes.

"It is what it is," Lilliana professed, "Now, let's talk about your man up on the stage. I think you need to take the lead with the boys' education, but make Phillip feel as though he's the one who came up with the plan." There was a sternness in Lilliana's gaze, a sharpness Georgia had never expected—it was almost as though Lilliana cared. "You want to avoid him putting too much pressure on the boys with rule setting and teaching of ideals, right?"

Georgia nodded. "That's part of it, yes."

"Give the boys two very simple rules that will express what both of you think of as important, ones you can spin to your side."

"I want them to be law abiding, and to look out for one another, yes. To love one another, and their fellow man."

"But remember that Phillip wants them to aspire, to Ascend from their one-fourth constitution."

"And crush others to get to the top..." Georgia frowned.

Lilliana's gaze softened. "Have they been tested?"

"Yes."

"And the results came back?"

"Yes."

A brief silence hung in the air. This was usually the moment where one person would tell the other what the test results were. Nobody was meant to ever tell. Yet, everybody told. It was the only real rule Nemes had that no one followed. People were keen to share, even if by doing so they were risking everything, their social status, their bearing in Silany, and for some, their dignity.

"They are both one-fourths. As we would expect."

"As we would expect. You are pure Silanese. He is half Nemerian. Everyone knows this."

"Yes."

"Georgia, with Joshua, I gave him rules that helped offset the extremes I knew he'd come up against if he was to Ascend, let alone prosper. When you say law abiding what does that mean to you?"

Georgia stopped and thought of Papa. He used to talk about man's laws. And God's laws. The laws men made to govern other men. They were unnatural. He used to tell her that you can do what you want in this world. But then she heard his voice and she remembered the time he said it to her, "As long as you don't harm anyone else." He was sat there in his chair with his paper by the window. There were flowers on the table. Blue house flowers. Lots of them.

Georgia did not answer Lilliana but instead announced: "The first rule. Never harm your brother."

"Good," Lilliana nodded.

"Rule Two, always obey the rules?"

“Rule Two, always obey the rules. I like the sound of this. They’ll look out for each other and it’s vague enough to mean they will basically follow the law...the law of the land, but from Phillip’s point of view...”

“He’ll interpret it to mean something from The Manifesto.”

Georgia forced a smile onto her face. She knew that the reality of raising the boys alongside Phillip would be far bleaker than she hoped. Peace, though, was possible through accepting the situation and throwing herself headlong into raising her children.

“Rule One: Never harm your brother. Rule Two: Always obey the rules. C’mon, let’s go back in there and pretend we love Nemes.”

Later that night, when the festivities were finally over and she was alone in their bed, she met in a dream a Leviathan-like creature, its skin hard and scaly, its eyes so blue they seemed black.

*

The Wise brothers, Richard and Norman, both learned how to shoot on the same day. One by instinct and one by instruction; One in Silany and one in Nemes.

The first Georgia knew that one of her boys had been playing with guns was when she found a dirty great hare lying on her kitchen work surface with a bullet hole bang smack in the centre of its head. It stunk. She’d come home from her shift at the café and it took her less than a second to let off a scream and a retch before shouting at Norman to *come down here right now*.

Norman slunk out onto the landing and down the stairs.

“Where did you get this?” She assumed one of the more outdoorsy of his friends’ parents—the bluff, beardy ones Phillip hated—had given it to him.

"Er...I shot it," he mumbled quietly, shuffling his feet.

"You what?"

"I shot it." He repeated, louder this time.

"You shot it? What with?"

He shrank back a little, until he nudged the fridge and couldn't go any further. Maybe he thought she was going to tell Phillip. Then again, for a strapping boy at twelve, Norman wasn't much scared of Phillip. He'd been scrapping with boys twice his age for about a year now, taking far more wins than losses. It wouldn't have mattered if she'd told Phillip; he wasn't there to discipline anyway. Phillip had taken Richard over to Nemes, where they were visiting Rusty, who talked about his new-found solace in his state-of-the-art shooting range: his compound on the edge of the city. Norman was also supposed to go, but at the last-minute Phillip had said he couldn't afford to take both of them. Georgia suspected this had nothing to do with money and more to do with Norman not exactly lapping up the macroeconomics lessons Phillip had been shoving down the boys' throats. Richard had started to call Norman a "philistine," a word out of the diction range of most Silanese boys his age. Phillip swore he'd never used it in front of them. Although, he'd seemed mightily impressed with Richard. Anyway, Norman wasn't a philistine. He was at least as good at chess as Richard and shaded him at boxing.

Norman was also the first-born twin, the bigger of the brothers. Stronger and less scared of their father, he was soon to become the man of the house. By default, then, Phillip would preach over Richard. Norman suspected it was so that Phillip could have someone he could control, influence, take to Nemes through his Rusty contact and mould to his liking to become a better and stronger man than Norman. In Silany, anyone who was still part Silanese needed a contact like Rusty to cross the Fal and enter Nemes.

Apparently, Rusty was allowed to take one person every three years, and that person was allowed a plus-one who was still a legal child, but only one. Norman didn't care. Besides, he knew Phillip wouldn't have asked him if he wanted to come. If he had, he probably would have replied with "prefer to go fly fishin'" or "nahhh." Who would turn down a free trip to Nemes in exchange for the Silanese woods, if only for a day? Norman Wise. Norman knew that even the idea of him turning down his father's offer was enough to irritate him and push him to take Richard instead. He knew he didn't even really want to take Richard, but Richard was nagging. Norman wasn't nagging. He may have been a dirty, sweaty little mucker who liked to hunt, but he never nagged his father to take him to Nemes. Norman was the type of kid to go and get something if he wanted it, like a fight, or a girl, or a hare.

"Norman, what happened?" Georgia's voice cut through his swirling thoughts.

He huffed. "I was over at Theo's, in the woods behind his house. He had the gun. That's about it."

"That's not about it though, is it?"

"Well, yeah."

"Yeah, the back of my hand yeah. There's a dead animal in my house and now you're into guns. My father had guns; he was five times your age. You want to play with guns, Norman?"

Norman raised one shoulder in a languid shrug. "I don't know. It's his dad's. He let me pick it up, and then we see this hare, big one, come out of the bushes, looking around. I don't know. I didn't think about it, Mum. I just lined up, pulled the trigger. I didn't expect to hit it. It was just shooting."

"Oh yes, you didn't expect to hit it. Is this about your brother? Are you upset..."

"What? No!" Norman scowled. "Nemes is for dicks. Anyway, I carried the hare home. Nearly broke my shoulder."

Georgia let out an irritated, high-pitched sigh and crossed her arms, but a few breaths later she was looking over the animal. It was meat. It was food and her son had gone out, hunted it and brought it back for them all. She had a son in front of her who was showing signs of being a man. No, he was a man. The type of young man that the Bear Man would have liked.

The Bear Man. Norman had a beat-up picture of him on the side in his room. In it the Bear Man's eyes shone. *If only they could have met.*

This was a good day for the family. She exhaled, releasing the tension from her shoulders and chest and then a smile. With her hands on her hips, she nodded her head.

"My boy!" she grinned. "This is impressive. You actually brought it all the way home. This certainly demands a celebration. We'll make hare stew tonight. We'll have a proper meal for the wanderers when they return from their trip. Give me a hand, will you?" And she rolled up her sleeves.

"Nah, you can get its head off. I'm going out."

An hour later, Georgia had dealt with the animal, the blood, its balls and stinking innards. Long ago she'd committed to memory a recipe for hare passed down to her from her own mother. The hare, in a pot now, reminded her of childhood. Good old Norman. She wondered how Richard and Phillip were getting on. Phillip would no doubt have been preaching on the perfection of Nemes, the electric cars, the plastic overpasses, the people in their glass castles watching the athletes train, the parks with the wrong kind of peace, the city transit network built to model the water cycle powered by the sun. "In Nemes, you glide on shimmering silver," she'd heard him tell Richard the other day. And what about the speech he gave to them, orated it like he was addressing the knuckleheads at Friends of Ascent.

"All the vehicles there are driverless and silent, from the giant Skimatiks to the lighter Skimvogels. There's no aggravated crashing or constant drilling in the background. Being there is like being in the place you can usually only reach through deep and continuous meditation. It's pure. Everybody in Nemes knows what to do. The Manifesto is the soul's guide. It is the apex, the end point of civilisation. And guess what else? You too can live with us!"

Did he actually quote directly from the pamphlet? *Second-hand garbage cribbed from the rest of The Manifesto.* He'd been stuffing it down their throats since they were four. She cringed as she removed the last of her browned hare pieces and placed them on a warm plate. The smell of fresh rosemary and salt made her think of the early days, when she still had the Bear Man and didn't feel the pressure to read The Manifesto. Part of her regretted that she couldn't reserve the rest of the stew for just Norman and herself. The Nemerian wannabees could fend for themselves. They'd probably had a pill of something over there containing some highly nutritious blue algae grown in a lab and teleported directly into the stomach to efficiently save the time wasted on eating meals.

After all, it was obvious that Phillip was favouring Richard. This had started when the boys were really little. He hadn't shown any interest when they were babies. It was she who had created the Milestone Book, a cream-coloured journal, a record of the twins' young lives that he could contribute to as well.

She remembered that about two-thirds of the way through the journal, when the boys were around two and a half, she had written:

> *Norman had Richard's toy truck. Richard was distracted by something else. Norman was curious about how the truck worked, and spun the wheels round and round, making a brumm sound as he played. Richard noticed, pinched then flicked Norman's face, but it was Richard that cried. Norman tried to give the truck back to Richard, but he didn't want it anymore.*

Next to this comment, Phillip had scrawled:

Richard is ripe for training. Nature is red in tooth and claw.

A little further down the page in the margin, he'd added the words:

Angels are brutes.

He kept his distance physically from them. It was she who decoded their baby language and then listened to their growing confidence with words. It was also she who taught them the alphabet and helped them with their speaking. Phillip's only contribution had been to chastise her for doing it wrong. When the boys were old enough to enjoy stories and ask questions, she found herself often saying to them, "Use your souls to help others, not your brains to put yourself first."

As she repositioned the pieces of hare into the pot, along with capers, parsley, and red wine vinegar, and set the stew to simmer in the hob, it struck her that it was more than annoying that Richard, so bright in many ways, seemed to have forgotten all she had taught him. All that her father had lived for. To trot after Phillip though, like a mechanical dog, seemed his natural course.

*

By the time Phillip and Richard returned, it was nine o'clock which was much later than they normally ate as a family. Rather than greet Georgia and Norman, Phillip scurried upstairs and into the shower. Georgia let her fake smile slip. There was no need for it now.

She glanced over at Richard, who looked like a current was passing through him. She suspected that he'd probably drunk a bucket of some energy water drink that came from underground over in Nemes, a natural spring that fed into the city for all its "Members." Members? *Silany doesn't have members. Man, woman and family, but not members.* As she assembled crockery and cutlery, he was gabbling about it all.

"And we had to get in and we had to be scanned for our thoughts and how worthy we were, and we were worthy, Mummy, we were worthy."

Georgia noticed Richard then, his eyes glazed over like he was high on something. Nemes. She couldn't help but notice the slight redness and pressure marks on the sides of his temples. The same markings she'd briefly seen on Phillip when he walked in.

"Then it began. And we sat down. And on the special train, we went in. And we were in and it was so wonderful. And we walked along the Avenue of the Ascended, and the Nemes Core, and saw the House of Gadd, and then we took this bullet-pod."

Richard bounced on the balls of his feet; his enthusiasm palpable. Georgia was glad Norman was not there to bear it, fearing he would out and out reject Nemerian ideals and resent his brother all the more. She gently shushed Richard as she lifted the stew pot onto the hob. As if summoned by the heat that flooded from the oven, Phillip appeared. He cracked his empty whiskey tumbler on the drainer.

"I'll take that," he said. "Richard. You must be starving. Go on through. Norman. Get down here, now!"

Around the circular table, they sat, Phillip at the head opposite Georgia, with the boys between them facing each other. Their table was so small, Phillip could stir the pot with the ladle without having to lean over. A rich and gamey aroma, one Georgia was confident no one had smelt before, filled the space between them. Phillip, now settled with a topped-up tumbler by his elbow, peered into the pot.

"What on earth is this?"

Georgia gave Norman a half-smile across the table and nodded at him.

"It's a hare," Norman said, then lifted his chin up indignantly, as though to tell his dad to be fucking grateful.

"Hare?" Phillip said, taking a piece of bread and dipping it into the stew. "How on earth did you procure it? I hope you've not been trading with the loutish."

"It's OK, Norman," Georgia said. "Tell your father about the hunt. And the gun."

Phillip's hands stopped moving. His eyes found Norman.

"Philistine?" Richard prompted.

"Aimed at it and shot it."

In that moment, Phillip's attitude towards Norman, soured. Georgia saw it—in the way his eyes narrowed, and his gaze darkened. It was a look she'd never seen before. It made her want to scoop Norman into her arms and protect him from it.

"That is wonderful news" Phillip said, his voice slow, steady, measured. "You saw a weakness in something, and you actually used your innate superiority to take what you wanted."

"Needed," Georgia corrected. "Please, dish up, darling."

Norman beamed. Whatever Phillip thought, Georgia wasn't going to overlook her son's achievement.

"You call that shooting," Richard scoffed. "A stupid hare, with a peasant's pop gun. Over in Nemes, I shot a gun, didn't I, Dad, a real gun, in Uncle Rusty's range. It was a proper Skimgun as well. Silver and gold. No one thought I could do it at first, not Uncle Rusty, and I couldn't, because it was hard."

Phillip was watching him as though hearing the story for the first time.

"I kept missing. It wasn't a stupid hare, but a man made of orange light a mile away. And then Dad, Dad tells me to concentrate on what I hate..."

"No one's really worth hating," Georgia said.

"Well, I hit the orange man first time, next time, took his head off, didn't I, Dad?"

Again, Phillip's expression was one of surprise, as if he was unaware of Richard's victory.

"Yes, you did, son. It was spectacular."

"What did you think of?" Norman asked.

Without skipping a beat, Richard coolly said, "You." He was staring right at Phillip as if they were collaborators and he was waiting for a sign of some sort. This unnerved Georgia, though she was relieved Phillip didn't seem to be encouraging it.

"Well, I don't think that's a very good joke," Georgia said. "Jokes are supposed to be funny. Congratulations for hitting your target, Richard. Now say congratulations to your brother. It seems we have a forest ranger in the making." She glanced at Norman, expecting to see a puffed chest and grin, but instead his shoulders were slumped, and his gaze didn't rise beyond his plate.

"Anyway, what are you going to use these shooting skills for, Norman?" Phillip asked.

"Don't know." He pushed a piece of rabbit around his plate with his fork. "Be a policeman maybe."

Nobody had started eating, it was all about winning at this table but only Phillip and Richard seemed to want to play. Norman just wanted to eat.

"And what about you, Richard," Phillip asked. "After what we saw today, what do you want to be?"

Richard pursed his lips. "Well, *I* want to study at the University of Nemes in Silany. I want to be a scientist, to help society and help the people of Silany understand the people of Nemes."

"Indeed, indeed. A very worthy cause." Phillip was beaming.

Georgia gave a terse smile as she stood up from the table, even though she hadn't touched her stew.

"Sit down," Phillip said quietly, putting his hand firmly on hers. "We've not finished yet." She sensed that Richard's desire had triggered an implicit criticism of her inability to understand Phillip, to connect with him on a deeper level. He had not said it in so many words, but it was there. Richard and Phillip had fused together emotionally in a way that she and Phillip never had. Somewhere inside her, her soul was hurt. The pain had been there all along, numb and dormant until the ageing of the twins had slowly teased it out.

Phillip removed his hand to massage his temples, where the markings were, and turned his jaw slightly.

"Well done today, Norman."

"Thanks, Dad."

CHAPTER 3
Failings of our Father

"Hey, handsome, you up for a bit of fun tonight?" The waitress snapped a lazy wink. With a coy, lopsided smile that stretched easily across her painted face, her husky voice rose steadily above the sound of the Pollen X DJs' bass, until it became distinguishable from the thunderous beat that pulsated through the throng of dancers just behind Phillip's booth. She slid another whiskey across the table to him and hooked her fingers under his collar, stroking him gently as she loosened it for him. He loved it. "There, now," she crooned. "That feels much better now, doesn't it? Aren't you feeling much more relaxed...?"

The titian-blonde cocktail waitress was not just a waitress. He'd worked that out already. She had other revenue streams, and he desperately wanted to support them. This was a place he could do that. Like nowhere else, it was here that he could do what he wanted, like a true Nemerian. A man unchained. She was to him a love goddess from an island so remote that even the elite of Nemes could lay no claim to it. Born into the upper echelons of sublimity, power, seduction, she looked at least twenty years younger than Georgia. In fact, she looked a little like Georgia had looked once, but only once. On that night Georgia had been at that party, talking about his mother. It had been enough to get him into bed. But now, Georgia talked in a dead language, there was nothing exotic or erotic about it. There was no surge to it. No heat. It was just Silany and their horse shit. Oh, but this girl made him feel himself, his true self. The heat. The flame of wonder, of passion. Her golden frame had an almost hypnotic effect on him. Even the memory of it was enough to send a rush of warmth through him, his pulse quickening until he felt himself explode and then quiver. Today, he found himself wanting nothing more than to feel her warmth against him, to trace the soft curve of her form. He had given too much ground to Georgia, too much of himself. Too much of his light. His Potential. And so he had recognised finally that he had betrayed himself. And now to reclaim himself and a semblance of his True Nemerian Potential, this is where it was at, here in this den. He knew it because he had visualised it again and again. Now he was here to live it out.

Up on the stage of Pollen X, her colleague moved: a lithe and lissom stripper with purple tits and the stage name, Miki-KK. Gyrating to the pulse, jazz, and percussions of a Silanese house track, under a blue light, she was to him an enchanting temptress, not good enough to be his type, but good enough to watch. She slipped her fingers into the hem of her cream knickers and started sliding them over her hips. Phillip dragged his eyes away for a moment to listen to the waitress, no longer imagining himself dominating her. Everything was muffled, a gentle murmur in spite of all the noise. He must have sunk half a bottle of brown already, but this was his right, what he was put into the world to do.

"I'm Jessi, slip that ring off your finger, love, and I can be your friend." She was the golden girl, so he took less than one ten thousandth of a second to decide they'd be *best of friends*.

By now, she had huddled up next to him on his seat and flung one leg over his. He wheedled off his wedding band and dropped it in his drink.

"My wife...She was beautiful once, now she's old and decrepit."

"You're not that old. You married an older woman? Why?"

"My intentions were to Ascend. Hers weren't. If she had been duteous, I would have gone up, taken the great step upwards. But even though I gave that all up, sacrificed it all to trust her, to trust us, she breached the contract and broke my trust. She doesn't want to be around me. She's more interested in our children than in me. And that's not how it works."

Jessi kissed him on the forehead. "How could she be more interested in them than in you? You're a king."

"She doesn't love me; I don't think she ever loved me" he said, woefully.

"I can make all of that go away, love."

Why live a little when you can live a lot?

"Ah, the rich red wine of the medium of exchange," Phillip muttered and eventually slipped into a gentle sleep.

"I am all yours, love."

*

At school the following Monday, Phillip slipped into a toilet cubicle at lunch time and let out a gush of piss. The pain was excruciating. He cursed as he winced. He'd had the pain for the past couple of weeks and was also finding it hard to concentrate for more than a few minutes at a time. Had he not been loaded up on whisky, he'd have lost consciousness by now due to the intensity of the pain. Inevitably, being drunk in school was proving increasingly hard to hide. Only in the last lesson, he had been explaining the theory of the Efficient Market Hypothesis to his senior class, when he suddenly became aware that he had blacked out for a short time. When he'd eventually come back to consciousness, the class was staring at him. The best of them were baffled and the worst sniggered.

While Phillip was washing his hands, his colleague Dr. Mani, Head of Maths, came out of the near cubicle and used the soap dispenser at the other sink.

"It sounded like you were in some pain in there."

"Really?" Phillip said, with feigned nonchalance.

"I also had a problem downstairs recently, so I know what it's like. The quicker you get to the docs, the better."

"Certainly worth getting checked out." Phillip was not convinced he had a urine infection, but it would make sense. His dick felt like it was on fire.

Stepping out into the wood-panelled corridor, Mani glanced around to check no-one was listening and then leaned over and whispered. "A couple of weeks ago, I was initiated into the Last Link of the FoA." He raised his eyebrows.

"I see," Phillip said, trying to keep his voice light. The Last Link of the Friends of Ascent. You were practically Ascended if you were Last Link. It was like sitting in the waiting room for a train that was scheduled to come. Phillip had tried to get into that waiting room for over twenty years.

"They won't let you in," Mani continued, "if you have a urinary tract issue."

"I'm sure they have a more rigorous criterion than that." Then again, looking at Mani, maybe standards had slipped again. They let Artie in and Phillip knew for a fact that he had bowel syndrome. June had told Georgia that. But she had said it differently—"his guts don't work." First Artie, now Mani, a fraud who had wormed his way in without investing a quarter of what Phillip had.

He tried to stand up to his full height but struggled to look down on Dr. Mani. *I'll show you bastards who's yellow. I'm not yellow–I'm fucking silver. I can use my mind in ways you CAN'T. I'll sort out the urinary issues. This is my business, anyway. Screw you all.*

Just like Phillip, Mani was said to be half-Nemerian, half-Silanese: a One-Half. Somehow, the Friends of Ascent had seen the Potential of Mani, but Phillip had not been invited into the Last Link. Why? What was wrong with him? Wasn't he earnest enough? Wasn't he dedicated enough to the cause? Nonsense! He was the most dedicated Ascender he had ever known.

Phillip's voice wavered and sounded hoarse as he tried to express an interest in Mani's success. He couldn't focus completely, not while his balls felt like they had been chopped off and his insides like they were being pierced by a fanged spider. "Tell me, what was that was like?"

"Oh, I'm not allowed to go into details of the ceremony, but within a few months my genes will be...anyway, it will all be confirmed by the testing. They'll add at least 50 years to my natural life span, and that's just the start." Mani's balding forehead was sweating profusely, and he shifted from one foot to another with excitement.

"How wonderful for you," Phillip said, his voice flat as a numbness took root in his heart and spread rapidly throughout his body.

That same evening, instead of going back home to his studies, Phillip felt a stir in his soul that pulled him towards Pollen X. The drugs he'd popped had dulled the pain, which had now moved to his lower back and head, and he was suddenly desperate for a gentle massage. Jessi soon lay on his chest, stroking his hair. He took her hands and turned them over in his own.

"You could be a pianist with hands like these."

"I can play with you," Jessi said, "whenever you like, love."

He slipped a small roll of notes onto her palm. Her fingers closed over the notes. So, now it was merely a toss-up between Ascenders Meetings and Jessi, the golden one. He was about to be accepted into the Last Link. He wanted to tell Jessi this, but he thought better of it—maybe she wouldn't want to know, given the nature of their relationship. Transactional. Clean. Ordered. Like in Nemes.

*

"How frequently do you drink alcohol?" The doctor glanced up from her clipboard.

"Not frequently," Phillip replied.

She raised her eyebrows. "How many drinks have you had today?"

Sighing, he averted his eyes. "Not much."

"Mr Wise. This is serious. The Virex 5-OQ is a brain disease—it's caused by a toxic liver, and drinking heavily is..."

"How the devil did this happen to me?"

"We're not sure how it is picked up. Research is being conducted in Nemes but they're not sharing their findings with us. The bottomline—You need a healthy liver to cleanse the Virex parasite from the brain. It's spread by human contact and the drug..."

"So, someone did this to me?"

"I doubt they did it on purpose, Mr Wise. And as I say, we know very little about this particular strain, but your blood tests indicate..."

Phillip interrupted the doctor again, raising his voice this time. "Well, isn't there anything you can do?"

"I'll prescribe you something to help manage the symptoms, but I'm afraid it won't cure the disease. In ninety per cent of the cases we have treated, we have observed patients lose their grasp on reality and their mental health decline rapidly. Your best chance of beating the disease is to receive treatment in Nemes. I'm sorry that I couldn't give you better news. I'll give you a few resources that explain more about the disease, which you can read in your own time."

*

It was early for Pollen X when Phillip shuffled in. No one was dancing yet. Ambient tunes played in the background and the faint scent of disinfectant lingered in the air around the only two bodies that were slumped at the bar. It bemused him that he was here, like a moth to a flame, he'd sought her out. After the doctor's, he'd cancelled his afternoon class to have a good cry. He hadn't intended to spend hours in Bar Tak Tak and, after they'd forced him to find another watering hole, the Maven's Head. A tumbler of brown, he lined them up, one, two, a dozen, more. Virex 5—the name rang in his ear with each sip, burrowing its way into his skull, and squatting in his brain like that insectoid bitch.

She was sat at the bar, in the short pink leather dress that acted as a waitress's uniform, her back to him as he marched towards her. Golden girl, how could she? This was the bitch who gave him the brain bug. He knew it "cause she was scum." A puffy-faced blonde man, no doubt a degenerate who would pay for sex was laughing at something she'd just said. *Probably about me,* Phillip thought. He came between them and poked Puffy Face hard in the shoulder, causing him to almost topple over from his stool.

"Listen you male prick, you may think she's going to fuck the brains out of you, but she's going to rot the brains out of you!"

"Phillip...what the..."

"Geddoffame, twatbollocks, I bloody work here." Puffy's eyes glared. He steadied himself and took a step forward and then a step backwards as if he'd changed his mind.

"Leave him alone," Jessi said. "He works the bar. He's my friend. What has gotten into you?"

"What did you do to me, you, you bitch!"

Jessi's expression remained calm. Apparently verbal bashings didn't come as a shock to her. "They'll throw you out."

"I should kill you for what you did to me." It was his hand, though it felt like it wasn't, that clawed at her. She jerked her head back.

"You fucked this poison into my head."

"You're drunk, mate."

"Virex, you gave it to me. You ruined...evvvryything!"

Jessi's head cocked, a smirk tugging at the corners of her small mouth. "Sweetie, I can't have. I'm as clean as a packet of chocolate treats. I'm tested every week. I'd never—'

Phillip felt his knees sag. His eyes grew hot. and he felt the tears cool on his cheeks even before the blow struck him from behind and he flew past Jessi. His knees slammed against the tiles with a thump and his head struck the foot bar. Somewhere deep inside him he still had the wherewithal to summon up the clear and clanging thought that he was going to Ascend, if he'd not actually Ascended, if he wasn't safely Ascended in Nemes, and this was just a nightmare he was having inside his new life there. In Nemes, he was having a nightmare about his old life in Silany, the sinkholes and fleshpots he'd had to frequent. It was entirely possible, he realised. Hold up, is that not how the mind works? He didn't have time to consider it.

The bouncer, who's head was a bald boulder atop a granite pillar, aimed the wide sole of his boot and hit Phillip square in the forehead. Jessi screamed.

"The lady says no, John."

They carried him out by his hands and feet and, swinging once, twice and thrice, tossed him into the street like a bag of rubbish. He rolled onto his back as he lay in the gutter and saw stars. If it wasn't the whore who had given him the death worm, it must have been his shabby slut of a wife.

*

"How could you do this to me?" Phillip hissed at Dr. Mani as they walked out of Radom High. For Phillip, it was the very last time. He held limply onto the formal notice slip. "This job was my life!" He could barely breathe.

"Didn't you always say to me: when one falls, another rises? I guess I have been putting your wisdom into practice, my friend." Mani patted Phillip on the back and unveiled a smirk.

"You snake," Phillip hissed, turning around and walking away without a second glance. His whole body throbbed with anger and the humiliation at hearing his colleague use his own words against him. Every member of staff knew that there was a financial shortfall in the school's budget, that money was tight. But did they come to Phillip, did they take advantage of his extraordinary understanding of economies and how to maximise resources? Did the Dean come to Phillip and ask him to draw up a plan to use innovative entrepreneurial techniques and latent semi-Nemerian intellect to generate more? No. Instead, Mani had used the handycam on his phone to record Phillip necking a few whiskey shots here and there. Admittedly he'd done this load of times, but still, what was the harm in downing a few shots? The shortfall was going to be made up by sacking Phillip and giving his classes to a cheaper, sober teacher who wouldn't come to school with what looked like a boot print on his face.

The boys must have left school half an hour earlier, and Phillip didn't have to concern himself with them. The whole way home, he replayed the recent events in his mind and agonised over how he could tell Georgia about the sudden loss in income. Above all this, a violent hatred for Dr. Mani spurted acid between gritted teeth. Mani was the "near perfect" being who had turned brute on him, and there was absolutely nothing he could do about it. He was only three quarters of the way to the summit, he was knocked out of the running, tumbling right down to the bottom.

By the time he arrived home, weak and tremulous, Phillip had worked out what he was going to say to Georgia so that he didn't have to actually see her or face her sickening sympathy when she found out.

Dear Georgia,

I am no longer an employee at the school due to the betrayal of a colleague. Please do me the honour of not seeking after me tonight as I am ashamed. It will not affect the boys unduly and they can continue at the school despite my absence.

I will try my best to find another job, but nobody is going to give me one because I will be unable to get a good reference unless I forge one, and that would be beneath me.

Yours truly,
Phillip

*

Knowing that Phillip wanted to be left alone, Georgia took a deep breath and shut down every impulse to seek him out. She was sure he was hiding somewhere in the house, at least for today, but she respected his wishes.

Half an hour later, she lay flat on her back on the sofa, swinging her left arm loosely in rhythm with *Notes Made While Falling* by Night Shadows Beautiful. The letterbox clattered as the twins poured into the house. At fourteen, they were now so full of energy they didn't know their own strength.

"Don't push me, philistine," Richard moaned, getting up off the floor.

"Come on, bro."

"Boys!" Georgia called out into the hallway, before their argument could escalate into a full-blown fight. "Come here, please."

A sharp twinge of pain shot up her lower back. She sat up, her arm reaching behind her to rub the sensitive spot warm in slow, circular motions. Georgia was a good 15 years older than most of their peers' mums. She was two years away from turning 60 and had grown used to the dull ache that now settled in her lower back after a full day of being on her feet at the cafe.

The twins growled and hissed at each other before sidling into the lounge, their faces flush from running and tussling. Richard perched on the chair nearest the door, and Norman plonked himself cross-legged on the floor, the muscles of his back protruding through his fitted white vest. Unlike Richard, Norman was practically a man, comfortable within himself. *Such a philistine*, Richard's face seemed to say. His body hadn't yet become athletic.

"Your father has lost his job," Georgia said. Norman seemed unphased. Just get another job, the bounce of his shoulders suggested. Richard was frozen.

"But he's a genius," Richard murmured.

Norman gave Richard a questioning look.

"I'm afraid I don't know all the details, but he says it was partly his fault and partly someone else's. You know what this means for us as a family, right?"

Richard lowered his head, as Norman responded. "We'll have to walk on eggshells around him till he gets a new one. Will we have enough to eat, Mum?"

"I don't know, I honestly don't," she said. She couldn't bring herself to lie to them. "But you boys can help me out around here, can't you?" She gave a wavering smile, trying to instil a sense of purpose in them. "You can help me with working out a tight budget—to think about what we really need and what are just luxuries."

"Where is Father? I want to talk to him now." Richard blurted. To find out that Phillip had lost his livelihood and most likely his chance to Ascend must have been a crushing betrayal of everything Phillip had taught Richard. He leapt up out of his chair and started to pace.

Georgia approached Richard and put one arm on a shoulder.

"Please respect your father's wishes. He just needs some time and space to himself right now. If you go barging in, who knows what it might do to his mind?"

"What about *my* mind?" Richard yelled and bounded out of the room, his stomping footsteps shaking the floorboards.

Sombre, Georgia and Norman looked at one another. She lowered her hands in the air slowly, indicating to Norman that he should give his brother time to calm down, but Norman showed no sign of wanting to help his brother.

That evening, Georgia found Phillip slumped in his green swivel chair in his study, spinning around and around with a tumbler loosely gripped in one hand and a whisky on the thigh of his grey slacks. She wrenched the tumbler from his hand, and he returned the favour by trying to tell her where she could stick it. "Can' you...le'... a man...enjoy...a d ...drrinkk?"

"You've had more than enough, Phillip. Boys, help me carry him up to his bed."

Half an hour later, with Phillip snoring in bed, Georgia came back downstairs to clear up the mess in the study. Scattered on the floor near Phillip's chair were pages of yellowing paper, ripped around the edges. Picking them up, she glanced at the words and her heart jolted. They were pages from The Manifesto. She held her hand up close to her throat and shed a tear. As much as she hated The Manifesto and everything it stood for, she knew what this meant for her husband. He had given up the fight. Now something else had to fill this void. *Perhaps, this time he'd choose the family.*

*

Sometime later Phillip woke up, yelling and screaming like he had pitched over an edge and was hurtling through a void. Georgia could make out a few words like library, mind and delete. She rushed up the stairs and poked her head around his door.

"Are you alright?"

"Why wouldn't I be, woman?"

"You were screaming."

"You put this in me, you did, you whore."

He leapt out of bed and raised his arm high. "Bitch!" he yelled as he struck her sharp across the face. Her body turned away from him at the hips but she didn't speak. Her legs found a foothold. She dug her feet in and turned to face him. Again, his hand cut across her face. She did not move this time. She just breathed and steeled herself for the next strike. Heat surged through her body, rising to her neck until it finally settled in her chest. Finally, his palm connected with her head, his wrist slamming into her ear...

She hit the floor with a sickening thud, and for a worrying second, she lay completely still and did not make a sound. Soon after, she rolled onto her back to find him towering over her, his chest heaving, the veins in his neck like coiled snakes, ready to spring.

With nostrils flared, she drew in her breath, filled her lungs and screamed. It was like something primal and desperate and unexpected.

"Who's screaming now?" he sneered.

She shuffled slowly, edging away from him until her back connected with the doorframe. Struggling to her feet, she turned on her heel and ran. "Get away!" Georgia whimpered, retreating slowly to her room and locking the door.

The following morning, Norman burst into the kitchen to give Georgia a quick "goodbye" before she left for work. She was bent down over the oven grill when he called out to say, "hey Mum, have a good day..." As he approached her, she clumsily tried to angle herself so he wouldn't see, but not before he caught a glimpse of the blue-back bruise across her face.

"Mum?" he asked her. "What...happened?"

"I fell," she lied. She knew her son, she knew he wasn't convinced. He had turned into a lie detector out there on the streets. His penchant for the truth often got him into scraps with the Chesser brothers and trading blows with Farmer Roger and his sons. He was streetwise now and could smell a lie from a mile away.

"It was him, wasn't it?"

The muscles in her cheeks twitched and she nodded slightly, turning to reveal the true extent of the damage Phillip had caused. The right side of her face was a dark ink. Norman's eyes misted over.

Georgia's expression softened and she cupped Norman's cheek. She couldn't bring herself to say the words, but she knew by his hardened gaze that he understood he was right.

School bag on shoulders, Richard stepped into the kitchen. His eyes flitted immediately to Georgia's hand on Norman's cheek and his lip curled. He looked so much like his father, so disapproving. She waited for him to say "philistine" but he said nothing and turned away.

*

Phillip flicked the edge of the business card with the tip of his finger and knocked on the door with the blacked-out windows. The night's darkness was heavy and steamy all around him after the short downpour. He glimpsed a persistent drip from a cracked gutter splattered on the tarpaulin covering a battered old pick-up truck.

The door opened a crack and a man in a black hooded tracksuit and a deeply-lined, slate-grey face peered out. Phillip held the business card up in front of his eyes and was beckoned inside. The room had sagging yellow patches on the ceiling and peeling paint hanging off the walls. There lingered a musty smell, like cat's pee, mingled with tobacco.

It was the ultimate insult stooping to this level. But, hey, on the bright side he'd be in Nemes tomorrow. *Stoop to conquer.*

"Look, I know this place is set up like we're Resistors," Slate-Grey told him, "But that's all part of the game we play. That okay with you, Mr?"

"Listen, Grey, I haven't got time to play games, I want out. I must Ascend. And we're talking days. I was meant to anyway, but it got snatched away from me by a..."

"Of course," Slate-Grey, replied. He'd seen it all.

"Don't look at me like that. I'm not one of these aspiring academic lawns mowing beard groomers you know. Since Bogod died you guys have had all the business. Don't think I don't know what the fuck goes on here. But I'm not one of those guys, okay?"

"Look, friend, I don't care who you are. I just get people into Nemes. What have you got for me?"

Patting his pockets to indicate that they were empty, he said, "I have my family fund—the money I was going to leave to my boy. He's a smart and driven Ascender, though. He won't need it. In fact, I'll be greasing his elbows and doing him a favour."

Saying this out loud made him feel light-headed. He found himself sinking... into dark water. The next thing he knew, his arm was being shaken and his knee slapped.

"Eh...what was that?" he said, grimacing as he raised his head.

"I lost you there for a moment," Slate-Grey said. He sat down with a sigh.

"Ah, that happens to me sometimes," Phillip said, trying to sound nonchalant. "Let's just say if I decide that this, that...Ascending is more important to me than anything else right now, how would I go about it? If my life depended on it? For medical reasons I mean?"

Slate-Grey smiled. "We do business. Then I play with your genes like they're plasticine."

*

Approaching the bulk of the Fal, Phillip felt the same reverence as always. It was a mystical thing to him, something more than a work of art. A passage of ethereal beauty, one made of precious stones by the greatest intellects.

Richard has the potential to be one of those intellects, he thought, slipping the photo of his protégé back into his wallet. *One day, I'll see Richard on the other side.*

Phillip craned his head to peer across to the side, but even with his neck outstretched, the top of the wall was hidden, and almost obstructed the sun. The wall glistened, as though made of ice, the sunlight reflecting off the Etronium, causing Phillip to squint. A camera on his right twitched and trained on him.

His mouth went dry. In his hand, he rolled the metal strip that contained his unique code over and over. It would allow him safe passage through the Fal-Nex checkpoint. Until he had gone through, he could not be fully certain that he had Ascended. Slate-Grey had explained it all, and it was exactly what Phillip needed to hear. Phillip relaxed a little. He knew he could trust him. Slate-Grey even offered him a white powder called Dream Sprinkle for free, to numb the pain and encourage the time to fly. Phillip had drifted off to sleep while Slate did his work, into an astral land of buttercups where dolphins throned giant purple chairs on a beach the colour of ice. He was a total pro and even played sea music during the surgery, which Phillip did not recall. That's how good Slate-Grey was.

The Fal-Nex was near the southern end of the vast stone panopticon, one of three entry points at Pano's Watch. It was not the main trade vent, where Slate-Grey sent him, but a black slit in the wall between Silany and Nemes. What it was used for, Phillip did not know. Only Silanese citizens with Nemerian heritage were allowed through with special licences or invitations, like the one Rusty arranged that day. On this occasion though, Slate-Grey had assured Phillip that he was not entering with a temporary pass, he was going in for good. He was now, by definition, Nemerian.

The entrance was heavily guarded by the tall Nemes security guards with their black and gold body armour and stubby, nasty-looking Skimguns. The guards, known informally as Mortalizers, were said to be sons of the bread-in-the-bone Nemerians standing up for what they believed in: the future. They stood at the edge of the line that separated the past from future. And this was that line. And when you had crossed over, you were no longer Silanese.

"I am Nemerian," he whispered, and he strode across the obsidian-black concourse, his confidence growing with each step. "I am. I am. I am." Smiling, he thought of his pathetic past life—the chaotic slum of Silany—he put it all behind him now as he faced true north. *How simple Georgia is. Not even worth a goodbye. Good riddance to bad rubbish.*

Mortalizers nodded in seeming approval and acceptance. They knew what he was as he passed them. "Yes, I am," he stated aloud to no one in particular.

Inside Fal-Nex was a line of twenty or so scan-booths manned by black-suited Mortalizers with short, ant-like antennae on their headsets. There was ambient music, accompanied with soothing chimes that pulsated through the air and made Phillip smile.

He approached a central scan-booth, nodded at the visored Mortalizer in his plexiglass cubicle, and ran his code key under a violet scanner-wand. Heart thumping, Phillip stepped forward. Almost immediately, the blue-tinted barrier ahead swished open.

The concourse on the other side was wider, vaster, and complete with long polished walkways with cascading tiers that seemed to be made of solid light. Phillip glanced from side-to-side trying to figure out which way he needed to go to find a transit point. He needed a transit to get to Rusty's compound. He'd never been there but he'd heard all about it. Heard so much about it he could darn well see it. Rusty could supply him with all the other things he needed. And Rusty was in Nemes these days, wasn't he? Rusty, who used to be called Torsten Job at school, could provide Phillip with a Nemerian job in Rusty's cyber-manufacturing business, and perhaps somewhere to live. Certainly a palatial apartment of the future, unsullied by guttural music and the peasant cavorting of Georgia's dancing; quiet without the constant noise of teenage boys. He had fifty, sixty more years of youth ahead of him now. He was younger and fresher and fuller than he'd felt in that tart, Jessi's arms. The Virex parasite will be flushed from his system, he will Ascend, and his life will finally start.

An electric jolt slammed against his neck. He jolted. And then he fell forward, crashing onto the marble floor and faded into blackness.

*

A craggy-faced man dressed in black and red body armour loomed over him. He was a Faj op—Nemerian secret police. Phillip was sprawled in some featureless marble room. No chair, no furniture at all, just a floor that beamed white. His knees and elbows smarted. A thicker, second officer in the same Faj uniform approached him from the other side, tapping his baton against Phillip's knee-high varnished boots.

"How very dare you," Phillip said. "I demand to see your superior..." Even as he said it, he knew that he had been *conned*. His voice was unconvincing. Phillip's spine tingled and he began to sweat profusely. Slate-Grey had played him and now his head was in the noose. He pissed his pants.

"Your code is corrupt," Craggy-Face said. "Your thoughts are impure. Our satellites can see your envy glowing from space."

Phillip's words exited in a jumble. "Officer, I have a brain disease. I think I have been the victim of a cruel deception."

Two hours later, Phillip sat handcuffed to a table in another marble-walled room, nursing what was, sadly, a cup of the best coffee he had ever tasted. His balls were itching in a rash now from the damp piss and he caught a glimpse of his own face in the back door mirror. He looked like a lunatic, an unhinged maniac or homeless alien from planet Nopus. Weirdly, he liked it. Craggy-Face was perched on the table while Thick-Boned leaned back in his chair, hands behind his head.

"Can you tell us the name of the man you claim took your money?"

"I don't know his real name." Phillip spread his hands. He had nothing to offer them.

Craggy-Face swiped a tired hand over his face. "For fucks' sake, help me out, here." He glanced at Thick-Boned with a sigh, his shoulders slumping.

Phillip bristled. "What do you expect from me?"

Craggy-Face suddenly banged his fist on the table, sending a pile of papers flying. He pinned Phillip with a glare, his earlier discontentment now magnified. He meant business.

"I don't know his real name, but I can tell you exactly what he looked like and where he can be found." Phillip took out the dog-eared business card with the moniker "Red Fish" on it along with the address.

Both men examined the card. Then they glanced at each other and chuckled.

"Regardless!" Craggy-Face said, his tone filling with condescension, "whether you were duped or not, you have committed a serious offence against the Faj. Stealing your way into Nemes and impersonating an

Ascended is not only criminal, but childish. We are putting out a warrant for your arrest. You will be arrested...in three days."

Phillip sat back as far as he could in his seat, his head pounding incessantly from the tasering. The muscles in his back were rigid as steel and his shoulders still ached from the fall. He knew there was no escaping such a warrant. Nemerian surveillance was, basically, omnipotent.

"Just arrest me now, please," he said, trembling. "That would be better than the other..." Seeing Georgia, the boys. Returning to face charges. Resuming unemployment. It was more humiliation than he could bear. His final hope snuffed out. His eyes drifted over to his reflection again. And he couldn't help but pity himself. "I think I've gone the wrong way." He spoke in an eery manner.

"We are not here to make your life easier. For this level of crime, that's the price you must pay."

"What about "Red-Fish"? Is he going to get away with it?" Phillip spit out, a last-ditch attempt to grasp onto any tendrils of hope.

The officers glanced at each other. Thick-Boned shrugged. "We'll send out a warrant for his arrest, too, though these smugglers are constantly on the move."

"How come you can't track his thoughts?"

"There will be a reckoning, we can assure you."

"Please, help me."

Confused, they eventually replied. "You are not a Nemerian."

"I am..."

"Time's up."

"Oh no."

"We'll escort you out. We'll see you in three days. Take care of any business you have to. And remember, your ass is toast."

*

It was two a.m. in the Bituva district of NEXUS-10. About a metre away from the door of the Cat in the Sack pleasure den, Phillip sat up in the chill air and couldn't for the life of him understand why he was still alive. Clambering to his feet, he swayed a little and watched as his breath came out in puffs before he stamped his feet. He shoved his hands into his pockets and went numb once it finally registered that all his money was gone and there was no way he could get any more. Not just tonight, but again, ever. He'd gone hell for leather, for the whisky, after they dumped him out onto the Fal-Nex concourse for all of Silany to see. There had been girls, a kaleidoscope of lips and tits and thighs and his money slipped under their straps and hemlines. How many girls? Three-four-five? One was painted lizard green with legs like a mantis and a tongue like an anteater. He headed in the direction of Port Maw Road. It was a long walk home, but he had no money to pay for a ride. It started to snow.

Having blacked out twice on the way home and bashed his head once when falling on the ground, Phillip was relieved to reach the darkened haven of his family home. When he opened the front door, warmth hit him.

He winced when taking off his shoes, his feet raw from walking. He struggled upstairs to his bedroom, where Georgia was already asleep. It was less than three hours before the boys would be getting up to go to school. Whether or not he slept in that time was irrelevant. Life would go on around him and he would spiral even further downward into his sinkhole and in three days Nemerian Services would find him and do what they did to criminals, study them while experimenting on them. It was a person's final way to be of service, according to the book.

He was exhausted yet he found no escape in sleep. No more dreams, please God, no more. But images and accusations pummelled him like merciless storm winds. "Phillip, Phillip. You promised so much. Look at me now." The word "look" was a lashing whip. He saw Georgia's cheek and on it, the bruise, a stark blueberry colour against her otherwise milk-coloured skin. "Look at me now!" He was staring at a mirror and in the mirror, he was shrinking into Richard. He continued to watch until Richard grew old and bloated, his shape losing form until it became a blob that lay in a heaped on the floor. The dreams had just begun. And though he was in his room, his scholar's cell, in his dreams, he was also inside the Fal. He was standing at the centre of the Panopticon, on a higher level than he had ever experienced. He looked around him, peering through the dark frames of prison door after prison door that circled him. Suddenly, he would hear screeching and moaning as lizard-monsters spilled out from numerous doors and slithered their way towards him. Phillip would feel their hot, stagnant breath on him as they closed in. They were serpent-like creatures, with bodies that squelched the closer they got to him. They were the girl with the lizard-green body paint and mantis legs and anteater tongue. As the serpents inched closer, one would coil itself up ready to spring and sink its fangs into Phillip.

They are not real, yet they are. They are the outworking of my failing, parasite-ridden psyche. Yet, as soon as he tried to close his eyes again, their faces and Georgia's injuries would loom before him, and his heart would thump hard against his ribcage.

Before he knew it, he would find himself tidying the bookshelves in his study again in a trance-like state. *"My envy is visible from space. I am a monster; I am a beast."* The voice in his head was loud. It was going to take one hell of a slap to silence it. To quell that rage, to calm it.

He opened the cabinet easily, having assumed that it would be more difficult to open. Suddenly, the shotgun had a real shine to it.

RICH

CHAPTER 4
The Colour of Money

Bouncing on the balls of his feet, Richard paced restlessly back and forth in his corner of the ring. Theo, the clingy suck up, was still chortling and praising Norman on the shine of his gloves. Richard hadn't needed a tagalong like Theo to flatter him. Besides, he knew he had the better gloves anyway. He wasn't necessarily as fast as Norman, but no matter—he was naturally the better boxer, or at least he deserved to be. When he was older, he was going to fight in noble crusades for the highest of purposes, like a knight on a white charger armed with a Skimgun when Norman would no doubt become the sort of lunkhead who'd fight in bars *because someone insulted an idiot for being an idiot.* Norman was an idiot. Theo was an idiot. Someone would reasonably point this out and Norman would start a fight over it. Unless he was careful, Richard already knew he could be marooned here in the world of peasant squabbles and the dreary, endless Silanese sadness.

Talking of idiots, Norman and Theo were still pissing about, giggling about something or other while Richard could hardly contain himself, full of expectation. There was no one else in the clubroom. He could do what he liked to it. It was crap. Old, tawdry and cheap in comparison with where he had been and what he had done. He had once shot a Skimgun in a gallery beneath a glass pyramid. Though his memory of that day in Nemes was diminishing, it was definitely what happened. The thinning of the image was just his mind telling him it was time for another trip. A trip away from here. And this clubhouse. He could set fire to the dump and someone from over there would give him a medal, or ideally, ascension points.

Norman was grinning like a pumpkin cut for the Day of Ghosts. Richard's fist twitched. His right arm wanted to swing. He wouldn't spare Norman today. They would fight properly. He needed something to fight, and Norman had suggested his brother needed a little exercise today. Richard didn't need exercise; he needed to fight. He remembered Nemes again, where thinking of Norman's boy-scout head had guided his shot. And he was even more angry today than he was then.

He was angry with Norman for getting him out of bed to come down here and spar in this filthy pit. Angry with Theo for paying for the session because neither of the Wise boys had any money now. Theo wasn't even his friend, he was Norman's, who had to be such a nice guy that he couldn't have cool friends; they had to be milksops and spanners. He was angry that Norman didn't act sad that Father had died; angry that Norman had never said he was going to track down and kill everyone who had set Father up and humiliated him. He was angry that Mother was wandering around like some sort of forgetful cow, leaving her trash and trinkets all over the place—in the oven, in the fridge. He was angry that the heating was only on for an hour a day and that he had to freeze his walnuts off for the rest of the time. He was angry that all those Salon women who used to flatter and brown-nose Mother now shunned her like she was shamed and dirty. He was angry that Silany was the graveyard of history, the dustbowl of ambition. If you looked up "shithole" in the dictionary, it read "Silany." Norman was so soft and kind and decent—a *nobody*—that he didn't even notice any of this.

Theo stepped away. Norman was finally ready and nipped forward, smiling, ridiculously happy, as if something good was about to happen. They bumped gloves and Theo rang the bell.

What did Father always say? "Nature is red in tooth and claw." Richard's first jab should have put Norman down for the count at least. Yet, strangely, Norman had the temerity to jerk back his head whilst keeping his chin tucked, landing a left-handed blow on Richard's chin, which was wide open. Richard didn't see it coming. He was too busy looking into Norman's eyes and imagining the lights going out as his kind-hearted brother collapsed and hit the deck. Too little, too late, Richard raised his gloves and pressed them together to protect his face. He circled round and found a gap. Norman was expressionless, like his mind was on something else, and this seemed impertinent. It was maddening, un-Wise even, to Richard. He attempted another strike, but his punch didn't connect. Norman took a sidestep and with one sharp jab pummelled Richard's ribs. Somehow, he knew that jab could have been harder. Richard's knees buckled, more out of surprise than anything else, and flailing helplessly, fell backwards against the ropes. The bell rang a second time. Round One.

Round Two was even better, as Richard found himself nimbler, more mobile, better prepared maybe, but he couldn't land the killer blow. Norman started to scamper behind him, making great looping runs around the ring like he didn't really want to fight, nor did he need to. Then just before the bell rang, he got in a couple of light jabs just under Richard's eye, again glancing and powerless, yet enough to gain the points he needed in this round. He was going to win, unless Richard took him down in the deciding third.

The second the bell rang for the final time, Richard threw a sly feint to the left and with his right launched a right hook, which, in his mind, should have trailed a comet's tail because it was so fast and brutal. Yet, Norman somehow managed to duck and then bearhug Richard so neither twin could punch the other. Was this some kind of joke to him? Horseplay. If Father had been here, he would have been appalled. An image of Father on his own and with a gun came up in a flash. *Father should have been there.* Fuelled by this thought, Richard's knee suddenly jerked up like a piston and connected with Norman's groin. Well, actually, his kneecap struck the inside of Norman's thigh, but it was enough to topple him backwards and cause him to land with a thump onto the mat, still laughing. Richard raised his gloves, poised, waiting for Norman to get to his feet so he could land the killer blow.

Theo, on the other hand, who was red-faced and clearly bent out of shape, hunched over and swiped his palms, one across the other.

"Disqualified," he said. "Foul play."

"Don't be a moron," Richard said. "Start the count."

"Foul play. You used your knee."

"No, I didn't."

"I saw you, Richard."

By now, Norman had gotten to his feet, "it doesn't matter."

"You can't win like that," Theo said. "It's cheating."

"He knows I could have won," Norman said. "That's enough for me."

"The angels are brutes," Richard said.

"No, they're not." Norman ripped off his vest and wiped his face with it. Richard took a step towards him and for a moment it was unclear whether he was going to apologise or restart the fight. But the moment passed, and he quickly turned back to his corner, hanging his arms wide across the rope, posed serenely like some sort of all-conquering emperor.

"Sorry, brother," he said.

"You missed my head anyway."

"Only this time."

"You Wise boys look like you're not getting enough to eat," Theo said. "Café's open upstairs. Bacon sandwich? On me?"

"No," they both responded.

*

When they returned home from the clubhouse, their mother was doing it again. Norman just stood and stared at her in the dining room. Richard sank into the armchair, defeated. At least the armchair was still here, even though their father was gone. His ribs and shoulders ached, but he refused to acknowledge them. They watched their mother's head arch and plunge as she attempted ballet exercises on her own, with no barre, or music. She used to dance to music, but they didn't have a player anymore, or any records for that matter. She wore rubber gloves and her waitress apron and looked more like she was practising a comedy sketch. She was in one of her trances. Norman clapped.

"Mum," he said. "You've still got the moves!"

Richard sighed. No, she didn't. What a suck-up Norman was. Normal Norman, so boring and annoying.

Their mother suddenly loosened. She crossed her arms and started to talk to the pair of them as if she had been talking to them all along.

"I didn't want to. I had to. We couldn't justify keeping them any longer..."

"What are you going on about now?" Richard asked her.

"Your father's books, Richard. I sold them all."

"What? Bullshit! His history books? Of *NE-MEZ*? They were for me. He was collecting them for *me*." Some people still called Ne-Mez, *Nemes* but they shouldn't. Instead, they should study history and understand the truth. Only the unloved, foolish, and hateful sell books and talk of history as kindergarten brats. Nemes will always be pronounced Ne-Mez, even though some people didn't know how to speak properly. She was so disrespectful when she pronounced it wrongly.

"Richard." Norman was trying to play good cop again with his take-it-easy gaze. Okay, Mother had early onset dementia, but it was only a theory.

"He was collecting them for both of you."

"Isn't there anything else you could have sold?" Richard screamed. "I'd have bought them!"

Mother shook her head, a distant look in her eyes. "I've asked Leo about taking on shifts extra, but he's said I'm struggling as things are. I don't know...he said if he gives me more work, I'll keep dishing out the wrong orders to the wrong people, but I never used to do that...before."

"Do you want me to talk to him, Mum?" Norman asked.

"Oh, he has nothing. We're not the only ones..."

"Look, Tony at the clubhouse says I can do some cleaning there, and Theo's dad says he'll pay us to help him build a stone wall. It'll pay for food."

"Goody-goody twat," Richard spat. "Spare change won't go far." He felt anger flare through his arms. He looked at Norman trying to be reasonable and responsible. He wanted to fight again. If he could climb back in the ring this second, he would. He'd dummy that left this time and then land a killer jab before the sucker punch to the guts. And then two, three more to genuinely hurt him, maybe even bust the spleen, anything, in fact, to break it and make him plead for mercy. He wished he'd hidden Father's books, Father's guns. Mother and Norman, they were trying to turn him into a nobody, bring him down to their level. Before either of them could complain about the outburst, he trudged upstairs, slammed his bedroom door shut, and went under his sheets where he brooded all night over how to go back to how it was before he saw his father blow a hole through his head.

Richard lay in bed with his eyes closed, trying to fall asleep, but his mind flashed back to Father laying on the study floor, dying. He finally managed to block out the images, but ten minutes after dosing off, the nightmares started up again. He saw it all as plain as day—Father was on the floor. Blood splattered across the walls. Mother had let loose a gut-wrenching scream, while Richard, on the other hand, remained motionless, unable to grasp the reality of what had happened; he told himself it wasn't real. In fact, any minute now, Father's shoulders would stir. His hands would grope around for the missing pieces of his head, and he would piece them back together until his head was whole and he was breathing again. But Father's head never again became whole. He replayed the images over and over in an endless loop until finally, he conjured up a girl to escape the madness. He imagined himself in her arms, their bodies intertwined as they moved together in the darkness. Her soft moans filled the shadowed room, and her voice erupted into a chorus of pleasure that called out his name—"Richard, Richard, oh Richard." Soon after, his body coiled like a serpent's, his gaze trained on the girl. He noticed how her skin shimmered in the dim light and how her presence stirred a desire that felt ancient and powerful. Somehow, he knew her spirit could devour him, unravel all his resolve.

Just then, a shadowy figure cut across his mind's eye. He focused his gaze, and the illusion shattered. She was no longer his lover but Mother. The mirror reflected a lean figure, ribs slick with sweat like the morning dew on blades of grass. A chill swept through him. His fingers traced the hollows beneath his eyes, gripping tightly as though to pluck his eyes out. Yet, though now blind, the echoes of her moans lingered—calling his name with a sweetness that turned sharp and strange.

*

Mother burst through Richard's bedroom door, tutting as she stepped over the piles of clothes. The room stank of sweat and days-old toast. He quickly turned his back towards her, his pants were wet from the dream. There was no way he could get out of bed while she was there. A blast of cold air struck his body as she drew open the curtains and unfastened the window to let out the odours. He pulled the sheets around himself with a sudden jolt. "It's cold!" he whined.

"Rich," she started. "Your brother is out there, working and helping out around the house."

"The perfect son..." Richard muttered, lazily flinging one arm out of the bed.

"No." Mother folded her arms and stood completely still. "Leo's cousin can show you what to do at the fish market. Get up. Get out there. I know you can do it. I know you're not like him."

Silence fell. God help him if the only way out of this is to be like Norman. To serve diseased people, smell fish in the market and step through grey puddles! Actually, the filth of that market suddenly appealed to Richard; there were hookers down there to amuse himself with, people to terrorise. Come to think of it, it had been a while since he'd terrorised the neighbour's dog until he lost interest and drowned it in the community pool.

"Mum, I can't go out there and work right now—you don't know what I'm going through." His stomach rebelled.

"I may not. But I do know a good day's work will take your mind off it."

"I'm only 14..."

"Come on. You want lamb, or bread and water? Seriously."

"OK."

"OK?"

"O-bloody-K, OK!"

"Wash up. I'll cook your breakfast; we'll play some music."

"Mum, we've not got a record player anymore."

"Chop, chop." She bustled off and on the landing burst into song as if the rosiest sunrise had just woken her up.

Perhaps she was better off now that he was gone. But how could she be? With the memories of that night and all? Of the blood, the torn flesh and the bits of bone? And the screaming? Maybe she wasn't. Even worse, what if she was happy because she thought the idea of Nemes, Ascension, the Manifesto thing was over. But surely, she knew that that was simply not the case, not with Father's genes and Richard's Potential.

"I will save them all, I will do what Father could not."

*

Yawning, Richard put on his face mask, hooking the white, elastic loops behind his ears. He then stuffed his gloved hands into his coat pockets, awaiting instructions from a burly man in dark grey overalls. It was 6am and he'd been up since 5am. This was unheard of on a Saturday. Struggling to stay awake, he blinked vigorously to stop himself from drifting off. Nothing was working. Burly man, Jonas, finished his cigarette, stamped it out with his boot and gave Richard a hefty pat on his back. Working men and women—dressed in overalls—busied themselves with setting up their stalls and hollering at one another.

"Hey, lad, time to get to work. Yer ma said you could work hard."

Richard shrugged. *Work hard at becoming a ruler maybe.*

"First things first. Take off that coat. It'll get filthy. Here, I'll lend you a pair of overalls." Jonas rummaged behind the counter and pulled out a spare pair of blue grey overalls, he flung them at Richard. Reluctantly,

Richard took off his coat and slipped on the ugly thing over his clothes. It smelt like Silany—rotting fish guts and weakness. He glanced at himself in a shop window. He looked like a peasant—grim and dirty. He stank like one too. And now, he was going to lift fish like one and apparently maintain some sort of dignity through hard labour. He decided that defiling the poster that Clara's used to promote their bubble soap would better serve the people of Silany, reminding them of what they could achieve if only they would free themselves from all inhibitions and simply be. Besides, the clothes in here were too big for him. *These people haven't got a clue about purpose and freedom.*

At the back entrance of the market, a lorry dumped a huge pile of wriggling fish into a slimy mess on the tiled floor.

"You know your salmon from your haddock, your cod from the mackerel?"

"*No,*" he replied, but only in his mind. He had turned mute, his nasal and throat passages blocked from the scent and cold air. His ears now felt like they were bleeding from the loud banging of the shutters. Combined with the grey of Silany and the misery of the cold breeze, it was enough to dampen his spirits. He wanted to go home. But instead, he was forced to listen to old Jonas crow, "You need to be sure of yourself to work here. This work isn't for lily-livers who buckle at the sight of some fish guts! Richard couldn't be more ready to go home.

Some minutes later, Richard tried to tackle a crate of mackerel that was full to the brim. He could barely move one end off the ground. It felt like a tombstone made of a slab of marble. Behind him, a tousled-haired woman stood a few metres away and called out, "Fresh bananas—10 strata a kilo!" And Jonas was nowhere to be seen near the stall. Determined not to give up at the first hurdle, Richard lowered himself right down to his haunches and approached the crate from the lowest possible position. Holding the handles on both ends of the crate, he leaned back and was able to hoist the crate up and walk with it. He stumbled about for a few metres, realising he wouldn't be able to keep it up for long. About twenty steps into his journey, two slimy fish slipped from the crate and fell, slapping the ground. He knew he'd never get the crate back off the ground if he put it down, so he staggered on without them.

As he approached the stall, Jonas was already deboning fish, using a fillet knife to prepare them for display. He lifted a rubber gloved hand and pulled back a loose lock of hair, pausing long enough to glance up at Richard and glare at him while the young lad struggled to balance the crate of fish. He rushed out from behind the counter and took the crate from Richard, leaving him red-faced and panting. He let his body collapse now that the weight had been lifted from him. Jonas laughed unkindly and shrugged.

Only three crates down. Richard's watch glowed 6:43am. Customers were about to arrive. Jonas' mood suddenly turned and he became twitchy and impatient.

"Where's the salmon, flyboy? The early customers, they love their salmon. Always, the first crate is salmon."

"You didn't say so. I'm not a mind reader."

"And you're not a weightlifter either."

"And you're not a brain surgeon, are you?"

"And you are?"

"No, but if you do want to know...I am going to negotiate as an economist between the states. I am going to Nemes to study how to."

"Are yar now?"

"Yeh, I fucking am."

"Nemes is a lie that fools only the foolish." The man was smiling, but the shake of his head was, to Richard, a display of arrogant deftness that led him to believe that Jonas knew something he didn't. It was a threat. "Here we work, we don't skim off the labour of others."

"I'll show you, you fuck. I'll show you. I'm better than this. I'm a negotiator. I can get people to do as I say. I can NEGOTIATE!"

"Well, you can do that somewhere else. I can manage things better on my own. You're a cost and a liability. So…negotiate that. Now, off you hop."

Richard ached and shook all over from muscle strain. He stared at Jonas, unable to believe that he had been given his marching orders, and even more preposterous, that he wasn't taking them, that he wasn't already halfway across the market by now. He took a breath. He calculated and weighed his options as a true negotiator would. He was letting Mother down here. He was showing himself unable to work his way up like a true entrepreneur. A record of failures, however low-level, would look bad in Nemes. They had a way of knowing everything about everything over there. Jonas was a problem that could be solved by the correct application of labour. If he appealed against this with cunning and guile, he could rescue this situation, not alarm Mother and deal with Jonas later.

"I'm sorry," he said. "I seem to have let the cold get to me as well as underestimated how much I have to learn. You are a master craftsman, Jonas." Richard bent his knee, slightly. "I'd be honoured if you could give me a second chance? I know what to do and expect now."

Jonas cocked his head. Slowly, his smirk stretched into a smile.

"That's big of you, Richard. Get on with it then. Let's see if we can make a fishmonger of you yet."

A lie that fools only the foolish. This phrase turned over and over in Richard's mind all throughout what he believed to be the hardest day ever of brute, physical labour.

"A lie that fools only the foolish," he muttered as he lumped boxes and crates together until his shoulders burned. He was unable to stop pondering this phrase as he swept ice from the ground around the stall with a crude, makeshift broom. "A lie that fools only the foolish, eh?" he said again later that evening in the alley alongside his shabby cottage, where he confronted Jonas and stabbed him. Only a fool would not have noticed that the boning knife, the so-called sharpest knife in Silany, according to its owner, had gone missing at the close of trade. Only a fool would have allowed it to end up stuck in his ribs. Richard scoffed at the thought and watched on as the life drained from Jonas' eyes and he slid down the brickwork to finally die on the cobbled footpath. When he'd stopped twitching at last, Richard was reminded of his father's philosophy, one that was more rarefied than that of Jonas: Nature is red in tooth and claw.

There was not a lot of money in Jonas' waste pouch, but it was enough to make the trip out here worthwhile and enough, Richard was sure, to pay for a couple of hours' company of that rather attractive slutty little thing he'd watched plying her trade all afternoon. Now, he'd teach her how simple commerce should work.

*

Mother was sitting on the sofa. Low autumn light refracted through the lounge window to coat her face in a warm, honey tint. Dust drifted through the air with a shimmer like fairy glitter and danced across her skin. Richard glared at the glow of her skin. He needed to talk to her about the fish-market humiliation and how Leo's friend, Jonas, was not very nice and since Richard was not made of rope and clay like most of the Silanese, it was below him to mix with low-grade Silanese men like Jonas. This was a pressing concern, and one Richard was eager to address. Especially as he had decided that for this reason, he would not be going back to the market. But here she was. She didn't speak and neither did he. They were locked into a silent standoff, protesting the other for what felt like hours but could have only been several minutes.

A sudden loud bang at the front door broke through and shattered the tension. Before Richard could react, Mother had padded over to the door in her bare feet and found herself newly tangled in the hard gaze of a scruffy, bearded man standing on the doorstep. Her senses heightening, Mother looked down at her blouse. She grabbed her long coat from the coat rack and wrapped it around herself.

"How can I help you?"

The man held out a beige sheet of paper. "This is a notice of eviction. You've not paid your rent on this property for ten months."

"I am Georgia Wise."

Richard managed to squeeze in beside her. "Richard Wise. How can I help?"

"We've sent you loads of warning letters, which you have chosen to ignore."

Instead of saying anything useful, Mother giggled like a five-year-old. The eviction officer glowered at her. But to Richard it was a lustful look, something dirty that told him the man could not be trusted to keep it in his pants. He'd be making his moves on Mother the minute Richard's back was turned.

"I'm serious, Ma'am."

"Oh," Mother said at last with a distant, unsettling gaze. "Please. Do come in."

"No. This is not a pleasantry."

"That's right," Richard said. "So off you go. On your way. Get off my land."

“Sir, I am instructing you to leave this house within five days. You no longer have the right to live here.”

It hit Mother hard. She shuddered like someone had just chucked a bucket of ice over her. “But...my husband has a PhD...”

“That won’t help you if you can’t pay up, ma’am.”

“I bet you haven’t got a PhD?” Richard said.

The man smirked. “Don’t worry, you’ll have somewhere to live. We’ll look at your income and provide you with something...more suited to your budget.”

Richard slammed the door in his face.

*

Two years had passed. With February ending, Richard curled himself up in bed, tucking the duvet around him. The smell of damp rose came from the corner of the room that he shared with Norman. However long he lived in Favela-7, Richard couldn’t get used to it. Life felt dense and purposeless. The air was thick with humidity, smoke, sewage, and the sharp tang of cooking oil—a smell so strong that it seeped into clothes and clung to skin, impossible to wash away. Sounds layered over one another: distant generators, the tired groans of miners returning from long shifts, and the incessant shrieking of dirty children racing through the streets. Women moved steadily along dirt paths or makeshift bridges, balancing baskets of fish or vegetables on their heads. Electricity was patchy, sanitation poor, and clean water scarce. Litter could be found everywhere. Yet, despite the harsh conditions, the people remained hopeful—jovial even—finding reasons to keep living. It sickened Richard and he told himself he should never accept it—he was destined for greater things than this grinding poverty. Going from the comfortable cottage home that they had been raised in, to this third storey flat felt like a giant step backwards. It had a corrugated roof, two bedrooms and one living space with only the sofa from the old house to serve as a drab, yet defiant reminder of their former lives. Mother had insisted on moving it into their new home, despite how difficult it had been to get it up the external metal stairway. The flat also had a tiny kitchen and makeshift bathroom with nothing but a tap and a bucket for washing in.

Through a gap in the duvet, Richard watched his digi-box with one eye. Modern digital projectors no longer needed walls—they hovered in midair. His device, sleek and compact, took the form of a black glove.

All this wearable tech had filled Silany these last two years after the state had successfully struck a trade deal with Nemes, thank God. The fact that people this side of the wall still had to negotiate through the Nemes Brain, instead of simply arriving at decisions, was, to Richard, an abhorrence—a clear sign of their stagnation and the reason they had been left behind. *Technocracy, technocracy, technocracy!* The voice on the digi-box called out. Digi-boxes, glove-screens, window-telly's, they were all over town and everyone was into them, apart from Norman of course—but no matter, some people were bound to be left behind. It was even prophesied in The Manifesto. Geniuses wrote The Manifesto, and it came into being in tandem with the SC1—the Super-Computer-1, or Nemes Brain as they called it for tourists from Silany, which was rather apt. Bogod and his associates were all amazing, and here they were—lapping it up, the future. But there was just this one problem; they were still here in rotsville Sil-ar-ny, the asshole of the world.

Richard had now moved out from under the duvet. The projection from the digi-box was broadcasting "The Making of Silany"—a historical documentary, which showed hovering machines moving sections of land under the commands of a small group of evolved beings. They seemed to float like they were somehow beyond any form of the human animal. A flying vehicle suddenly arrived beside them, and they didn't even need to move, they just sat, and the machine itself transformed its design to accommodate them. These were the elite Richard knew of, his nameless heroes, the children of the Ascended Ones, the Leaders of Nemes.

An acidic burn sizzled in Richard's guts. He didn't want to name it for what it was—an insidious, misplaced hate for her, his own mother and what she had allowed to happen.

He turned the box off and slipped out of bed to shove a doorstop under the door. *No locks.* He returned to the edge of the bed, leaning over to read The Manifesto, page 18. While he worked, he kept an ear strained for Mother's or Normal Norman's return – he couldn't bear their scorn for this great book.

Page 18 had a note stuck in it, as did several other pages that he had marked. He reread again the highlighted words of Odo Myler:

"For eons we have known that the Silanese conditioning is invariably inferior. It's a thing of genetics, a condemnation for those who will not yield to the wisdom of Nemes. Your so-called values can no longer sustain you. But alas, today we can rejoice. For we can justifiably hold the belief that the lands of Joy now exist, and that the past bindings and the frustrations of existence have been in large measure surmounted in Nemes. We can transcend our bonds, each of us unshackled by negative emotions, free to unleash the winds of power distilled from our now pure minds. Each an Ascender, each, benevolent."

Footsteps on the stairs. If they stopped at a distance, it would be one of the neighbours; if they continued getting louder, it would be either Mother or *Normal Norman*. The growing sound of footsteps signalled to Richmond that someone was getting closer.

Richard slid The Manifesto under the duvet, his heart pounding as though he had engaged in some shameful activity. He knew what Norman would say. He parroted Mother's philosophy as if it were his own. But Richard didn't feel like engaging in a debate today. Certainly not with a lesser man. The front door creaked open; Richard had neglected to oil the hinges even though Mother had asked him to last weekend. Spending time on house chores or contemplating the teachings of Odo? It wasn't even a question he'd ask himself. Dedication, discipline, faith. These were his ways now. He heard Norman's sigh and a dull thud as something was released from his hand onto the floor—probably his boxing gloves. Then, the fridge door swung open, followed by the clinking of glass from the kitchen.

Richard decided that now was the time to make his presence known. It was always best to pre-empt criticism than to invite it. Being caught lounging in bed would only achieve the latter. He swung out of bed and strode into the living space, where the kitchen occupied one end.

Norman was gulping down a glassful of milk. Wiping the white from his upper lip with the back of one hand, he grinned as Richard burst into the kitchen.

"Where've you been?"

"Fishin', walkin' the dogs."

"Oh." Peering over his brother's shoulder, Richard cast his mind back to the first time he met the dogs. Back then, Norman had insisted the dogs would be good for the family—good for *Mother*. "Where are they now?"

"The dogs?"

"Yeah."

"Theo's. He keeps 'em."

"Why?"

"You said you have allergies."

"Yeah, but I don't know if it's from the dogs." *Filthy mutts. Don't know why Norman has them.*

"Well don't worry, they'll be back here on weekends from now on. The place is pretty small for them. What you been up to, anyway? Studying?"

"It's cold in here," Richard said, rubbing his hands over the gas storage heater—the only heating they could afford.

"I hadn't noticed." He was rinsing out his glass, when he suddenly angled his back, and offered Richard a clear view of the breadth and definition of his lower back. It was solid. Come to think of it, Richard recalled hearing whispers of his brother's nickname as it circulated through town—Ox Man or something similar. It wasn't important.

"You know, you don't have to spend all your time studying, Rich. Give yourself a bit of a break to do something fun..."

"It's the only way I'll reach my Potential," Richard said, snorting to release some built-up phlegm and eyeing up a sofa to slump on.

"Potential! You're already at the top of the class in all your subjects."

"I can do more. I can do what Father did not do. Rise above my limitations, be more than I am. Norman, I can be Nemerian."

Norman abruptly fell silent but quickly resumed. Only, what he said next irritated Richard.

"You sound more and more like him each day," he said quietly.

They both sat on the couch together.

"Is that such a bad thing?"

"He lost all our money and then blew his brains out."

"That's because of...But he...He burned with *aspiration,* Norman, to be better than himself, to be an even more useful, productive member of society. To serve Nemes and all human beings; to fulfil his purpose!"

"I just think, our flaws mark and shape us, and navigating our flaws, well that just makes us human. We should be focusing more about making peace with who we are—accepting *what* we are, whether as human, as Silanese or Nemerian. But they don't get that about us—that we're okay with it all—with just being us. Well, it's their issue, it's their bullshit. It's like what Mum says Granddad used to say, "They just need to make us feel lesser, so they can believe they're upper." It's just like how folks are with their dogs. They treat 'em bad to remind them that they're in charge."

"Bullshit. That's justification. Have you not read Bogod? It's been scientifically proven that we're lesser beings, genetically. They've explained this. Part of us wants to be like this—governed by them, I mean. What *they* are saying is that *that* is half the issue. They *want* us to be with them. YOU TOO CAN LIVE WITH US. Not be here, in this shit. Like DOGS!"

Norman exhaled. He looked at Richard as though he didn't understand.

"And they have struggled to get us the texts, guidelines for us to follow. All we've got to do is let go, keep the faith and continue."

"I don't know," Norman said, "it all sounds a bit radical."

"No disease, no pollution. No State. Yeah, radical alright."

"Rich—just don't forget your roots, yeah? We've got our spirits here, blood and flesh and that's okay. For me that's what is missing, ya know—the real. Nemes is all about brains. Not heart."

"Bullshit. Do you think Nemerian woman end up like *Mother*? Not knowing if they're wearing clothes or not, she's going mad. Her tits were hanging out the other day. You think Nemerian women are this dishonourable? Thinking they're eating ducks when they're eating cabbage. *We could be better if we chose to be better*. We could save her, Norm. Come on, man, wake up!" Richard leapt to his feet. His already tight shoulders tensed all the more and stiffened the palm of his hands until they felt like metal clamps. "With gene modification we can be stronger. So much stronger, so much less likely to get ill and so much more prosperous because of it. Father could have lived, you know. Of course, he killed himself. But *he* didn't do it. We all did it *to* him. He dedicated his life to get there, but we failed him and held him back. And because of our collective ignorance, he, the poor man, was chained to this hell, condemned to remain a lesser version of himself. He wanted out and he deserved to go to Nemes."

"Just calm it a little," Norman said. "Let's go fishing or something? Get into the forest?"

"Here in this filth, you're sinking rather than living. I hate it. I fucking hate this place." He marched over to the bookshelf, grabbed the glass lamp off it and raised it above his head.

"No, Rich, don't," Norman warned.

Richard threw the lamp against the wall and turned to face his brother. "Free yourself, Norman—I know you can join me."

But all Richard saw was pity in Norman's eyes. Behind those eyes, Richard saw a smugness in his brother and in a flash, was reminded of the young, self-inflated boy he'd always known his brother to be. He blinked and sensed his fingers twitch as he wondered whether he, too, was sinking. Before he could process what he had seen, Norman stood up and took a step towards him. Without another thought, Richard swung a punch. Unlike the failed boxing match, this time, he connected squarely with Norman's chin.

"Aww, fuuuuck." Richard clutched his hand, wringing it to minimise the shock of impact from busting his hand on his brother's jaw. If their last boxing match was anything to go by, Norman clearly knew how to take a right hook—tuck the chin in, pull it down, and embrace the impact. But not this time. Shocked, he toppled sideways and dropped to his knees He wrapped his hands around the back of his head and squeezed his biceps to block his neck and face. Meanwhile, Richard, pumping with adrenaline, bounced on his toes and paced around him. Despite the shock, Norman seemed to quickly recover. Within seconds, he was back on his feet and pacing in a circular motion like a nimble wrestler.

"You're toast," he growled.

He sprang at Richard, placing his arms around his neck, and held him in a chokehold. Richard panicked and thought he must have wrestled Theo and the Chesser boys in the forest earlier on in the day, because these were new moves to Richard. It wasn't fair. Norman wasn't being a true sport. A few moments later, Norman drove Richard into the bookshelf. Then flipped him onto the couch, causing them both to sit down together. Norman stood up in Richard's spot.

"Leave it out, you little psycho. If you want to fight, we do it in the ring. I've been scrapping all day and I'm not fighting here," Norman spat out, panting heavily.

"Who says you get to make the rules?" Richard shot back.

"Why don't you stop pretending to be Dad and do something good for once? Face yourself and stop avoiding the truth—You'll always be Silanese. And dad filling your head with his talk of Ascending was because he saw you as a project; someone to save, but who doesn't need saving."

"Someone like you, you mean?" Richard scoffed.

"Like, I don't know, anyone."

Richard raised an eyebrow. "Help me understand, Norman. You've lost me."

Norman shook his head and exhaled.

"Look, Richard, I've signed up. Fal Institute of Law Enforcement—Trainee cop. I'll be bringing in a basic wage now."

"Right?" Richard was still breathing heavily, the veins in his temples bulged like taught ropes, but Norman was calm. His arms hung loosely by his side, relaxed.

"I can make more money than you. I'm an entrepreneur."

"Oh, just stop it Richard."

Norman shook his head and walked into the bathroom, lightly tapping the side of his face. Richard watched on, scornfully. So Norman was going to be the Sheriff of Silany, was he? Fat chance of that, Richard thought to himself, certain that his brother had a greater chance of catching lice and ringworm from the streets than catching perps as as a Silany police officer. Who cared? Norman didn't know it, but he had lost. His first mistake was forgetting that life was war and that every action was all about winning. Richard let him think he had won this round. But this was a battle of wits, and they were playing chess after all. One battle did not win the war. All that mattered was the end, because in the end, Norman would wallow in filth of the Favelas, while Richard would Ascend.

*

Lurking by a window in The Cobbles Pub on the corner of Lead Walk and Rise Avenue, Richard watched Lucio, a street kid with a face streaked with dirt and a bandana tied around his neck, pirate style. Lucio was making his way to the market, taking two steps at a time. He was fresh pickings; the newest recruit of one of the most notorious pickpocket gangs in Silany. For two years, the introduction of face scanners, body sensors and AI-Spy-Flies in Silany had reduced the crime rate, causing the street crawlers, sex workers, thieves and dream-dealers (the DDS) to lay low. That wasn't the case anymore. The new arrival of Pig Chump, a well-known officer who had transferred from Bow Lane put an end to the quiet. He was as corrupt as they come, and predominantly responsible for putting crime back where it should be—on the streets. The police needed crime to keep people in line. Why? It was a distraction tactic, meant to prevent people from venturing where they weren't supposed to. Whatever that was, nobody knew and nobody cared. So long as Pig Chump had an area to patrol, Magie got her curb back, and Richard got to employ a few child-thieves and manage a few projects of his own, life was bliss again.

Richard climbed the few steps of the wet metal staircase next to the pub. It led him to an abandoned storeroom filled with old boxes and rubble nobody used, apart from Magie, every now and then. That's how Richard knew about it. Once inside the storeroom, he closed the door behind him and waited. Lucio knocked once and entered. Richard gestured to a seat he had prepared. Richard pulled out a blade and Lucio's eyes widened. Trying to compose himself, he took a big breath and drew his own blade. His hand shook clumsily, and the tremors moved along the length of the blade, betraying his fear of Richard who was twice his size. Bretty the Scrawn, a ten-year old with frayed shorts and odd socks, clattered into the storeroom carrying a bulging backpack... Richard put the knife away and decided he wanted to trade.

With the threat eliminated, Richard helped Lucio and Brett unload their loot onto a giant thick cloth. There were boxes of luxury chocolates, his favourite tins of pineapple, quality T-shirts with crisp logos that looked like they were the real deal, a pair of high-end jeans, a selection of lighters, a knife, and a small gun. And then the prize collecting gemstones—some silverware, a watch, VR specs. It was all good loot and he planned to take it all back to the house. Mother was at work, breaking her back for pennies, and Norman was at the academy learning how to herd plebs. Better they didn't know what he was up to because Norman would probably arrest him.

Lucio bounced up and down on the balls of his feet. "Oi, One-fourth, pay up."

"Stop calling me that, Lucio."

From his bag, Richard pulled out two handwritten copies of one of the pages of The Manifesto and gave one to Lucio and one to Bretty the

Scrawn. Lucio looked at the sheet of paper with shining eyes and folded it up into four meticulous quarters. He stowed it in his pocket as though it were a precious sheet of gold. Bretty put his in his now empty backpack.

"No trouble today, boys?" One-fourth Nemerian wasn't actually a bad name. In a way, he kind of preferred it to Richard. It was just important he maintain his position and remind the little shits he was in charge any chance he could. They were, after all, toe rag pickpockets from Silany; they were beneath him.

They looked at each other. "Your friend Big Jim..." Bretty began.

"He's not my friend," Richard said, sharply.

"He was standing near the stall I snatched the lighters from, talking to the stall manager. He stared at me real hard, but I pretended like I was just walking by super casual, and he didn't notice a thing."

"Well done," Richard said, putting a firm hand on Bretty's shoulder. "When you boys have been helping me for four months, you'll get a real payment—not just pages, precious though they are." The boys looked at each other again, with uncertain eyes. "I am a man of my word," Richard promised, and their mouths relaxed into grins.

"Now, listen closely. I'm not meant to give you what I have. It's against the 10 Principles. But I like you boys, so I'm going to tell you what you need to do here. I've told you before, but I gotta drill it into you." Richard's open hands gestured downwards as he delivered the news to the young men. "You're no good." He nodded at them to make sure they understood the words. "On this side of the track, you're a bottom feeder's dinner, but not just in life—your blood is low-grade, so you're bound to the streets. But I've got it in me, the one-fourth. I do have the Potential, but you boys are stuck here and will amount to nothing. It's even certain that your lives will be cut short, as you will catch diseases and die. But I'm not going to. They say that with Potential in my genes, I may get to live for thoooousands of years. Time is like gold. With that much gold at my disposal, I can change things, create a new world, build an even better society. Show people how they ought to live with meaning and impact. My friends, there is hope for you yet. There *is* new science. One that now helps pure the Silanese-born with no Potential to transition into a one-fourth. It's a chance at a new life with new realms of possibility. So treasure these pages I've shared with you and read them every day before you sleep. The knowledge will seep into your bloodstream and flow through your veins. But you've gotta do as I say because you will join me. Soon, I will share some philosophies of my own, develop my own science to help others, the less advanced to become their greatest selves… These teachings will help you. You know that man they made a statue of—over at Bogod Falls?"

"Monocle Man?"

"Yeah, Monocle Man. He was a writer, and he had new ideas. Those new ideas are already old. And someone's going to replace him. I'm that someone. Put your trust in me, and by the time I'm four-fourths, you boys will be one-fourths. But you've gotta do as I say."

*

After three months of "running projects", the pile of loot stored at the bottom of Richard's wardrobe, covered by a dust sheet, had become impossible to hide. From every stash that the pickpockets brought, Richard would only take one or two items for his family's personal use. He didn't want Mother or Norman to start asking too many questions.

Mother was becoming more and more forgetful, oblivious to anything beyond the routine. Richard decided that it was more manageable to keep the prizes he brought home to a minimum and avoid disrupting her routine. Norman was immersed in his new training in co-operation with the Faj.

During the week, he was barely at home, leaving after breakfast and returning no sooner than 9.30 at night, by which time he was so exhausted that he just rolled into bed fully dressed.

One evening after school, Richard sat in bed leafing through the glossy pages of the University of Nemes' prospectus. He flicked back and forth between the section on funding and the course profiles. The more knowledge he fed himself, the more his desire grew. The more his desire grew, the more he felt the hidden, yet rawest part of himself—a purity he had only experienced once before—was unveiled. He didn't fight it. Nor did he fear it. He bided his time and waited for its full manifestation, believing that one day he would meet with himself again. Only this time, he would savour the experience. The only way he could afford to go to the university would be if he could get a scholarship. This meant passing the entrance exams and his school senior exams with the highest scores. Unfortunately, simply passing was not enough. Sighing, he dropped on his back and let the brochure slip from his hand. An idea was forming. It was thorny and it prickled, and he was certain it would involve teaching those thieving kids through tough love.

*

Strobe lights flashed and the bass pounded the ground. The stripper with the hour-glass figure and the silver kit was eyeing him from the stage, staring into his booth. The look on her face told him she actually wanted to devour him. Richard's jeans tightened around his groin. He knew he had her hooked. He looked sideways at his bald friend, Jim, and winked at him. Jim gave him a thumbs up. Jim had told Richard about Pollen X a few weeks ago. With a couple of hundred strata under his belt—newly acquired from the loot that had since become lucrative on the black market—Richard felt like a street hero. Not only could he blow a few strata here, but he could put some aside for his future course expenses and give some to Mother, at least, just a little bit more than Norman gave her. It was the least he could do. Yeah, he was supposed to share it with Lucio and Bretty the Scrawn. They were just going to learn the hard way that self and family come first. They were only kids. They would get over it. And what would they have spent it on anyway? No, he was becoming a man here. He had earned this, through hard work natural charm and his brilliant mind. Yes, he had earned this. And he had a pocket full of hard cash that needed emptying to show for it.

The dancers finished up on the stage and bowed. The men cheered, stamped their feet and hollered desperately. Richard closed his eyes and imagined he was in Nemes where the gentleman's clubs did not resemble a cock fight or pub car park. Instead, they were clean, sophisticated and the bodies pure, not like this filth. These ones basically stank. He visualised the glass floors and the cosmic zen nature of Nemes, the water features and the butterflies. He recalled an open restaurant called *Lavender Butterfly* where naked women stepped...among...the butterflies. He saw it on the digi-box. And in his dreams—bosoms as black as night, and white as the moon. Within minutes the hour-glass blonde had sashayed across to Richard, fluttering her lashes at him and swaying her hips. He grinned as she leaned over him, a musky scent stinging his nostrils and the heat of her body evaporating over him. "I'm Jessi. I can be your taste of sunshine."

Throwing his head back, Richard chortled and said, "How's that for an intro!" Then he leaned forward and whispered something in her ear. Within minutes, her hand was on him beneath the table, slow and deliberate. He sank back in his chair, exhaling in uneven bursts, his pleasure rising in silence until it crested and broke. But the haze lifted, replaced by the weight of an old shame—Father would have disapproved. Paying Silanese women for this, just like the girls down The Cobbles, when it should have been the other way around—them paying him. When it was over, Richard said nothing. She kissed him full on the lips anyway.

"What do you do?"

Richard gave a wry grin. She clearly thought he was older than sixteen.

"Oh, you know—this and that. Mostly working hard though."

"And what makes you work so hard?" Jessi sat on his lap and traced her slight fingers along his jawline.

Swallowing hard, Richard pondered how much to tell her. Honestly, what did it matter? She'd never remember him.

"I'm planning to rise, baby, rise—until there's no falling back down again!"

"And where is it that you want to rise so high to? Nemes?" Jessi was curious.

"I'm a one-fourth. According to the writings, I will ascend. It's just a matter of time. Faith, persistence, and time."

Jessi frowned. "You don't like it here?"

"Don't be stupid." Richard smirked. She was wearing a silver bikini, the top offering minimal coverage.

"It's about fulfilling your true potential, can't you see that? I want greater than this. I want to be someone who betters society, and cures disease. And mark my words, brother, they will build statues of me."

Jessi's face blanched. She unpeeled herself from Richard and stood back. "yeah, no. You're freaking me out." She shook her head and walked away.

Richard didn't care. She'd given him what he wanted and that was enough. He had only one more thing to do that day, mail Lucio and Brett each a little essay he'd written: *Why the End Justifies the Means.* He had orders for them too.

*

Richard pondered his next move. Norman had just plonked his black queen in the open; it had to be a ploy, surely? His eyes roving the board with laser precision, Richard realised that if he took the black queen, he would expose his king to a checkmate. Oh no, no, no. He gave Norman a wry grin, then moved one of his pawns a step forward.

"Have you been following the latest news? About Nuvo?" Richard asked.

"Nuvo? That mind-messing drug?"

"The mind-*enhancing* medicine." Richard shifted his leg position to stop the pins and needles. They still played chess on the floor with the board between them.

"Not had the time. Working my ass off," Norman replied with raised eyebrows, and made his next move. "I can see you're dying to tell me, though."

"OK, so there are these drugs in development. They can change your mood, delete memories, even help you cheat death."

"Death is part of life, Richard."

Richard drummed his fingers impatiently on the floor. "I keep thinking of Father. At the end, his mind was totally screwed. His brain was diseased."

Norman kept silent, as always.

"Don't you see? If only he'd had access to this technology, then, he wouldn't have lost his life. That's why he tried to break into Nemes, Norman, to get this medicine." He climbed up off the bedroom floor and paced backwards and forwards, jiggling his fists. He'd not behaved like this during a game before. "He'd have been able to get rid of the negative emotions and continue forward with his push for societal development. It was his inability to control his emotions that led him down the wrong path. Physical degeneration is a symptom of a sick mind. Father was not truly sick. He was brilliant. He was Nemerian. He just had two-fourths Silany left. But he gave in to his urges and lost his focus. That is the battle everyone with Potential must wage. Yet, I fear that everyone who has Potential will lose. It's a curse. To be Silanese is a curse, but it's, it's like a test or something. Without the base Silanese condition there would be no testing, no pruning process. Nothing to determine whether we are fully formed—ready for our life's mission. You need to *earn* the Nemerian status. Only then will it present itself in the genes. Norman, wouldn't it be amazing to explore the yet undiscovered possibilities of the mind? And to evade pain and death like the Nemerian have? We could change the world by preventing man from ever falling sick again! These drugs, this is what they have there. This is what Father wanted. They keep us sick here in Silany, they keep us inferior. And when we've had enough of it, we can choose to Ascend and become like them. They test us, they...they...they enslave us, but, equally, they help us by giving us something to long for to help us push on. These are powerful forces at work, Norman. It's—it's important. Life has meaning, because of Nemes. Nemes exists because of Silany."

Norman sighed and shook his head. "I'm not convinced that technology is *such* a good thing. Also, think about the reality of living forever. I think Grandad was meant to pass on, you know?"

"Norman don't be a fool, these men died because they were too weak to grab life by the balls. They chose to die, but we don't have to. Death can be overcome. It's just like the Nemerian Mystics say. If the mind is perfect, the body can live forever. The Manifesto says it even better: "The goal is not to die; it is to Ascend". Because the goal Norman is to *transcend*."

"And they want to release the drugs into the market, they want us to join them. *You Too Can Live With Us!* Norman, I will become Nemerian. I will go to Nemes. But Norman, don't worry, I will come back for you."

"Rich, I think there's something dangerous about these drugs." He paused, staring at Richard with something akin to sympathy. "Look, I've never told you this"

"Why not?"

"It doesn't matter."

"You agree with me, don't you?"

"I don't."

Richard stiffened. How could this man who calls himself his brother be so blind?

"What is it?"

"I'd prefer to live out my time and then die here, basically."

What a peasant, how typical of the Silanese to remain as they are—unlearned and unevolved.

"Norman, don't be spineless like the rest of them—you are one-fourth like me."

"Well, if you believe it."

"What are you talking about?"

"I mean I'm good with the simple stuff. Besides, is there any evidence for it?"

"What the hell are you talking about, you degenerate?"

"Norman let's be real. This science, as far as I can see, is all about hating people. Now, that don't sit right with me. As a matter of fact, I think you gotta love each person no matter who they are, you gotta love yourself, too," Norman said.

"How dare you spit on the one-fourth heritage. I will never accept the base Silanese condition. I will never accept what I am, I hate what I am, I hate you!" Richard blurted out. He looked back at the chessboard and noticed a new move. Richard moved the pieces around in his mind, trying to see the board like Norman would. He then moved his bishop across the board. "See. I will always be better. I will always win when I choose to use my mind. You're afraid to engage your entire mind because deep down, you fear who you are—a dull-witted brute, content in your filth as you feast on rotten scraps. You're destined to rot away like a diseased mutt and die a pitiful death." Richard sniggered.

"Checkmate."

UNIVERSITY OF
NEMES
ACCEPTANCE LETTER

CHAPTER 5
Wise Men

Norman stood up and gestured to Richard to approach. Shaken by his claustrophobia, Richard walked with purpose towards Norman, his breath laboured from his frantic escape from the elevator. The neurology unit waiting room was a cold white cube area.

"Where is she?" he demanded.

"Rich, come in."

"I asked you a question."

"I don't know much, Rich. Someone's coming to talk to us."

"Look, I have just come out of an important exam. I won't get to Nemes if I—"

"Rich. I was in weapons handling training when they rang. She didn't do it to inconvenience us."

"Got knocked down, did she? How? I mean, when...? What's she doing in the neurology unit? There's nothing wrong with her brain."

One of the doors off the waiting room suddenly flew open and a man in a white coat beckoned them to him. Strangely, Norman did not feel comforted by the man with the dark eyes and the neck that was both tight and far too thin. He guided them into his office.

"I'm Doctor Winbow," he said, and held out his hand. Richard looked down at it for a moment, as though he didn't know how he was supposed to respond. Reluctantly, he picked up his right hand and shook it.

"Please, sit down," Doctor Winbow said. He sat at his desk, glancing left to right, from Norman to Richard. "Twins?" He smiled. "I'm also a twin."

"What is the matter with her?" Richard asked. There was no sense in beating about the bush. The sooner he knew what was, the sooner he could get back to more important matters.

Flicking gingerly to the relevant page in his file, Doctor Winbow summarised the report.

"Mrs Georgia Wise—your mother—was brought in three hours ago. It appears she was knocked down by a car."

"No," Richard whispered, as he ran both hands through his hair.

"Fortunately, she was relatively unscathed—it was just a bit of bruising." Like Norman, he noticed Richard's changed form and intercepted his question. "But it quickly became clear that something was amiss; we brought her down here for further tests."

"What do you mean? She is fine, isn't she?" Richard pressed his right foot into the floor and sensed, rather than saw, Norman's warning look. In his mind, Richard reeled off his mother's list of symptoms. What was he missing? To his knowledge, his mother suffered from memory loss, the lack of proprioception, vision, exhaustion and drowsiness.

"Rich, we both know that she's not been herself since—"

"Don't patronise me, you smug—" Richard's jaw clamped.

"Doctor Winbow, none of us have truly recovered from the day our father committed suicide." Norman filed away this obvious fact into the archives of his mind. He understood the role it played in his mother's condition, but he wasn't ready to face it yet. There was a moment of silence before the doctor continued, his face filled with something new—compassion and worry.

"Boys," the doctor said. "I'm afraid to say that your mother is suffering from dementia."

Norman's skin chilled. He wet his lips and let out a croak. "Go on."

"I'm afraid this particular type of dementia is caused by a build-up of the PK-11 protein in the brain. It is a progressive and complex disease and the most likely cause of her significant memory loss, prolonged and disturbed sleep and the steady decline of her cognitive abilities. At this point in time, there is no known cure. The latest studies indicate that the PK-11 protein is produced by a gene carried by people of Silanese ethnicity."

"That's not possible," Richard said. "Our family have...excellent genes." Dejected, he spoke without conviction.

Norman knew what he was thinking, that Mother was Silanese, through and through. Conveniently, their Mother's Silanese heritage was the cause. Damn it Richard. *This only reinforces the belief that we are cursed.*

Norman winced.

"I'm sure you both want to know how your mother is doing. I believe she is awake now if you would like to see her." Doctor Winbow pressed a leaflet into Norman's hands and ushered the brothers out of his office, towards the ward where Georgia shared a space with three other patients.

A blue PVC curtain was drawn around her bed. Richard perched carefully on the edge of her bed and squeezed her hand. The skin around her eyes tightened as she smiled feebly at him. There was a yellow hue about her that accentuated her frailty.

Until now, Norman had always thought her as invincible.

"Mother," Richard said. "Why'd you have to run in front of a damn car?"

She laughed sheepishly, like a small child who had just discovered that she had done something silly. "Where's Norman?"

"I'm here, Mum." Norman came forward until he was behind his brother and his mum's eyes didn't need to search for him anymore.

"I was leaving home," she replied. "I saw beautiful lights on the other side of the road—twinkling, fairy lights. And...I don't know...My head hurts, Norman..."

There was a brief pause, and then, "What happened to her?"

"To who, Mum?"

"June."

He'd heard the name before. Sometimes Mum would mutter it to herself while she bustled around the house. Norman hadn't had the heart to ask about it.

Drawing back the curtain, a petite nurse came up behind Richard, smiled warmly at Georgia and felt her pulse with an experienced pincer grip.

"Boys, I'm afraid you need to make a quick decision about her medical and professional care. We have to take more blood to conduct more tests. Separately, we need to wash her and feed her before she can get more rest."

Norman could feel Richard's rage pulsate beneath his unusually quiet demeanour. If it wasn't for the humdrum of the medical equipment and the constant buzz of chatter, the cloud of death would have settled in the room and a grim silence would have fallen, punctuated only once by Richard's frustrated screams.

"Rich, she's just doing her job."

Richard suddenly halted up and turned, barging past Norman and into the corridor, both fists balled at his sides. Norman didn't bother trying to call him back.

"Norman. That day you shot the hare."

Norman couldn't believe it. It was her again, all of a sudden. It was a miracle that only demanded that Richard leave.

"Well done, my son."

But she wasn't back. He could see that now. She couldn't possibly be lucid with all of these drugs passing through her blood. Her eyes, though—they were clear and shining. Though her body had been reduced to a shell, her eyes sparkled still.

"Mum?"

"Norman, listen to me, son. I want you to hear me now. I don't want you to forget. I want you to remember. It's what my father taught me to do. I've done it all my life and it's the only thing that's worked." A brief silence fell, along with a sense that whatever she was about to say was important.

"Go on, Mum."

"You have a fire in your belly, Norman. Do you remember that day? When your father and brother came home. I want you to try to remember."

*

"Richard." Norman caught up with him in the corridor.

"Norman, we need to be solution oriented. We can save her. These people are about old thinking and old systems. They don't know the mind like I do. All of this is to do with how the Silanese think. There is new science, Norman, even the Silanese can die pain-free if they dedicate their final hours to the..."

"Rich, I won't allow any of that manifesto shit near her. It is what killed Dad. And you know it."

Richard grabbed Norman around the neck, his hands gripping the collar tight and rammed him against the corridor wall. Norman wasn't fazed; his eyes were locked into Richard's like a hungry predator locked onto its prey.

"I don't give two shits about what you allow or don't allow. Just 'cause you're the one who came out of her first, doesn't give you the right to play "good cop." You're as dark inside as I am—Angels are Brutes, Norman. *Angels. Are. Brutes.* I've just got the balls to admit it and live my truth. Mr. fucking good cop. I bet you have dreams too. Fantasies. Things you wanna do to me, to *her*."

"What's the matter with you?" Norman was too strong, and his wrists were thicker now from the weapons training. He manoeuvred out of Richard's hold and twisted his brother's arm behind his back, pinning him against the wall. "Stop this madness, Richard" He pushed his face against the wall. Becoming increasingly aware of his actions, Norman exhaled slowly, released his grip, and stepped back into the corridor. Medics and patients watched on, their murmurs a distant, disapproving, hum. Meanwhile, Richard steadied himself, smoothed out his shirt, and stepped into the center of the crowd. Norman watched him—his gaze unsettling. The manic energy in his brother's eyes bled into the red-rimmed edges—dark and consuming.

"The knight and the dark prince. It could be the story of our times," Richard sneered.

His fist smashed into Norman's nose, the hardest blow he'd ever landed. Norman dropped to the knee. But it would be the last time.

Picking himself up from the floor, Norman covered and pinched his bleeding nose with one hand.

A security guard Norman hadn't noticed appeared at his side with hands spread towards Richard. "Sir, I need to ask you to calm down. We're going to have to call security."

"It's okay. We're brothers." Norman told the man.

It would be the last thing he said about Richard before he turned on his heels and walked back to his mother.

That night Richard walked the streets of Silany alone. It was a cold night. Though the rain had stopped, the streets were nearly deserted. He moved through side streets and back alleys without hesitation—tracing familiar paths. Water pooled in the cracks of the road, reflecting dim street lights as he walked, his steps quiet against the wet pavement. He wandered until sunrise, past puddled lanes and over bridges, slipping deeper into the FDS. Here and there, a DS unit prowled—Dog-Scanners, the new Wolves of Silany. AI hounds with demon-red eyes, restless but harmless, their metal limbs gliding soundlessly through the dark. The city had seen riots lately, bursts of violence that left the air heavy but the streets calm. Crime had dipped, and the DS Pups, as they were called, had little to patrol. At this hour, they weren't even programmed to bark. Nemes needed Silany to sleep. If the people were to wake, to mine Etronium, to keep the empire running, they had to rest. And that meant silence—no barking, no sirens, no noise at all.

So, when Richard injected the White Milk into his vein, only one DS Pup watched, silently recording. He didn't care. If anything, the lone machine was company—it wasn't much, but it was something. Not that it mattered. Neither the pup nor the drug could fill the void. White Milk, as they called it, was the heroin of the old world—only better. A synthetic refinement, stripped of its filth but not its purpose. No rusted needles, no infections, no rot. Just the high—pure, clinical oblivion. Some genius had started bringing it over from Nemes last winter and asked the one-fourths to help them, as part of their research. Richard admired them, so when the DS watched him do it, he thought of himself as doing good work. Despite being illegal in Silany, White Milk was part of something bigger—though it never gave Richard what he truly needed: real company. That's what Rainbow Penny was for. She was the best because she let her customers piss on her. And right now, Richard needed to see her. By the time he stumbled into her place, eight Dog-Scanners had already locked onto him—not that he noticed. He was too far gone, so high on White Milk he couldn't even remember Penny's name. He kept calling her Alina. Or Allana. Or Alexa. Penny tried to correct him several times but failed and the whole thing spiralled. Before he knew it, Old Man Price—Rainbow Penny's husband—had him face-down in the street. Price usually let men do just about anything to Penny. But the moment a hand was laid on her face, that man met the back of Price's vehicle.

Richard woke up a few hours later to the sound of angels, but they weren't real. He must have somehow slipped his Digi-Glove on. It was morning now and Richard watched the tube as he lay there in the middle of a park like a homeless bum. Runners passed by, bin men wheeled out park trash, and somewhere in the distance, a real dog barked—a rare sound in a city overrun with machines. Richard barely noticed. His eyes were fixed on the shifting screen in front of him, adjusting automatically to his movement, tracking his gaze with seamless precision. Like everything these days, it was an upgrade. Najak-Globe had just developed a laser sensor that linked the iris to the glove, making interaction effortless. The tech had spread fast, especially down The Cobbles. Richard had five of them. With a flick of his eye, the screen responded. He could watch Nemes TV—his favourite channel—anywhere. And right now, that was all that mattered.

On the screen, Richard watched as a white-haired female being moved across the screen, clad in a sleek, skintight spacesuit. As she stepped forward, the world around her shifted terrain, reshaping itself, colours bleeding into one another, even her outfit adapting to match each new environment. She strode barefoot over glowing green-glass floors, carved effortlessly down neon-blue mountains, and walked through shimmering waterfalls of AI-generated snow. Every motion was precise, fluid, otherworldly. She was a Nemerian—flawless, captivating, a living embodiment of the future.

Come to Nemes. Where freedom and technology unite the light of the soul.

You can make a family here. Swim with Dolphins. Abandon your old beliefs. Perform ceremonies at night in the Tower of Obe. In cities like Jiwa and Bersag and Mito you are neither free men nor slaves–you are Members. Come and see for yourselves the beauty of smart living where oneness simply "is.""

All our resources have been surveyed; all our Members' thoughts excavated. And the Central Star–our computer, is the Nemes Brain–a cerebral AI Mind, which connects with all our inhabitants, to create lifestyle synergies to advance the future. Mobility, transportation, safety–you can find it all in Nemes. Where our grass is green and lush and consumption is a form of regeneration. This is Nemes. No longer are the animals and natures of old misunderstood. Understanding? The machines do all of this for us. They comprehend. And as we feed them, they feed us, so we have time to meditate, and use our minds for creative work. This is our "contribution" and once our time is done, we give ourselves back to the earth to be used for our greatest purpose–nourishment for the soil. In Nemes, we are diplomats, we are analysts. In Nemes, we are Nemerians–students of The Manifesto; disciples of the 88.

After the speech, an illustration of Nemes appeared, the map scanning into view. It separated itself from Silany with a bold divide—the Fal, the great wall. All of it contained within the elegant, looping curves of a figure eight.

New cities are in a state of perpetual evolution, like our bodies–they upgrade themselves. We hope that you will join us, and help us use Etronium together, a universal gift. Help us etrone.

Handshakes, laughter, and people running through sunlit meadows filled the screen. Then she turned back to the Silanese viewer and invited them to follow. Richard hesitated only for a moment before following, mimicking her playful, effortless bunny hops as she led them along...

Yes, we are radical in our approach to achieving self-perfection, but we believe that every Member who loves themselves, should love their mind. The joys of introspection outweigh time spent with other Nemerians, but interactions still hold value when they serve a purpose. Relationships here are transactional, built on mutual benefit rather than sentiment. Even the concept of family is different, as is language itself. In Nemes, communication–whether between people or machines–operates on a system of fairness, ensuring equality among all Members. Why? Because disease has been cured through tough love: a redefined approach to the very "idea" of love, where suffering fosters growth, and rehabilitation is the only true medicine.

She fired a laser gun, leafed through ancient books in a giant hall, and sat in silent meditation on a raised white beam.

There is still hope for the Silanese. And now with the new science, it's better than ever. Your life. It is now a choice. Your Choice.

You too can live with us...

Richard looked to himself, the muck and the puke. How dare Norman do this to him, hold him back, keep him here. *Keep Mother here.*

Every passing moment I am here, I am missing it there.

*

A month later, a letter arrived addressed to Richard, stamped with the University of Nemes' coat of arms. He had won the Basil Black Scholarship—8000 Strata per year to cover the cost of his Nemero-Enconomics course. But, of course, Richard had cheated on his exams. He didn't care. It was just a means to an end. What he didn't know was that Norman had seen him meticulously translating quotes and formulas from textbooks into a coded script, scrawling them onto long strips of till roll paper—before tucking them away inside his uniform.

On the shooting range, Norman thought of his brother often. Since that day at the hospital, he'd been shooting non-stop. The range was where he came to ground himself—boots planted in the dirt and dust; fingers wrapped tightly around cold metal. The bullet. The target. The sharp crack of the shot. The exhalation that followed. In those moments, there was nothing else—just the rhythm, the focus, the fleeting sense of peace he needed to get through these strange days.

Mum was getting worse. The doctors had decided to send her home but told Norman that he needed to find a new home for his dogs—Juny, Ram and Tan. She was too vulnerable now. With an increased allergic intolerance to everything, including dog hair, it was too great a risk to keep them around. Though devastated, he took them to a good home up in the hills—Mr. Johnson's place. It was open, peaceful, the kind of land where dogs could run free. Besides, with all of Norman's training, he barely had time to care for them anymore. There was no time for long walks through endless fields. So he consoled himself, reassured that they would be better off with Mr Johnson. That didn't make it any easier. Norman threw himself into sterilising the house, wiping away every trace of dog hair—trying to keep the grief at bay. But without the dogs, the air felt too still—the atmosphere, hollow. While the twins still lived under the same roof, they were like hips passing in the night. Their mother was sinking in an oceanic expanse between them, her own boat riddled with holes. Norman knew that her end was drawing nearer. There was little he could do but stay strong—for her, for all of them. To be strong also meant to forgive, he realised that. He had to forgive their Father. He knew that now. And so he did, out there on the range. Somehow, he knew that if he anchored himself, he might regain his bearings—chart a new course for himself and ride the storm instead of drowning in it. The biggest wave was already forming on the horizon—their mother's death—he could sense it. He also sensed Richard's desperate, futile attempts to keep her from slipping away. They were helpless.

But out on the range, the gun helped to ground Norman. It was a strange choice for a gun—the Zlock 43. It was a single stack, 9mm Jak-Pin calibre. No one else used a weapon quite like it, but Norman had his reasons. It was compact enough to hide in the back of his jeans, yet large enough to puncture a hole through any skull. It felt right in his grip, lightweight. The built-in beaver tail letting him hold it high and tight—just as he was doing now. Thinking, between each exhale, that he didn't want to be here. Didn't want a brother like this. But here he was. And yet he did. So he fired, squeezing the trigger again and again and again.

Days passed. Norman would sit on the step watching the sunset, then hitch a ride home with Tad Lowman, the trainer with the halitosis. He had said Norman was so far ahead he could finish his two-year training course in a matter of months. That wasn't the plan, but plans change. Norman didn't like the idea of taking a shortcut. It felt like cheating—like bribing someone to get special treatment...He knew those things happened, but that didn't make it right. Besides, Norman wasn't that kind of man. He didn't need to be. His aim was excellent, and his arm was steady. Tad didn't know where it came from, but Norman knew. It wasn't the eyes. Sight was one thing, but true vision came from somewhere deeper—the gut, the ground. He was anchored. One with the earth. Ready to ride any storm.

*

Although the University was still in Silany, access to it required an invitation. Gated and secluded, it sat on a vast patch of private land—the closest anyone on this side of the Fal could get to experiencing Nemes. The hedges that lined the swan lakes were so well-groomed, they put Norman on edge. Richard made a point of walking ahead of Norman and their mother. His matriculation gown billowed behind him as he adopted the gait of a vampire count. This grand, almost theatrical approach was known as the Ascent of Nemes. Although they were still technically in Silany, it felt like they had stepped into another world, away from everything Silany stood for. Gone was the thick, cloying scent of hot tar, fried food, and urine that clung to clothes and clogged nostrils. Here, the air smelled crisp and clean, like the plushest public buildings Norman had ever set foot in. The greenery was richer, more vibrant. Grasses, vines, and lush gardens climbed the sides of elegant buildings, thriving in a way that seemed almost unnatural. And the sky—compared to the low, suffocating canopy of Silany—stretched vast and open above them.

The other thing Norman noticed was the absence of noise. Despite it being in the city, there were no engine sounds. All vehicles on patrol were electric, driverless and silent, from the hefty Skimatiks to the light and nimble Skimvogels. There was no crashing, no drilling from manufacturing or construction to plague the potential new Members of Nemes. Inside, the hall seemed like a carefully curated illusion. Norman thought it was just like the ads, but he kept that thought to himself. This was Richard's big day after all. Richard had explained everything to him before: In Nemes, you can think. You can contemplate real things. Being here is like reaching the place you can only find through deep, focused meditation. Norman had taken him at his word. He was thinking a lot—that much was true. Norman had noticed that there were no signs plastered across walls, no peeling posters with strict admonishments, or reminders of what to do. For many here, this here was Nemes. But Norman knew better. While it was the end of Silany as an idea for Richard, for Norman it was a callous reminder of the path his father had taken, forsaking his family. And that path had led to shame, poverty, and ruin.

In one corner of The Great School Hall, under the classical white coving and cornices on the ceiling, Norman stood with his mother, waiting for Richard to appear. The portraits that lined the walls watched on in silence, their painted eyes surveying the scene. She had been quiet since they arrived and seemed more docile than elated. That morning, she had told them that she would wear the same green dress that she'd worn when she first met their father. Now, as she stood there, she looked misplaced, as though she had stepped out of another era. "My smart young man. I'm so proud of you." She'd repeated this several times today already—before they'd left. On the Ascent. In the campus grounds. Norman had naturally assumed she was talking about Richard, but now, watching her closely, he wasn't so sure. He couldn't tell where she was or what year it was in her head.

"Who are all these young people on the walls?" she asked.

"I think they're the previous recipients of the Foundation Scholarship," Norman said. "They all look a bit Richard-like, don't they?"

Mum giggled. "Ooh look," she said. "They're bringing him out now."

Gowned individuals were shuffling across the stage. The PA was as clear as a bell. When Professor Alder, Head of the School started, there was none of that grinding feedback you'd get at a Silanese event with its antique equipment.

"Without further ado, let me introduce you to this year's recipient of the Basil Black Foundation Scholarship, a future Leader with outstanding Nemerian Potential—Mr…Richard...WISE!!" Professor Alder stepped back from the lectern and lifted one hand into the air to welcome Richard on stage. Cameras flashed and snapped. Thunderous applause shook the hall as Richard stepped up to the lectern. Norman simply watched on. All he wanted was to be back at the range, his feet in the dirt, hands wrapped around his gun.

Looking out over the sea of upturned faces like he was already their king, Richard quelled the quivering in his hands and attempted to pull off what he must have thought was a grave and dignified expression. He lifted his head, so it looked like he was focusing his attention on the back row of the audience, giving the impression he was engaging all of them and not just the bigwigs. He seemed to catch Norman's eye, though Norman wasn't sure. He'd seen Richard practise this speech in front of the mirror at home at least once a week ever since that day he'd shot a hare, and Richard came back from Nemes full of dreams of steel and circuitry. *The trip Mum didn't think they went on anymore.* Richard cleared his throat and began.

"Ladies and gentlemen. It is an honour to be here among you today as the second Silanese recipient of the Basil Black Foundation Scholarship. As my family will attest..."—at this point, Richard did cast a brief glance at Norman and his mother—"I was overjoyed to receive the scholarship. It is a privilege to undertake this course as a Basil Black scholar, particularly at such a critical political-economic moment for Nemero-Silanese relations."

"When questioning whether I was even worthy of applying here, I kept asking myself, why? Why does this scholarship exist? Surely, it exists, because Silany is saveable. Its decline is not yet final, its stagnation not yet irreversible, even though most Silanese accept it as such—or worse, embrace it as a way of life. To live in Silany is to be trapped in a state of inertia, where ambition is mocked, poverty is normalised, and dull, brute labour is mistaken for fulfilment. Basic survival skills—like gutting a fish—are treated as grand achievements. Each person views life through a narrow, back-slanting keyhole, peering out at a romanticised vision of servitude that never truly existed. But this scholarship stands for something else. It is proof that change is possible. To live in Silany is to be bound by the past, forever tugging one's forelock to dead traditions. It is to prefer the company of dogs to the comradeship of the elite and the productive. It is to live in crumbling, neglected buildings—untouched by repair for centuries—and to walk streets in cities and towns frozen in time, their rural development and economic standing unchanged since time existed. Silany's roads are scarred and potholed. No Silanese owns, let alone flies, an aircraft. Some may handle muskets with skill, but they wouldn't recognise—much less operate—a laser shotgun. They are strangers to knowledge, to opportunity, to self-advancement. Strangers to long life, free of disease. Strangers to the hero's life, to a life unshackled from peasant morality and group fealty. Strangers, ultimately, to life itself. So, here's to Nemes. The Basil Black Scholarship says you don't have to stay this way. You can be saved. You can save Silany. You can become Nemes. And Nemes...Nemes wants you."

Richard's vision had blurred somewhat, so focused was he on driving as much charge and passion into this opening salvo. He paused, drawing a slow breath, to let the weight of his words settle. It was then he realised—the room was his. They weren't just listening, they were *rapt*. An especially gorgeous green-eyed girl was so transfixed she looked like she wanted to roll him up in precious, silver paper and take him home with her.

"Here, in this enclave, we glimpse a fragment of Nemes. And Nemes, like the mirrored shield that turned the gorgon's gaze back upon itself, does more than contrast with Silany—it confronts it. Here, we revel in the triumph of reason over superstition, of strategy over disorder, of mastery over quantity. Here, the relics of dead generations hold no power. Weakness is rooted. Decay is ended. Lifelong health is the norm. Mental dexterity is sharpened, propelling every Nemerian into high-achievement cohorts where the best and the brightest clash and compete, driving innovation, optimising markets, and forging the future. And from across the Fal, from the dark, stagnant streets of Silany, Nemes already looks like a myth—a distant, unattainable paradise, an almost-afterlife."

"A hard-working—though, I must say, rather challenged—Silanese artisan once told me that Nemes is a lie, a fantasy that deceives only the foolish. And what did I say in return, good people? Nothing. Being Silanese—at least in part—I was humble, I was reverent. I held my tongue. But later, I came across the words of Odo Myler: "*We can justifiably hold the belief that the lands of Joy now exist, and that the past bindings and the sad frustrations of existence have been in large measure surmounted in Nemes... We can transcend our bonds, each of us unshackled, unchained into the winds of our pure minds, each an Ascender, each, benevolent.*" I memorised those words. I carried them with me. And the next time I saw that artisan; I recited them to him. Did he listen? Not much. But I am certain that with time—and the right treatment—he could be saved. All of Silany could be saved. Silany can be saved. And it is my aim, through the knowledge and opportunity granted to me by Basil Black, to help save it. The goal is simple: to bring the two worlds together. To involve. To evolve. To...solve."

He gave the audience a beaming smile and stepped off the stage as another roar of applause erupted. Various faculty members slapped him on the back, yet he made a beeline for his mother and brother. Her eyes were misty. His hands were stuffed into his pockets.

"Norman, there was some stunning girl staring at me. Green eyes...you see which way she went, detective?"

"The next Skimpod back is in half an hour—we'd better go, Mum is a bit tired," Norman said, tilting his head to one side.

"The Skimpod—what's that?" Mum said.

"Mum," Richard said, drawing out something hidden in his gown, a brown leather-bound copy of The Manifesto. He gave Norman a don't-you-dare-say-anything glare and handed the book to her.

"Don't listen to Norman, Mother. Please, use the money for your medical treatment, and...read the pages I've highlighted. They are the cure for you."

Mum took the gift, placed it close to her lips and kissed it. "Thank you, my son. I will do. Such a dear, kind heart you are."

She beamed, a grin cracking her face. But it was gone as soon as it arrived, replaced by something stern, something Richard hadn't seen in years. Her gaze swept the room, scanning it with quiet disappointment. When her eyes returned to Richard, they held a depth he hadn't expected. A kind of pity.

"Don't be like your father, Richard. It's all in our minds." She gripped Norman's hand. "Take me home now, Norman."

CHAPTER 6
Four Amoral Capitalists

Richard crossed the immaculately clean, white-tiled floor of the Erik Xenoi Building—his new home for the academic year. An ankle-high Skimdisker, a flat robot with huge baby eyes glided behind him to clean up the footprints. "The day is yours to seize," the bot chirped, blinking endearingly before it arced around his shoes. He smiled back at it. Dad would have loved it. It was, however, easy to love robots.

Nerves fluttered around Richard's guts. He was about to meet his three new roommates. He knew their names, and that one was a geek in quantum security, but nothing else: Ares Yi, Miles Peter and Tom Freeman. These were, after all, people he was going to spend the whole of his first year with—a daunting concept when he'd never lived with anyone other than his family before. Much as he wanted to trust the sophistication of the personality test he had to fill out as part of the application process, he knew there was always an element of uncertainty when it came to human relationships. To him, that uncertainty was far more challenging than addressing an audience of hundreds. That was it! Just then, something inside him clicked—

something sudden, sharp, palatable. He could not trust people. He nodded quietly to himself as though in a trance. *One cannot.*

On the fourth floor, he found what would become his new home: Apartment 415. When he knocked, a young man with sparse ginger curls, an egg-shaped head and thick, triangular glasses flung the door open. "Richard!" he bellowed, sticking out a veined hand.

He lifted his head to peer over Richard's shoulder and chortled as though he'd said and done the funniest thing.

"I've heard you're a one-fourth."

He stepped back and Richard wheeled his case into the large, light-filled open plan living space.

"Yes, I am a one-fourth."

A muscled black kid with huge shoulders, and an understated elegance, lounged on one of the sofas with his stockinged feet raised against one arm of the seat. He was attractive, though arrogant, and didn't look up when Richard entered, but kept his nose in the textbook he was reading: *The Future of Futures.*

Seconds later, a third roommate stepped out of a bedroom. She had a slight build with short, spikey black hair and dark wide-set eyes. She sidled towards the man on the sofa and perched herself on the arm of the sofa, near his feet. Her skin had the warm, golden undertone of someone used to the sun. "Already studying hard. You need to lighten up." She pushed his toes back against the bones of his feet, willing him to pay attention to her. "Hey," the girl said, glancing at Richard. "Nice speech."

"Thanks."

"You've got the room over there at the front. The views are amazing everywhere, the rooms are all the same size. I'm Ares by the way. This guy is Miles." She lightly prodded the knee of the morose man on the sofa. "In case you hadn't noticed—we've all got significant levels of Potential, that's why we've been placed together."

"I hadn't noticed," Richard said, giving her a wary look. How much Nemerian each person had in them was the only thing people cared to know. The total volume of Nemerian Potential in a human's genetic makeup was fundamental to their life journey, their potential in this world to do anything.

"One-fourth," Miles said, shifting his body to a sitting position.

"Exactly. That's one-fourth Nemerian," Richard said. "Not three-fourths Silanese."

Tom sat down on the sofa next to Miles. "We're all wannabes or misfit Nemerians then. That's what a Sub is. To a Silanese, you ain't no Sub, but to a Whole One, we're Subs, alright. I take it as a badge of honour! Rather be a Sub Nemerian than a Silanese Hopeless. Not that they're ugly monsters like some say. They just need our help."

"Right." Except, while here he hadn't been prepared to be second-class *anything*, even if he was supposed to take some pride in it. Learn humility or something. He wondered what Father would have thought of this, how Father would have been better prepared than he was, how Father wouldn't have felt as cheated as he did now.

"Richard—where are you actually from?" Tom asked. "What do your people do?"

Such a strange way of asking, Richard thought.

"What do *you* do?" Richard demanded.

"You first," Ares cut in, turning her dark grey eyes his way.

You cannot trust them.

"Come on Mr. Scholarship. Who are you? Apart from an aspiring bureaucrat?"

He didn't want to admit that he was the son of a waitress. On the other hand, he *was* the son of a genius. His father's suicide was to him, these days, a sacrifice, something he had chosen to do for the good of his family. Only because he sacrificed himself could Richard now climb higher. It was a gift, really. A tough gift to have parted with, but nobody said that becoming a genius was going to be easy.

He didn't want to think of himself as an aspiring bureaucrat, either. To be honest, this made him laugh. He didn't really know what the Basil Black Scholarship was for, only that it would allow him to network and climb up the ranks of the Nemes enclave. Sure, he knew it was to study interdisciplinary and holistic systems and things of that nature, but he didn't really need to know all that. After all, Father had played by the rules and had tried to show them what he thought they wanted and all he'd gotten for it was betrayal, loss and humiliation.

Richard, on the other hand, hadn't played by the rules. He hadn't earned the scholarship—he'd taken it. He knew he couldn't be what the board was looking for, so he played the system. After all, the end justifies the means and that's all that mattered.

Jock Koch had been the perfect mark. A studious Nemes fanatic, freckled and earnest, the kind of kid who practically bled doctrine. Richard had watched him for a year, learned his routines, until he'd figured out exactly where to sink the knife. White Milk had been the key. He'd started small, slipping Jock just enough to take the edge off. Then more. Before long, Jock was chasing the high, and Richard was walking him right into the trap. Every time the kid passed out, blissed into oblivion on his bedroom floor, Richard got to work—rifling through his notebooks, copying his essays, stealing every thought Jock had carefully sculpted for the scholarship board. Then came the final move. A heavier dose. A little fire in Jock's room—just enough to destroy his work, but not enough to kill him. When his parents found him, dazed and useless, surrounded by ashes, they didn't bother asking what had happened. They just packed him off to some third-rate agricultural college in the wastelands of Silany. Richard submitted the stolen work under his own name. And just like that, Jock was gone. And Richard was on his way to Nemes.

He toyed with the idea of telling Ares all this to test her. He was curious to see if it turned her on—if he'd be lucky enough to get laid on his first night. He remembered the self-negotiation techniques he'd homed in while dealing with Jonas and cautioned himself. Timing was everything. Better to wait and get to know her first before playing that particular hand.

"My mother is...retired now," he said. "She is...Silanese. You know how it goes. And I've got a twin. He's more like her. In that unnatural way. Training to be a policeman. My Father—he passed on. He was a great teacher. I guess it goes without saying. He was a half. He wanted to make it *Whole*. But he died in the struggle."

I heard he blew his brains out with a shotgun, he heard someone say.

Richard's voice faltered and he shook his head. The image of his father's broken face appeared in his mind and stung all over again.

"We are all halves here," Miles said, "though I actually question the new doctrine. I'm sorry to say that, actually, it irritates the hell out of me that the Pure Silanese think they can "discover" Nemerian values, Potential, for themselves. I don't think they can. I think they just *think* that they can; they're poor by nature in contrast with us, by virtue of the natural selection process. I think they're being misled if I'm honest. Sorry about your dad by the way."

Richard's head pounded. Bollocks. His mind wasn't weak, but he was only a one-fourth. "What about the One-Fourths?" he asked, stepping forward.

Miles thudded the arm of his chair. "Only with the right sequence of coaching! Yes, they can Ascend. But it has to be done right, I'm certain of this. If you were fed *The Manifesto,* the teachings from young, say, as a child then, yes. You wouldn't be here otherwise, right? In our company?"

"Right." He relaxed a little.

Tom picked up the train of thought. "Subs. Sub Nemerians, genetics aside, let us all unite. As it stands today, we all retain some link to the Old World of Silany, yet we have chosen to move into the future."

"Of futures!" Miles shook his book.

"Yes, perhaps," Tom continued, turning his curls as he paced, nodding to the ground as though to channel Bogod. The Ascended "We have either inherited our wealth from, well, you know—filthy, dirty Old-World industries, or have become Nemerian by Ascending. Nevertheless, to those who have gone before, let us pay homage. We all have Potential, but we are all Subs, still. Even a three-fourths is still a Sub. But never fear, we are not what we will become." His proud stance wavered, giving way to the less assured student he was beneath—the one simply trying to find his way. "I'm a Sub, yes. But for now, I accept that. My grandfather built his wealth in oil and cement—made a fortune, more than he could ever spend. I inherited it all, but more than that, I inherited the chance to Ascend.

Ares cracked her fingers on the edge of the table, staring at Miles the whole time as if challenging him to say anything.

"My grandfather," he said, glowing, "was a plastics tycoon, although these days he just sits in a chair and shouts at everyone about Etronium." She gave a laugh of resignation.

"How old is he?" Richard asked.

"A hundred and twenty-eight, so not as old as some Nemerians. He's stationed here in Silany, part of some old programme to help accelerate development." He stopped pacing and the four of them congregated in the middle.

"And you Ares, who are you?" Richard asked.

"You can call me the rebellious baby. For now, that's all you need to know."

"It's our first night," Richard said.

"And you know what that means?" Ares was nodding to the group, bouncing around like some type of kickboxing catwoman.

"Richard, you might not be familiar with the new blend of White Milk."

"Nemes, here we come," Tom said, squinting through his glasses and rubbing a small yellow spot pink.

Ares squawked, then jumped and landed on Miles' back. After licking his cheek, she turned her gaze towards Richard.

"Time for Milky."

Richard's vision blurred as a bead of sweat traced a slow path between his eyes. He steadied himself, lining up another ping-pong ball at the scattered remains of the triangle of cups. Across the table, Ares watched him with a knowing smile, her grey eyes like dirty pearls, glinting under the low light. They were all high—floating, weightless. The Milk was better than good. The old stuff Richard was used to was missing the sweet comedown that this kind had. There was no messing around, a quick entry into magic land and then a gradual return back to boring reality. That said, the come down came with a deeper thirst. The milk acted as a numbing agent, dulling the senses to the stark contrast between the Silanese existence and that of Nemes. While the high slowly dissipated, their conversation took an interesting turn. In their shared hallucination, they agreed they were no longer in Silany—but in Nemes. That in fact, Silany wasn't separate from Nemes, but rather its foundation, its unseen support. They paid homage to Silany, acknowledging that without it, Nemes could not exist. The wall was merely an illusion and the connection between both civilisations ran much deeper. And one day, they decided, Nemes would rise from the earth's crust and float above the clouds, directly over Silany, anchoring itself with large shafts of hollow blue glass. The rings of the Eight would separate and the shafts would become gateways for Silanese Ascension. One day they would all be together. Richard simply watched. Someone needed to *hold the room*—steady the energy, make sure they stayed connected. These were his people now, his new special friends, and he would take care of them in his own special way. When they emerged from the ritual, they thanked each other, recognising that on some deeper level, they had created something real. Their own Future of Futures. It was at around this time that the beer games began.

Plink! He flicked the ball. It hopped three times—clipping the rim of one cup, skimming another—then shot straight up. All four of them held their breath as it hung in the air, suspended for what felt like forever. Then, with a perfect drop, it landed dead centre in the middle cup, sending up a tiny splash.

The others hollered and whooped.

"You spawny git," Tom said. "You havnnn gotten enough milk down ya..."

Richard was sure he could drink them all under the table. He picked up the beer cup, proud that there were now more full cups at his end of the table than on Miles' and Ares.' He guzzled the drink in one go. It was fun but it was lame compared with the trip they all had. Everyone wanted more.

"Where'd you get it?" Richard asked Miles. There was a sudden, awkward silence. Nobody seemed to want to talk about, let alone acknowledge the trip they'd all just had. The question just sat there, unanswered, until

Ares picked up her ball, rolling it between her fingers before pressing it into her palm. She blew onto her fists, like a fighter preparing for a match. But her legs were too slender to belong to a boxer. She was probably into Tae-Kwon-Do or Muay Thai or something. In any case, it didn't matter. The silence pressed in, suffocating Richard and making him feel small.

*

Ares was sitting on her own in the corner of the room. The men were drinking now.

"Yowza!" Miles said. Even he had loosened up with a bit of booze inside him. Tom was up now. If he landed this shot, Miles would have to sink his own to keep the game alive. Tom took aim—pong. A perfect shot. Miles stepped up next, aimed, but his throw was off. The ball bounced wide, and victory was accorded to Rich Wise & Associates.

"I hate you and your Silanese blood," Miles said, turning to Richard.

"Me too," Tom said with a grin, raising an empty cup in mock salute. Ares giggled from the corner and rolled over backwards, spilling the rest of her drink on the carpet. It didn't matter if there was any staining as the cleaning Skimbots would be out in seconds if their sensors detected any excess moisture. It was like living in Nemes here. But that was the point, to eventually merge the two cities. "You're still the Subbest Sub of us all," she teased.

For a moment, Richard's heart felt strangely full. Something had struck a chord in him—an affirmation of his otherness. Their "hate" felt closer to love, which was more than anything he had ever received from Norman. Ares sauntered toward them—catlike in her movement, sly and calculating. Richard admired that about her, the way she didn't bother to hide that streak of mischief the way Silanese girls did. It wasn't that he fancied her—he didn't fancy anyone at the moment. He'd decided it was wiser to spend this time learning what love was all about. Ares placed her hand on Miles' shoulder.

"Bring on the future revolution," Tom slurred.

"What are we talking about now?" Richard asked.

Miles shook his head. "It ain't just going to be a revolution," he said, "it's going to be war!"

"One day these tight-arsed Nemerian leaders will realise that their carefully constructed lives and all its mess can come undone at the drop of a dime," Ares said.

"So, let's toast to future chaos." Tom held up his glass, and the others clinked their almost empty glasses against his.

"To chaos!"

Richard wasn't quite sure how they had arrived here, or what exactly they were raising their glasses to, or if in fact they had come down from the hallucination at all. There was a blur between what was real and what was fantasy—Nemerian. He floated through another hallucination. This time, Richard stood alone, atop a castle on a hill in Nemes. The castle was built from pure light and a purple cloak was draped over his shoulders. It was then he realised. He was the King. And the illusion faded as quickly and gently as it appeared. Tom lurched forward and threw up on the floor. Somewhere in the apartment, a bot whirred to life.

*

One night, about two months into his first university term, he dreamt that Mother had lain face down under a bus. When the bus rolled over her, she lay there, softly singing to herself. Her face had been stripped of its outer skin, revealing layers of subcutaneous tissue where worms writhed and burrowed.

On the following day, after his final lecture, Richard packed a weekend bag and hopped on the Skim. With a pang of regret, he thought about the time Father had taken him to Rusty Barnfather's compound. It was hazy now. He wished that his Father could be here to see him. He would have been so proud. He stuck his long fingernails into his palms and squeezed hard. Boy it hurt, but it felt good to experience the pain. He dug his nails again and this time, he drew blood. Good.

The first thing that hit him upon returning home was the sharp, unmistakable stench of pollution. He had grown so accustomed to the crisp, green air of the university grounds that his initial reaction was pure revulsion. In his mind, the suffocating smog became a swarm of vile, microscopic insects, wriggling into his lungs, gnawing away at the bronchi. *I can't believe I put up with this for so long. If only Mother and Norman weren't so stubborn.*

He unlocked the door and was surprised to find Mother standing right there. For a moment, she didn't seem to recognise him. She stared at him as though he were a stranger—just for a moment—then, with a sudden cry, flung her arms around him. "My boy!" Richard felt the sharpness of her ribs beneath his hands, a stark reminder of time's toll. Yet, despite that, warmth flooded through him. He was home. Holding her again, he tightened his embrace, as if he would never let go.

"You didn't tell us you were coming home..." she said. "If you had, I could have made...I would have made..."

"I only decided this morning," Richard said, releasing her at last. "It's enough for me simply to see you."

Out of the corner of his eye, Richard spotted it—the Manifesto, tucked away on the top shelf of the bookcase in the living area. He recognised it instantly: the electric blue cover, the bold yellow italics, the only book there without an author. His eyes had a way of locating it in all the right homes.

And yet, here, it was clear she hadn't so much as touched it since he had given it to her—the special edition, newly printed and bound with such beauty for them, the people of Silany. Gold, free gold. It didn't matter. People couldn't be talked out of an illusion. The Manifesto said so itself. Still, he sighed inwardly. No matter how much he tried to accept it, the knowledge that his own family was suffering unnecessarily always stung. But he remained hopeful that they would get there. According to the teachings of the 88, all would eventually Ascend—even if it meant Silany enduring a thousand rebirths of its people. All would Ascend and evolve. It was the natural way of Kings and Queens. And Richard's Mother was a Queen.

*

No food appeared, not even when Norman returned home. When Richard asked about dinner, Norman simply glanced up and said nothing. Soon, they were on the floor in their room over a game, just like old times. The chessboard was the same one they had used since they were kids, its worn edges a quiet testament to years of battles fought in silence. Richard knew playing was better than talking to Norman. Their conversations had a way of turning into something else—something exhausting. And by keeping his focus on the game, he could avoid the moment Norman would inevitably shift, his voice taking on that sanctimonious tone, the Holy Loser of Silany in full form.

Norman picked up a pawn, turning it over in his fingers as if noticing for the first time how small and unassuming it was—almost delicate. Then, without a word, he set it back down. Richard understood. He had always liked the chess pieces too. "Seems like you're getting on well over there,"

Norman said, his tone carefully neutral. Richard exhaled through his nose, bracing himself. He knew this conversation was inevitable. With a grunt, he pulled his attention away from the board, sat up a little straighter, and met his brother's gaze.

"Love it, bro. Love it."

"You've got to have more to say about it than that."

Reluctant, Richard gave a quick rundown of Tom, Ares and Miles—the wild times they'd had so far, their philosophies, their group ethic, their aspirations. He spoke easily, letting the words flow, but Norman remained silent, offering no reaction, no judgment. Still, Richard could guess what was going through his brother's head. He was probably deciding which one of them he'd arrest first.

"I think it's great you're so happy," Norman said, at last. This was the longest conversation the twins had had since Richard punched Norman in the hospital. "Just be careful with these guys. They're going to take you on a path that is darker than you know." Richard's head lifted, his mouth opened, and a pong of trapped air fell out in shock.

"What do you know about paths, dark or otherwise?" Richard's head felt tight now. A flicker of hate burning at the back of his mouth.

"Misfit chaos bringers?" Norman said. "I thought you wanted to work towards peace."

"Checkmate." Richard brought his knight out of nowhere to hem Norman in. "You think you're so measured, but in reality, it's you who's hemming yourself in. You choose not to activate that inner...*Potential* that you have so you'll never develop your mind the way you could. Fools want to remain fools. Because you are faltering in your own development, you diminish your own role in serving the greater good. This world has less goodness because you refuse to be who you truly are."

"Did you copy that out of a book, too?"

"You think you're so righteous training as a police officer but let me tell you, you won't change a thing that way! I mean, think brother, why are there no crimes in Nemes? Good policing is just another sign of a broken system. You're treating the symptoms instead of curing the disease. In a truly sane society, crime wouldn't exist at all."

"Let me guess, we are the problem? The Silanese? We're our own worst enemies?"

Richard sighed, shaking his head. "Ever the victim! Shake off your selfish Silanese compliance and wake up! If you just take a moment to think about the teachings, you'll easily see that there is a better way. You'll understand Father more. You'll understand yourself more."

"You can beat me in chess, as you always do but that doesn't mean you can leverage your victory as an opportunity to recruit me. Or maybe you're just practising. Fake leaders need disciples, I suppose."

"Look, Norman, I only meant—"

"I may not have your intellect, but I've always accepted myself as I am. You want me to emulate you to make you feel better about who you are, but there's nothing wrong with who you are." Richard exhaled, ready to reply, but before he could, Norman added "Those people are no good, Rich."

Richard held up a hand, covering his eyes. "You haven't even met them...forget it...I'll sleep on the sofa tonight."

As Richard lay on the sofa that night, stewing over the events of that evening, the familiar sounds of the favela murmured around him—soft footsteps overhead, distant voices, the rustle of life pressing in through thin walls. A plan began to take shape. It was one that relied on Norman trusting him, and that was the point at which he faltered. In the end, Richard realised that if trust wouldn't motivate him, then it's more fragile sister would: naivety. Norman was nothing if not naïve.

Feverish with excitement, Richard slipped out of the makeshift bed and pulled out a scrap of paper from the notebook Norman had left on the table. He scribbled a few words on it and slid it under Norman's bedroom door.

He drifted off to sleep, having set his phone alarm to wake him up at 7am, so he could leave nice and early. He wanted to say a proper goodbye to Mother, but the thought of facing Norman again filled him with dread—like the prospect of a long and unbearable boredom. In contrast, Ares and the gang would be up early, shooting White Milk into their veins early, then stretching their evenings out while they sprawled out on the grassy fields, watching Nemes TV. They had their routine down at last. Strawberry mousse delivered fresh while the movie warmed up, followed by lemon jet desserts to chew through the Milk comedown. No matter how much they trained their bodies, the craving for sweetness never left them. It was their only indulgence between the heavy weights they were pushing because beer was off-limits these days.

Those were the Sub's rules during testing season, and no one dared to break them. Not just because of discipline, but because the gang had devised some god-awful punishments for anyone who did. But they wouldn't break. They had sealed their pact in blood to make sure of it. It felt wrong for Richard to be away from them.

A week later, Norman opened the front door of the boxing club and called out to his brother, his voice echoing in the arena. Richard watched on through a peephole in the cleaning cupboard door.

"Are you there, Rich?" For a moment, he must have wondered whether he had misread Richard's message and took the piece of paper out of his pocket. The message read: November 18th. That was today's date.

The only light on in the club hung over the ring itself. As Norman approached, a lithe female figure stepped out of the shadows.

Norman opened his mouth to speak, but the girl went first. "You must be Norman." It wasn't a question. "You're the spitting image of your brother, but I reckon you're hotter..." She laughed and flung her head back.

Norman laughed politely. "Is Richard around? I was supposed to be meeting him here."

The girl came forward and held out some gloves for Norman to take. "Afraid not. He sent me instead."

He shook his head. "I'm sorry, but..."

"You don't want to fight a girl, right?"

She moved forward to give him a testing punch on the shoulder. Frowning, he looked down at her. Maybe he'd already figured it out—who she must be. Ares, Richard's kickboxing roommate. The one he'd described as "superior" in every way.

"I don't need those; I've got my own. Who's going to ref us?" Norman asked, warily.

"We'll have to do it ourselves. Trust me."

Richard knew that Norman believed her. Relief and disdain churned inside him. Norman had fallen for it. Ares would crush him. Her enhanced body and mind guaranteed it. It was in the genes. Richard's heart pounded so loud he felt convinced it could be heard through the door, but he quickly forgot it all, enthralled by their first few punches. He began to measure the agility and strength of each player as they danced around the ring. And then she did it, threw a powerful jab-cross combination to the guts, then swung a left uppercut under Norman's chin, causing him to lose his balance ever so slightly. She prepared herself for a knockout finish but at the last second, her hook only clipped him. Norman, on the other hand, having taken a fair few punches to the chin, was pretty accustomed to them. But he hadn't expected this slight woman to throw them quite so well. He exhaled and re-focused, looking in her direction while bouncing on his toes.

"Okay then," he said.

By the end of the first round, Ares had the upper hand. Had this been a real match, she would have had a 10-9 lead. Not that anyone was keeping score. She won again in round 2 and then 3, leaving Norman breathless and shaky. What he couldn't do, Richard could tell, was work her out. Instead, he was surviving, taking small but ineffective shots to slow her down. He felt his legs go first, his movement losing its sharpness. Then his arms drooped as if weighed down by invisible sandbags. All he could do was take quick, shallow, breaths and throw the occasional one-two combination to stay in the game.

After thirteen minutes, Ares gave up on playing by the rules.

"Hey, Norman," she called out.

She shifted her stance and struck him with an illegal flying knee-kick. Before he could react, her legs coiled around him—two bands of muscle crushing his diaphragm—squeezing the air from his lungs...

"What the fffuu..."

At some point Richard heard Norman cry out, "stop."

Ares had released Norman from the headlock and was now on top of him—full mount—her fists raining down on his face in a relentless assault. His attempts to block his face proved futile as rivulets of blood ran from his nose. And as she smiled, Norman's eyes burned with new-found resolve. With a deep, guttural roar, Norman hoisted Ares away, his strength fuelled by something deeper than anger.

"Crazy bitch." He lifted himself off the ground. It was obvious that he no longer saw her as a normal woman, some of whom he'd faced in the past sparring in different clubs, but saw her only as a violent and hateful freak.

"Stop!" Norman yelled.

It was quite funny to see him outraged after losing hard, like the loser Silanese man he was. Richard almost wished his brother could see him grinning.

"Oooh, temper, temper," Ares said, wagging her finger at him. Good. She'd remembered how to goad Norman further.

Against his desire to see Norman defeated, Richard's respect for his brother surged. A new strength emerged from Norman, and Ares, blinded by her ego, lost focus and in turn, one of her hard-won points.

Mesmerised, Richard watched the contraction and expansion of Ares' chest—the slenderness of her torso and the tilt of her small chest as she inhaled, sweating and glowing under the full beam of the ring light. He realised that despite her strength she wasn't invincible. He had thought her unstoppable but had seen her falter. His pulse raced and his palms were damp. Norman struck her in the face. It was a straight right punch, and it connected well. But for some reason, rather than landing a knockout punch Norman let her bounce it out and regain her strength—probably to teach her some respect for the rules of boxing. Typical Norman, always teaching.

Trying a new tactic, Ares began with quick, light jumps, mixing in feinted kicks as she moved. She appeared to be circling him, keeping her rhythm unpredictable—then, in a split second, she wrong-footed him and switched direction. He braced himself in the centre of the ring and sent the occasional classic punch her way, but it was all so predictable because she was so *un*predictable. Norman kept his arms tucked into his chest mostly. Richard could see Ares wanted to hurt Norm in ways he wasn't used to.

"Now the end," she told him.

She worked her way behind him, and channelling all of her fury, climbed on his back and put him in a chokehold. She curved her spine so that her back took some of the weight away from weakening her lock, and she clamped her right arm against his neck, squeezing with the left. Norman was exhausted but used his elbow to fling her off of him. She clung on tightly, her heels digging into his hips like vices around his thighs, as she attempted to break his back.

"Tiger," she spat.

Norman gasped in defiance, his pipes losing air as Ares squeezed tighter. Just when he thought he couldn't hold out any longer, she twisted her body, and pulled him to the ground, allowing gravity to take them both down. They crashed into the ropes of the ring. She was still hooked around him like a snake, when she decided to release him, unable to squeeze any harder. Norman wheezed.

Watching his brother being choked to death, Richard unexpectedly felt his own windpipe constricting and flung his arms out in a panic. He inadvertently knocked over a broom, which clattered to the concrete floor. Ares must've heard, as she released Norman's neck and, instead, kept him pinned with her foot. "Yield?"

Gasping for breath, Norman took some time to reply. She was about to kill him. *I asked her not to go this far.*

Richard wondered what Father would do. Would he utter "philistine" over Norman's body and leave?

"You're like Richard," Norman spat. "You che-eat."

Even though it was true, the accusation hurt. Richard would never willingly make known his role in today's action, but this deceit against his own twin brother—the one with whom he had shared his mother's womb pricked his conscience more than anything else ever had.

Never harm your brother. His mother's rules had been the soundtrack of his childhood. The memory made his eyes sting.

After Ares left, Norman was spitting blood, rolling into the floor and calling out for help. Nobody came. It took an hour for Norman to find himself, find air and water and stop the bleeding. He had been beaten before, but this was almost murder. But in the end, it wasn't Norman who was suffering.

Richard waited to hear Norman leave before stepping out of his dark corner, his hair tousled and damp with sweat. "You were fantastic, Ares. That showed him," he whispered to himself, a tear running down his cheek.

*

Richard lingered by the canapes table. Music hits bellowing in the background. It was someone's twenty-first birthday party. He wasn't sure whose. A Two-Thirds', apparently. Sometimes they were split that way. He even met an Eighth yesterday and one person claiming to be a Three-Tenths. He'd been at a seminar. He'd given a presentation. People had slapped his back. They were always slapping his back here and saying, "good-work One-Fourth," "go on One-Fourth," that sort of thing. Someone had invited him here yesterday and here he was, wondering who that person might have been. Maybe he'd invited himself once he'd heard about the party. The details were fuzzy. The White Milk was clouding his mind. Leaning casually against the table, he made a half-hearted attempt at nonchalance, occasionally reaching for a caviar snack.

"If you lean too far back, you'll end up with fish eggs all over your jacket." A woman stood partially in the shadows near a large Yucca.

"Maybe that's what I want," Richard said, turning. "Who wouldn't?" She wore a long, silky red A-line dress, with offcut shoulders. A queen couldn't have worn it better. Her shoulders were both broad and slender. Richard's heart did a flip-flop as he recognised the dark cinnamon-skinned, green-eyed beauty who mesmerised him from a distance during his pre-enrolment speech. If he was honest with himself, although he had had many sexual encounters since that time, no one made his heart pound like she did. He knew he liked her because he didn't want to hate her.

"Ah, you're Richard—the Scholarship King."

"I'm impressed that you remember my name," Richard loved that she said the word, King. "And you are?"

"Arora...Gamble. I'm in Chem. Guessing that's what you were going to ask next."

"Nemerian?"

She was close to him now, her breath warm against his cheek.

"You'd think so, wouldn't you? I'm Jiwanese born but emigrated here at the age of two. My maternal grandparents were Silanese. I love being mixed; it's part of who I am."

People always had stories like this, and the recurring theme: nobody was here who was from there or who had gone there, it was a one-way traffic lane. People were travelling from Silany to Nemes, and if they were here despite being born there, they were en route back. The Young-Nemes—those who were born in Nemes but found themselves in Silany before age two or three—were rare. Mostly, if you were born in Nemes and had more than two-fourths showing on an N-Test, you stayed in Nemes. It all depended on the parents—and the story—what had happened before the divide and before the wall was built, before the Ascended scribed *The Manifesto*. To call it rare was an understatement. Richard had never met a Jiwanese before.

"But you're still a Sub," Richard said. God she was cool. He knew it. She knew it. The air between them fizzed with unspoken understanding. His mind ticking as he pieced their futures together. They'd fit together effortlessly like a puzzle coming together. He could see it all so clearly. Somehow, he knew he'd never feel like he was trying to prove something to her. He knew she was his safe space.

"I'm not the biggest fan of that term, but I guess you could say so. Just not such a Sub as some. Mr. Wise, I'm a one-third." He didn't ask why she was so low, something must have happened there with the grandparents, but she was higher than he was and that made him feel her heat. All he could do was wait for her to speak again.

"Are any of your friends here tonight? Parties are great fun, aren't they, but it's always better to share the fun."

"I came alone. My roommates had other plans. The climbing wall to test the new weight jackets they bought."

Arora offered a warm smile, tossed her hair, and said, "I guess we'll just have to dance as a twosome, become each other's climbing wall?" She grabbed onto his arm and led him onto the floor. As they gyrated under the kaleidoscopic disco ball, Richard gave Arora one of his rare smiles and her eyes locked onto his. She swayed closer and closer to him, pressing her body against his. Taking the lead, she leaned in for a kiss and their mouths met—soft, yet searing, blistering. Whatever this was, it wasn't a passing fling. It was something more.

*

"I came as quickly as I could," Richard said, breathing heavily as he burst into yet another cold cube of a hospital waiting room. He'd run all the way from the station without slowing down. Norman had called him only an hour ago to tell him Mother was in hospital again and not looking good. He'd immediately jumped into the shower, thrown on a change of clothes and a textbook on *Applied Nemero-Economic Policy* into his weekend holdall despite the fact he had been looking forward to enjoying his fourth date with Arora that evening.

Norman put down his coffee, straining like he was in pain. He stood back and gave him a searching look. Richard lowered his eyes. He couldn't bear to be scrutinised after what he'd done in the boxing ring. If Norman didn't bear any grudge against him, he *ought* to. Norman was clearly still in pain, and though he was recovering, he still sported two black eyes, broken ribs, and a mangled back. But the real blow wasn't that he'd been beaten—it was that he'd been beaten by a girl.

"So, how's Mother?" Richard asked. If they could focus on the issue at hand and nothing else, then they could avoid arguing metaphysics, right and wrong, or the stitch-up in the ring.

"Her muscles are struggling to hold her up. She can barely cope with everyday activities. The doctors are telling me she's going to need round-the-clock care, and because our home is not practical, she'll likely need to be admitted into a care home."

"Can't you look after her?" Richard asked.

Norman shook his head. "I've just finished my training. I'll be working full time soon, nights, too."

"Any ideas for fundraising, for care?"

"You're the money."

"Not yet."

"My salary will help, but it's not enough. I've done some calculations, and we'll still be 500 strata short per month."

Richard sat down on one of the frayed reception area chairs and tapped his foot, anxiously. A worm of an idea squirmed its way into his mind, but there was no way he could explain it to Norman. "I'm in school. Then I'm going to Nemes to work. This wasn't meant to happen yet. But it has and I'll deal with it. Leave it to me, Brother. I'll figure something out."

"How lovely!" Mother's eyes filled with tears as she accepted the single orchid Richard handed to her and held it up to her nose. "You know that they're my favourite, don't you?"

Richard hadn't known, but he smiled, blinking his eyes at her, feigning intuition. Propped up against the pillows with her hair in white waves around her head, she looked a lot older than 63. Her skin was blue and papery as a result of the ravages of her degenerative condition. Keeping up his cheerful facade for her sake, Richard felt his spirit sink. The drug treatment he had suggested to Norman could have helped reverse her ageing if nothing else.

Five minutes later, Richard and Norman sat in the office with Doctor Winbow as he shuffled through the case notes and then looked over the rim of his glasses. "So, I presume your brother told you about your mother's need for social care? Do you have any questions?"

Richard gave Norman a subtle dig under the table to forestall a reply.

"Not right now," Richard said, pushing his bottom lip out. "I think everything is clear. We'll have to look into our options in terms of location, obviously."

"And we have some leaflets to help you with that." Winbow passed them across. "I also want you to be aware that although her mental degeneration is currently slower than her physical, the slip is inevitable. She may seem lucid at times. Hold onto those times but remember that will not prevent her eventual descent into complete memory loss."

Richard forced a smile.

*

"Pull!"

The recoil reverberated up Richard's arm. His shot was clean and the disc exploded.

"Nice!" Adonis stepped forward and clapped Richard on the back. "A true marksman."

Richard smirked. Shooting with Rusty and Father was paying off.

Adonis levelled his shotgun into his shoulder. He was well over six feet tall with a thick beard and a web of tattoos up his right arm. They'd been shooting partners now for months, ever since they'd first met on the grounds.

Richard opened the chamber, and the empty cartridges fell out in a cloud of smoke. He slipped two new cartridges in.

"Pull!"

A disc hurtled up from their right side. Adonis followed it with the shotgun and fired. A clean hit.

Richard offered him a smile and took his mark. The first shot shattered the disc. He took a breath. His mind wandered to Norman and the hare and how Mother had praised him for it. If only she could see what a good shot Richard was. If only she could have come with them to Nemes.

The second disc flew. Richard fired, but there was no satisfying shatter. The disc fell somewhere into the grass.

Richard's stomach clenched. He never missed. He stepped back and met Adonis's concerned gaze.

"That's not like you," he offered. "You seemed a bit tense on that last one. Everything alright?"

Richard emptied the chamber. "I got some bad news. About my mum."

Adonis's brows furrowed. "Is she unwell?"

Richard nodded. "Dementia. It's terminal. Unless my brother and I can get the money for treatment."

Adonis paused thoughtfully. "I'm sure you'll figure it out."

Richard slung the barrel over his arm. Adonis was a one-fourth like him. He knew the struggle of bettering one's circumstances. He would know that sometimes risks had to be taken. And Richard was willing to take whatever risk was necessary. "I know. I always do."

*

Watching the numbers scroll down the screen, Tom turned from his computer and glanced over at Richard. "It won't take long for the money to show up. The University might not notice it's gone for some time, and by the time they do, the encrypted pathways to your account will be so jumbled that they won't be able to figure out where the funds have gone. I think they'll just figure there was a technical error with routing the funds and won't guess where the money has been sent."

Richard opened the Nemerian banking app on his A.I smartphone, which talked to him through an earpiece, and he watched the income increase by 3000 strata within a moment. He grinned wryly, and patted Tom on the back.

"Looks like the university chancellery can indeed afford to help out your mother." Tom flicked a loose bit of wiring into the bin. "What will you tell your brother?"

"Norman? He'll believe whatever I tell him. He's naïve that way; kind, but a dumb brute."

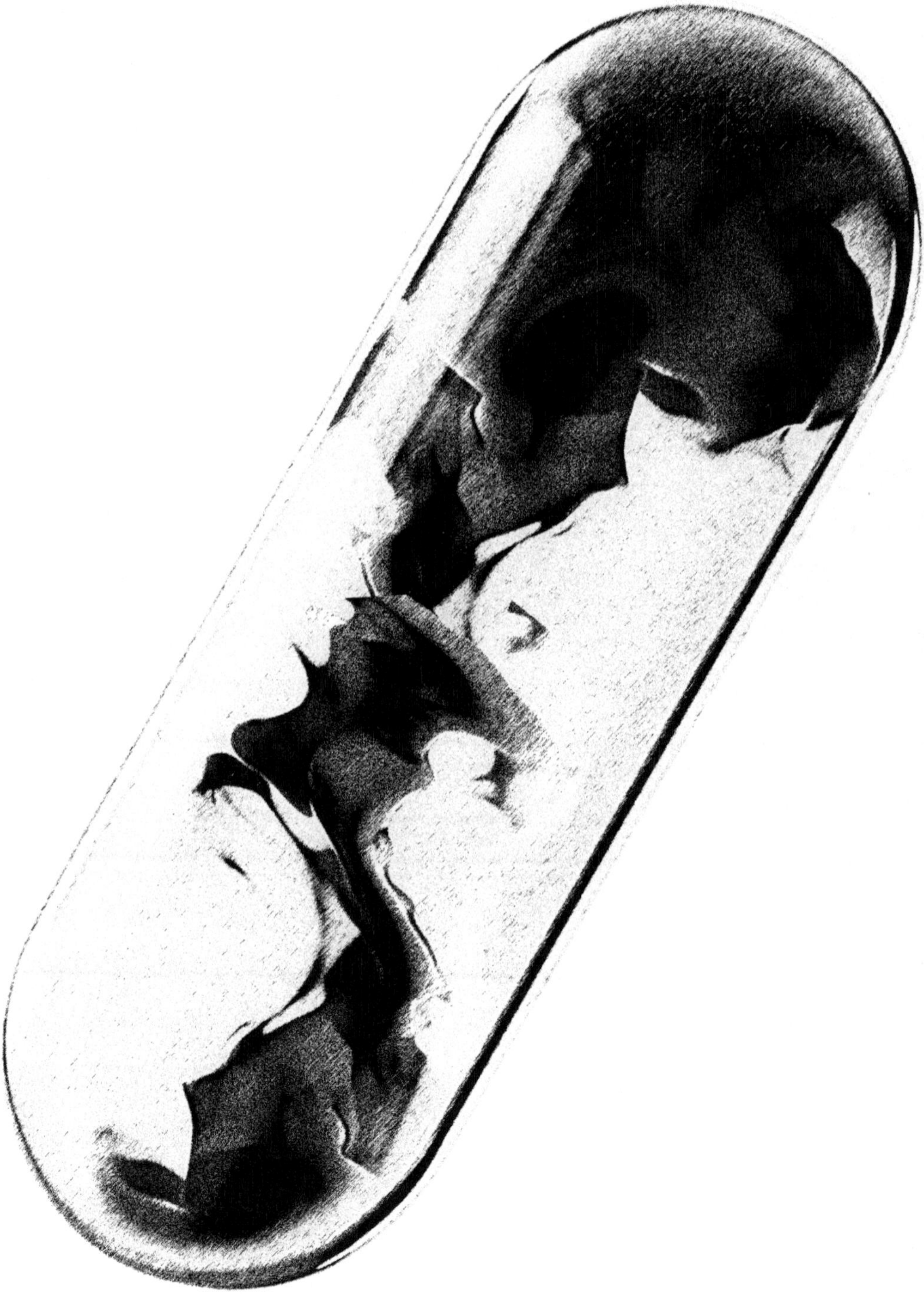

CHAPTER 7

Stroke My Ego, Swallow My Pride

Superintendent Victor Shepard gestured for Norman to sit down on a nearby chair.

"How have you found it so far?"

"It's been an education. I spent two days manning the enquiry desk next to Atherton, I've been out on patrol with Brown, alongside all the mandatory get-to-know-the-admin processes."

"A young man of your calibre must be getting bored with the routine?"

Norman, bemused, was careful with his answer. It felt like a trick. "I'd hardly expect to be running point on major investigations during my first few days on the job."

"So, you wouldn't be interested in the assignment I've got lined up for you?"

"I don't know what the assignment is."

The Super leaned in and passed a heavy box file across the table. "The drugs business," he said by way of introduction. "If you can imagine a slow-growing tree root that's weakening walls and threatening to topple whole buildings then you've got a complete picture of how the drug business is crippling the state. Folks everywhere are into these goddamn hallucination trips—it's got them all by the damn throat. I don't understand it. And now, it's got to my wife's sister's kid, oh, Norman...it's a damn mess."

The Super got up, came around and propped his heavy bulk close to Norman. "They take this stuff, and away they go to keep company with the funny people. Norman, it may not look like it, but I notice a lot more than you think and I've noticed something about you already. You're a man, Norman. With a natural instinct to know what is right, what is wrong, and what is in between. You're the type of man who can smell a rat. Who knows the lines to cross, and which doors to force open. Now the question you've got to ask yourself is a hard one. When you find the right key and you open the right door with it, will you be able to walk through it even if you find something in there that you don't want to see?" He turned to a framed photograph of a man and then settled his gaze back on Norman, who in turn shifted his eyes to the man in the frame. He was a big old boy, smart looking, and clean shaven with a strong face and a sharp suit. Few men these days could wear a suit like this. "Integrity is a tough moral code to stick to. It's one of few virtues all police officers naively believe they can hold onto without paying the cost. Naivety and inexperience make them think that when the time comes to choose between one path over another—and the time will certainly come—the decision will be easy and the toll, light. But I think that the ones who make the best police officers are the ones who understand that discipline has a significant part to play in keeping to a strict moral code. And as for that discipline, I think either a man already has it, or they don't." The Super drummed the palm of his hand onto his chest. "If you got it, you could make it far in the force—hell, in the whole of Silany! With these virtues, a man can take on the biggest of the bad. They can look death in the face and laugh. The ones who love to hate. Because men with a code know they ain't big boys. They're just little boys trying to be big."

Folding his arms, Norman questioned him. "What's the assignment?"

"To give Silany what it needs, not what it wants. This folder contains documents on the biggest drug cartel in Nexus-10. They refer to themselves as The Luminous, but our sources tell us they also go by Party X. Track 'em down Norman. We're looking for the head of Party X. Help us take 'em down and put an end to this drug epidemic. We can reclaim the streets of Silany together, and you'll be known for your code. Youngsters will follow yar, learn from yar, and have themselves a new role model—a real hero."

Norman stared at Shepard. This was huge, well beyond his experience. It was tempting to buy into it. But something didn't feel right, though he didn't know what. The task sounded noble, promising invaluable experience that might otherwise take him years to acquire. He could hardly refuse based on a gut feeling alone. But wasn't that instinct the very thing he'd just been praised for? Could he accept, knowing that something felt off? Pieces were missing—he wasn't being told everything. Doubt gnawed at him, but was it enough to walk away from the biggest challenge of his life? Then, as if Shepard had read his mind, he blurted out, "There's always *something* fishy going on, Norman." The Super drummed his fingers on the table. "Look, how about you take this file home and read through it tonight. It'll buy you some time before you have to make a decision."

"It's OK," Norman said, "I'll take it on."

For a moment, the Super's brows relaxed. He took the cigar from his mouth and clapped Norman around the shoulders. "I knew you had it in you! We can talk more tomorrow once you've read the file. You can have Ant Atherton for this, if you like?"

"Sure, if you can spare him."

Winking at him, the Super grinned, awkwardly exposing stained, cavity-filled teeth. "Care to join me for a celebratory little drink at Pollen X tonight?"

Neither Norman's father nor his brother had ever openly talked with him about their experiences at Pollen X, so he had only heard about the place from colleagues and acquaintances. He was as hot-blooded as any other young man but chose to abstain until he found the right woman.

"I'm not interested in those places."

The Super's mouth fell. "Puritan, eh!"

*

As Atherton left the office at 6:30pm that day, he placed a plastic cup of coffee on Norman's desk. "You look like you need this more than me, kid."

Norman looked up from the file, surprised. "Thank you, Officer, but you really don't have to."

"Call me Ant." He was ten years older, with soft, blue eyes and blond mussed-up hair. He had a nice guy's face and the gentle posture of a man that made Norman doubt his dependability in the field. "Don't stay up too late, Norm. It won't do you any good in the long run. Oh, and if you need anything, feel free to rifle through my desk. I keep at least everything!" With a chortle, he let the door close behind him.

Yawning, Norman sat back in his chair and stretched his arms behind his shoulders, pointing his elbows upwards until his neck cracked. He looked at the clock on the wall. 8:29pm. He'd decided against taking the file home. Where possible, he would maintain a separation between work and home, having decided very early on when he started this job, that he would finish any work off at the office before going back to rest. He'd been reading through the Party X file for two hours, jotting down key dates, incidents and people on one page of his notebook, trying to get everything into a semblance of order. He was puzzling over one thing. Two years ago, one of the

Party X perpetrators had stolen a kilo of opium from a legitimate supplier of codeine and morphine for the pharmaceutical industries. There was no record, however, of the supplier's name in the overflowing box of files, and Norman wanted to know who they were. He went over to Ant's desk and rifled through the manila file labelled "Unresolved." He flicked through the stack of papers, scanning for the date: 15th August 2220. His eyes widened at the discovery. The name of the supplier was Ganopolos-Tramp. Norman jotted the name down and resolved to do some further research on the company tomorrow. He returned the document to Ant's file.

No sooner had he closed the file, the telephone rang. He answered it but heard nobody on the other end. *Strange,* he thought. Just as he set the phone down, his eyes caught a name faintly printed on a sheet of paper near the top of a file. It was conveniently positioned right beside the phone. "Richard Wise," it read. The top edge of the page had slipped out at an angle, but it was just enough to be noticed.

Norman clenched his teeth in concentration. Perhaps it was another Richard Wise? His family wasn't the only Wise family in the whole of Silany after all. He picked up the sheet and carefully read through it. It was a list of online thefts that had taken place in the past month. There was no mistaking it. 3000 strata had been pilfered from the University of Nemes with the source identified by their own sophisticated tracking systems. Either the university was turning a blind eye, or the intel had not yet filtered through to the relevant authorities. Three thousand. The exact amount Richard had contributed for Mum's care.

*

Richard tucked his legs under him and moved his queen into the centre of the board. In his mind's eye, Norman could see several steps ahead of what

Richard might be planning. He might have a chance of winning. There was no doubt that the investigative work he was doing was sharpening his wits.

"Do you remember me mentioning Miles?"

Norman nodded, concentrating on the board. He couldn't look Richard in the eyes just yet.

"As part of his course, he has to do a six-month internship at a bank. So, you know what he does? He calls and gets through to the CEO of SS—the most prestigious bank in the whole of Silany—and says, "My father is Delaney Adebayo Peters, I'm a second-year business student at the University of Nemes and I would like to do my internship with you." Just the mention of his dad's name was enough. "Oba Adebayo-Peters, most respected sir; we'd be only too happy to oblige." And that's it. He's in!"

Norman moved his bishop away from the pathway of Richard's queen. "Checkmate," he said, moving his queen. He sat back, allowing a half smile to form. "It might be my first time ever!" he said, surprised and delighted, without a hint of smugness.

"Did you cheat?"

"Me, cheat?"

"You must've done."

"Of course I didn't."

"Then let's go over the moves again."

Norman swiped his hand against the standing pieces that remained. They clattered across the board.

"Richard, did you steal money from the university to pay for Mum's care?"

Shifting his position on the floor, Richard looked at Norman. "You may have beat me in chess, but let's have one more go in the ring."

Norman shook his head.

"I'll take that as a yes. What are *you* doing to help her?

"I'll fight. If you promise to return the funds. And fighting you means fighting you, not one of your galvanised sin-bots from over there."

Richard stared him in the eyes and nodded, grimly. "No, I'll come alone, brother."

Richard pummelled Norman, not once, not twice, but three times in the face, and Norman lowered his body and twisted around to step away. He knew Richard was wasting his shots with his hatred. It was the type of energy that would burn out quickly, and he was already breathing laboriously.

Meanwhile, Norman conserved his energy. He didn't even smile. He stepped backwards keeping his head level, his stance grounded as he shifted his weight onto his hips. Light on his toes, he bounced and weaved around his twin. Richard's head darted frantically, his movements erratic. Then, in a sudden burst, Norman threw all his weight into a short bolo punch from an awkward angle, Followed by a sharp left-uppercut. That was all he needed. Richard toppled backwards, crashing into the floor with a heavy thud. The second punch had clipped his chin just enough to leave him dizzy. He lay there, wheezing, unable to move.

Lowering himself to the floor next to Richard, Norman spoke, his breath hot on Richard's face. Richard couldn't even smell him; all his senses were shaken. "Return that stolen money or I will report you to my superiors."

Norman shrugged on his jacket and cast Richard a backward glance, who had managed to get on his feet, his legs still somewhat shaky.

"So, what do you want me to do? Pull her out of the care home?"

"You're the clever one. You figure something out. And I'll tell you what, Richard, I'm done with fighting you, but you can tell Ares the broken rib has healed. I'll be here waiting for her if she wants to go again."

*

"I can't believe you've got this whole place to yourself!" Richard spread out his arms across the back of Arora's vast, grey-leather sofa. The huge wall-sized window in the living room overlooked the fountains in the grounds of the Mansa school. He was sitting, slumped in his rightful place. His wallet slipped out of his pocket onto the floor.

"My parents had wealth, I guess," she said, shrugging. Noticing his wallet on the floor, she picked it up and flipped it open. Her boldness was refreshing, even if slightly discomforting. "Old school," she said. "They say nobody has them over in Nemes. Is this your dad?" She took out a small ID size picture.

"Yes. Good looking fella."

"I thought you said he'd passed?"

"What does that have to do with anything?"

She frowned and handed him back the wallet and photo. "Sorry. I guess I was thinking..."

How dare she ask me about Father? Richard was confused and somewhat surprised that he wanted to hate her but couldn't.

"Sorry Richard. My parents, I never met them in the end."

"It's okay."

Arora paused, seeming to contemplate her next words, carefully. Then her shoulders relaxed, and she said, "When I was brought back here, I was adopted. I'm still finding out new threads to that story and I recently found out that when I was eleven, I was also offered a scholarship to a specialist school of medicine for girls of sixteen."

Richard wanted to respond, but there were more pressing matters. He was mulling over how to phrase the question that troubled him, which was hard. He hadn't slept with Arora yet, so he needed to hold back as much of himself as he was able. "Do you think I should pay back the money I took from the university?"

Arora's jaw clenched and it was another few seconds before she replied. "I guess you could think about The Tawandra's Principle."

Richard plucked The Tawandra's Principle from his memory of The Manifesto. It stated that plundering resources from wealthy corporations to better society was a greater good. "Of course," he said. "Does the University of Nemes count as a corporation though?"

Arora's high cheekbones gleamed in the flickering candlelight as she pondered. Richard knew she didn't agree with what he was doing. He masked his panic with an inscrutable look. He decided that if she was going to have any access to his mind, she would have to prove herself to him.

"I'd say they do, yes, not so much in name, but as far as their source of wealth is concerned."

"You're beautiful," Richard murmured.

Arora's expression softened and he took her slender hands in his.

Her body was enticingly close as he became aware of a small hole in the seam of her trousers near the front of her upper thigh that exposed a tiny patch of her taut and tender brown flesh.

"You've got a hole in your trousers near..."

"Show it to me."

*

Arora stroked the length of Richard's ego with deliberate grace, traced it with her tongue like a prayer, worshipping every inch, until, with a final surrender, she swallowed his pride whole.

*

Arora leaned her head against Richard's chest and walked her fingers up and down his ribcage, blinking at him. Richard knew, looking at her, that he loved her in ways he hadn't felt before.

"We were a timebomb waiting to happen," he said. "I don't know why we waited so long."

Arora laughed softly, and then she went quiet. She sat up in bed and slipped on a T-shirt. "Richard, I need to speak to you about something. At the beginning of the academic year, I got nominated as the head of the Pharma Society. We're looking for volunteers to trial a new drug. It's called Nuvo 7. Our sponsor is working for Nemes. I was wondering whether you might be interested?"

"Depends."

"They're calling it the final end to psychotherapy, basically. By allowing patients to enter and bio-hack their own minds, they can modify memories and parts of their personality."

"I've heard of things like this," Richard said.

"You may have heard of earlier versions of the same thing."

"How does it work though?" Richard got out of Arora's bed and went to sit on the windowsill where the window was open. There was a slight chill in the air tonight, but he didn't mind. His skin was still warm from being entangled with Arora's body.

"The drug allows you to explore and re-organise the mind's architecture. This has a domino effect on the biochemistry and in turn the physical body. The body and mind are one thing, but the focus has always been on the body when it comes to surgery. Working with the psycho-architecture is common in Nemes. The Manifesto is no longer the only way to Ascend.

The sponsor claims Nuvo 7 to be an accelerator. When the mind is perfect, The Manifesto principles take immediate effect on a person's life. It is as natural as breathing. Instead of working with the book to sharpen the mind, now we can enter our own minds, organise it and write our own manifestos. This is what is happening over there, they say it's a new age of wisdom, of development." She walked over to him, where he was sitting by the window, and ran her hand over his chest as they looked down at the water fountains. "Under sedation you'd be going into your own mind."

"Go on..."

"I've seen diagrams. They show how the mind appears like a library, with your memories represented as books. It's like going into a long, extended dream. Only in this "dream" can you confront aspects of your personality called "Traits," all of which will look like little versions of you. Each trait learns and grows stronger, more influential, by studying and learning your memories in the library. With this understanding, you can improve your own personality; for example, if you have problems with time keeping or anger management, you could tidy those aspects up. In principle, you could even ban anger from the library so he knows less about you, or get rid of him entirely! Ha! Who knows, we could use it to eradicate disease one day and heal some real hurt. Leave something more for this world. And of course you would receive a cool 10,000 strata for your time."

"All for the use of my mind?"

"All for the use of your mind. Then there's the bonus point, if Nuvo 7 is what our sponsor thinks it might be—perfection, life extension, Ascension—Then it's a free ride to Nemes, baby."

Richard was silent for a moment, staring at the empty street below, and thought about Arora's proposal. A way to change his mind. A way to revolutionise Ascension. A way out of Silany.

Arora leaned into his side and stroked his hair. "People respect scientists, Richard, but they fall in love with artists." She turned his head to hers. "All you gotta do to kick the Silanese in you is say, Arora, baby—gimme that pill."

Her thick eyelashes fluttered around the light of her eyes. He traced his fingers over her back and under the cups of her breast. Her warm skin made his body tingle. When she met his gaze, eyes darkened in the dim light, his breath caught in his throat.

"I love you," he said, drawing her close to him in an embrace, savouring the sensation of her heart pounding against his.

"Is that a yes, then?"

"Yes."

"Just be warned. It's a confidential operation. You might need to go through a few hoops to get there."

"Don't worry, I can do acrobatics, gymnastics, semi-pro boxing. I can do anything I put my mind to, you know that."

Later that night he flicked through his wallet and came across Phillip's picture. He thought about how he'd responded to Arora, always so quick to defend Father. But the memories of his death were still too sharp, too vivid. If he was to be truly Nemerian, he couldn't linger in the past, he needed to let go. He needed to be exorcised. Turning the photo between his fingers and thumb, he hesitated for a moment before stepping onto the balcony. Then, with a quick release, he let it fall into the wind. Just like that, it was gone.

*

Richard entered his mother's room. She sat propped up in bed against the pillows, her skin papery and her face drawn. It was as if she'd aged ten years since his last visit. Norman sat beside her in his police uniform, holding her hand. She glanced between him and Richard, a flicker of confusion crossing her face—almost as if she had forgotten they were twins. Blinking hard, her eyes welled with tears.

"Ah, Rich," she said. "Seems like you've remembered you have a mother after all."

"It hasn't been *that* long since I visited," Richard groaned. "Are you off to work then, Norman?"

"I've still got an hour or two before I need to head off—I'm doing a late shift."

Richard looked around the room for an additional chair and pulled one over from the corner. Most of what he wanted to say required Norman's presence as well, so he was relieved he was there.

"I've missed you, Mother," Richard said, stroking her frail hands. "How are you doing?"

A distant look clouded her face. "I'm not getting any sharper."

Tears slid down her cheeks. Aghast, Richard took a handkerchief from his pocket and gently wiped them away.

"Pesky water gates," he said, forcing a lightness to his voice. She tightened her grip on his hand—it was gentle, weak, like the tug of a newborn.

Bracing himself, Richard took a deep breath and said, "I'd like to apologise to you both for my behaviour towards you over the past few months. I'm sorry if it seemed like I was more interested in my studies than in your health, more interested in my own life than in yours. And Norman—I'm sorry for dismissing your concerns. I've been self-centred."

He let out a shuddering breath and allowed his eyes to fill with tears. Drawing on strong emotions to produce a physical response had always come easily to him.

"I've been seeing someone, Mother. Her name is Arora. Isn't it a beautiful name? She's reminded me of what really matters in life. I've got a part-time job now." He hesitated, choosing not to mention what it was. "Every cent I earn will go toward taking care of you."

Their mother pinched her face. "Tssk, don't spend money on me. I'm not going to be around to enjoy it."

"Don't say that," Richard said. "I don't want it to be true!"

Norman kept his distance from it all. His expression was inscrutable, but Richard knew that beneath it all, his irritation was bubbling. But it didn't matter. Not right now, because this moment was all about Richard and his mother, not about Norman.

"Am I not going to get any sort of response to my apology?" Richard's voice sounded strangled, even to his own ears.

There was a long silence.

They're tight as two thieves. I'll never worm my way into their little party.

Arora was his refuge now—his place of acceptance and security.

"I've got to go," he said stiffly. "Study and work calls. I'll be seeing you again soon."

*

Arora was right about the hoops to be jumped through before entry to the Nuvo 7 trial. Even before dawn had broken, Arora had driven him out to a slab of concrete between the University of Jiwa's Outer Labs and Overmend Purplex. He stepped out of the Skim, the ground slick with dew. A breeze pressed against his back, and he made a mental note to tread carefully—one misstep and he could slip. Turning, he caught a final glimpse of Arora's Skim as its taillights faded into the distance, shrinking to two orange specks. When he faced forward again, she was standing right in front of him—a young woman in a short red dress—completely unsuitable for the chill. She was built like a fantasy, all curves and allure, but her face was obscured. A slim, obsidian-black visor shielded her eyes, and a facemask hid her mouth, leaving her beauty just out of reach. Even he knew; the most beautiful part of a naked woman was the face. For a fleeting second, he wondered: was this some kind of gift from Arora? A provocative surprise? More likely, it was a test. Was he supposed to take the bait? Allowed to indulge in a faceless girl behind Arora's back? Should he? Could he? Would she leave him if she found out? Or would she admire his buccaneering spirit?

"Hi, I'm Foni," said the woman.

"Can I use you?" said Richard, in a way that he hoped had sounded like a joke but had not, in the end, sounded like a joke.

"I am your guide," she responded, unfazed. "I'm sure you appreciate the need for discretion and security."

With both hands, she presented a new visor and pressed it against his temples. For a moment, it simply cast an indigo sheen over her image—now he had an indigo mask and an indigo dress that clung to indigo curves. Then she adjusted the visor again and a second screen slipped downwards. Black. It wasn't protection. It was a blindfold.

Richard wasn't sure how long he remained unable to see. He tried to count the seconds but soon grew bored during what seemed to be at least three Skim changes and three take-offs. One leg of the journey had seemed so long and disorientating, he could no longer tell what was up and what was down. At some point, he felt a searing heat—like the intense flame of an acetylene torch—pass dangerously close to the right side of his face. He was down on one knee, steadying himself, when the visor was removed. Blinking rapidly against harsh, white, lights, he found himself in a marble-walled room, the kind that wouldn't look out of place in the foyer of a corporate HQ or a boutique hotel—at least, the ones in Nemes. But something wasn't quite right. The marble wasn't still. It swirled, as if fire flickered just beneath its surface. It shimmered, shifting in a way that felt almost alive. Some kind of LCD effect, he guessed. A cool one, at that. Behind him, he caught the faint trace of Foni's scent—that lilac-tinged perfume. But when he pushed himself to his feet to ease the strain on his knee, she was gone. And where she had stood, he expected a sliding glass door, maybe a revolving entrance leading out to an industrial estate. There was nothing. No exit at all.

When he turned, the red marble wall stretched endlessly, its surface flickering and shifting like a living flame. It transfixed him. Richard stared the way he might have stared into Arora's eyes, the woman he loved. His mother's. He stared until, deep within the swirling red, a shadowy oblong began to take shape. It darkened, going from red to black, until it split in two. Somewhere close by, he heard elevator doors ding open. The ground suddenly shifted, and he felt his body plummeting downward. Unable to see, panic clawed at him, and he scratched frantically at his head until his fingers caught on fabric. A blindfold. He tore it off. He had no idea how long he had been falling and no idea how long it would last. But one thing was sure, he had been falling long enough to start doubting that there had ever been a surface world to cling to.

He came to what was clearly a crude laboratory constructed in some chasm under the earth. There were workbenches and generators, defibrillators, fans, glass cabinets with glass shelves where mineral lumps sparkled and goo-like substances floated in transparent tubes filled with coloured liquid, changing shape while rising and falling in a smooth, hypnotic motion. He was greeted by a tall, bony man in his late thirties. Despite a visor identical to the one Foni had worn on the surface, Richard could still see ocean blue eyes and extremely high cheekbones.

"I am Doctor Cynar," he said, "but Richard, please call me Cynar. I'll be taking you through the procedure today."

"That's a relief," Richard said, "for quite a while I've been wondering if I was being sent to hell."

"What for?"

"My crimes, I suppose." Unlike with Foni above, this time he managed to keep the jokiness in his voice.

Cynar raised an eyebrow without commenting. He waved his hand towards a red plastic screen imprinted with a white moonflower emblem.

"Please undress behind the screen and adopt the protective clothing provided. Sanitize your hands before you put on the gloves, just in case you are carrying anything on your shoes or clothing which could pass through your respiratory system."

*

Richard soon found himself dressed in surgical scrubs with a mask and cap, gloves and plastic casings over his feet. He was strapped to a bed that was more like a gurney.

While Cynar bustled around the bed, taking readings with a scanner, Richard noticed two small, metallic, circular orbs in a kidney dish on the table next to the bed.

"What's that?"

"A Cognitive Mirror."

"What does it do?"

"It allows two or more people to undergo the same procedure we're about to go through, but through one mind and at the same time. We won't be using that today. Please, try to relax. Think of what calms you."

The doctor sat next to the bed with a tablet in hand.

"I don't know what you have already been told, but Nuvo 7 allows the patient to access the virtual world of one's own mind. When you take the pill, you will sleep and enter what will appear as a dream world. Some people say that there's an adrenaline rush like plummeting on a rollercoaster as you enter it. Please be prepared for this. That dream world will be sharper and more real than any dream you have ever had. Now, listen carefully. There are three essential components to this world. The first is The Library. The Library contains all of your memories organised onto bookshelves. It's an infinite storehouse of everything you've ever seen and learned." He paused. Though this was new information, he could tell his words were having an effect. He watched Richard's intent eyes drink in the information and savour it. Cynar had seen this before.

"The second component is The Courtyard, which is where all your personality and character traits exist. Each trait will look like you *physically* and you'll be able to identify the traits by how they behave and what they say to you. What you change here in yourself, for example, the order of the books in The Library, or your relationship with your traits, will express themselves within you when you wake up. Whatever you do in there will impact you on the outside; the person you design yourself to be will become real.

"The Clerk is the one person inside the virtual world who does not look like you. In fact, he might even resemble me as I'm the one guiding you here. After all, the Clerk embodies the guiding principle within your mind. He helps to organise the books in your library and can give you insight regarding yourself that you may not be able to work out on your own. You need to trust him the same way that you trust me.

"The final component of the virtual world is the most important. It is a kind of "safety check" to protect your mind from descending into madness. Cognition is complex, and such a holographic compartmentalisation of the psyche is designed to protect us from ourselves. It's a maze which we've named *The Maze of South Bend.* We believe on the other side of the Maze is your subconscious. Whatever you do Richard, do not tamper with it. Don't burn, destroy, or alter this maze. Do you understand?"

*

Lying back on the bed, with a series of sensors attached to his scalp, Richard took a deep breath in readiness for the pill. His heart rate had skyrocketed as though he'd been running. He was as excited as he was terrified. An EEG machine encased in a sunburst-shaped steel frill would monitor his brain activities while the procedure took place, but the key aspect of the trial would be Richard's own testimonial on re-entry from the virtual dream world in his mind.

Cynar placed a luminous orange capsule with a blue strip around it on the table next to Richard and handed him a glass of water.

"Are you ready?" he asked, his hand balling into a fist that belied his calm tone. "Remember, you can stay in the Nuvo world as long as you like, but I'd recommend no longer than forty-five minutes the first time around.

"You've done this yourself?"

"I'll call you after forty-five minutes to prompt you to come out if you haven't already emerged."

"I'm ready."

Cynar pushed the start button on the EEG machine. Richard took the pill and rolled it around on his tongue. He swallowed it dry, noting Cynar's body stiffen. There was no way out of this now.

Within five seconds, the pill had taken effect. Richard drifted off to sleep and as he slept, he became aware of an exhilarating, falling sensation. The sound was muffled like his ears were stuffed with cotton wool. Opening his eyes, bright colours flashed as he plummeted through what looked like a kaleidoscopic mine shaft.

*

Hitting the ground at high speed, but without impact, Richard arrived in the land of his own mind. He looked around, and true to Cynar's words, the realm of his psyche felt sharp, its edges crisp and tangible—it was far more real than any hazy dream he had ever experienced. Once his vision came into focus, he noted that he was in the "Origin" of The Library. There were stacks and stacks of books upon bookshelves on all sides, panoramically, for what felt like miles and miles.

He walked up to the shelves closest to him and noticed that they were neatly filed by category. The first row he approached had a wooden sign above it labelled "Second Year Economics study." This had three levels on it with each book the same height and weight, although some like "Welfare" and "Economic Theory and Practice: Understanding Altruism" were tucked away much further back on the shelf and they were dustier than the rest. Richard grinned. These were certainly topics he valued less, or had given less attention to than others. Next to his studies, there was a row of shelves labelled "Sexuality." He was fascinated to see a whole book dedicated to "Arora Gamble," along with another one, "Sexual Fantasies." The one on fantasies had slipped further back on the shelf than Arora's book, which held first place at the front of the shelf. Despite its prominence, it was still quite a small book, a mark perhaps of the little time he'd known her. While he watched on, the "Arora" book floated away from the "Sexuality" shelf and drifted through the air. Intrigued, Richard followed it. He wanted to grab it and put it back where it had come from, but he had the feeling that the place it was going to was equally, if not more, important. A short distance away, the book landed on a shelf labelled, "Significant Relationships." A warm sensation filled him like he had just drunk some warm milk. Arora wasn't just going to be a temporary fling; he'd been hopeful about that, but this transition made him even more certain.

A little further away from the centre of The Library, Richard came upon a shelf labelled "Trauma and Pain." Inevitably, there was one book called "The Death of Father." He was relieved to see that it was on a shelf further back. His memory of *Father* was slowly being buried, but it was still there.

A tall man approached Richard, whom he knew was the Clerk since he looked like Cynar, though dressed only in blue. He had his nose in a book, but he lifted his head and spoke to Richard. "You are the sum of everything here. You can completely destroy that book if you like, then it would no longer affect you at all." The Clerk then wandered away to give him the freedom to do as he wished.

Richard stared at the book. In his mind's eye, he saw the blood on the wall of Father's office. He knew that despite his disquieting memories of Father's death, he wouldn't want to remove them completely.

Richard could have spent hours looking around The Library. It was a cornucopia of detail about his life, even down to long forgotten memories from his early childhood that were tucked away on one dusty back shelf. But the thing that struck him as most personally significant was that he would never have to cheat again. Not even to squirrel his way into Nemes like he had done with the university. All he needed to do was ensure that the information he wanted to access and remember clearly was placed at the front of the appropriate shelf, closest to the centre, the Origin of The Library, where he had landed only moments ago. The further back and dusty the memory, the more difficult it was to recall. The link was clear.

Right at the centre of The Library at The Origin, there was a wooden signpost labelled with the points of a compass, which Richard hadn't noticed when he'd first landed. It comforted him that there was a familiar navigational system in the world of his own mind.

Knowing that it was time to move on, he passed through an archway that looked remarkably like the one that he so admired at the entranceway to the University of Nemes with beautifully wrought plasterwork.

The Courtyard was almost as big as The Library but somehow felt more crowded and less ordered. The floor was laid in heavy stone slabs surrounded by rustic looking sandstone walls. While Cynar had told Richard what to expect, it was still disconcerting seeing so many versions of himself wandering around. Although they were all him in appearance, in manner and demeanour they were all very different. With no warning, the Clerk approached him from behind (in any other circumstances this would have made Richard jump) and murmured in his ear, "Remember, don't interact with your Traits unless they initiate contact, or you could cause unnecessary confusion to your own existence. The way to deal with your less attractive character traits is through education. Point them in the direction of relevant books within The Library that could be of help, rather than a hindrance, and be careful not to expose them to memories they might be able to use against you."

One of Richard's Traits caught his attention because he was completely naked. He shuffled around the room with his head hung low and his shoulders hunched. Richard noticed that he was murmuring to himself and twitching involuntarily but couldn't hear what he was saying. "What's he saying?" Richard asked the Clerk.

Without any comment or judgement, the Clerk told him, "I'm not like Perfect Norman. I'll never be like him. I'm a cheat and a stinking liar."

Richard swallowed hard, recognising the words as the worst of his anxious, self-critical thoughts.

Another Trait was wearing a suit and a tie—a dapper number like one of Father's—with shoulders squared, hand strutted like a peacock from one corner to the other. His words could be heard loud and clear. "I will achieve every goal. Nothing is going to stand in my way. I'm an indestructible force of nature."

I'm not sure which is worse: the arrogant ambition or the self-abasement. Aware of what Richard had seen, the Clerk spoke again: "Those two keep each other in check, mostly. There are more Traits, but this time you might want to explore the final part of your mind as you only have eight minutes left before the alarm will sound."

Frowning, Richard spoke back: "But I thought the final stage was dangerous. Is it safe for me to go in there?"

"It is dangerous, but so long as you don't actually burn the maze down or attempt to fight with any of the monsters you encounter, you'll be fine." The Clerk spoke as casually as if he were talking about a springtime walk through a meadow. "And if you don't want to go down there, that's also fine. Stay here and learn more about your Traits or familiarise yourself with your *memories*. These are the choices available to you."

Knowing that he would regret it if he didn't face the worst, Richard steeled himself ready to enter The Maze of South Bend.

The entrance to the maze was through a tangled mass of brambles over in the western corner of The Courtyard. Chills settled in the base of Richard's spine. "Is there any other...?" he began to ask the Clerk, but he knew from the impenetrable expression on his face that the answer was *no*. Taking a deep breath, Richard plunged in.

The initial stretch of the maze-like corridor was a pale, brownish hue, resembling sandstone. Yet, when Richard stared at it, an eerie, sickly glow pulsed beneath the surface, as if the walls themselves were hungry for something fresh. Ripples of dust scattered with each step Richard took, stirred by the disturbance of his movements. Brambles twisted across the roof and hung like tangled fronds, their thorns digging into his skin as he forced his way through.

"Ouch," he winced. Despite knowing that the pain was only of his mind, it felt disturbingly real.

Once he'd made his way past the brambles, Richard pressed on through a dim corridor. Light filtered through the tangled hornbeam hedges that formed the walls and ceiling, their unruly branches twisting together like grasping fingers.

He took a right turn and instinctively glanced back to see where he had come from. The path behind him had vanished, swallowed by shifting branches that had curled inward, erasing any trace of where he'd come from. His heart raced; his palms were cold. A creeping sense of abandonment settled over him, stark and familiar. It felt just like that day in the forest when Norman had split off down the trail to the river, leaving him behind. He had desperately tried to find Norman without success. Back then, just like now, the fear had overwhelmed him and he had cried.

Trying to slow his breathing, Richard figured he'd just have to trust in the process and avoid panicking. The Clerk wouldn't have sent him down here with less than eight minutes spare if there was no way back.

He concentrated hard on his surroundings, acutely aware of a cacophony of sounds coming from the other side of the maze. A bull's maddened bellow merged with a breathy groan too human to be safe. Screeches, clicking, growling, and something wet and suckling. It was as if a thousand mouths lapped at bone, sinew, and dirt all at once. Chittering simian laughter curdled with porcine snorts. From deep among the chaos came a ghostly trill—like a dolphin choking on its own scream. Nothing born of ocean or earth could make that sound. Each sound clawed over the next, competing, overlapping and devouring the other until a single, mournful note stood out—the song of a creature that had never known silence. It came from neither man nor beast, yet it carried the layered anguish of both. The maze listened and was still.

Richard proceeded to walk slowly, and the screeching and clicking suddenly engulfed the darkness as though whatever was making the sound was getting closer.

I'm not sure I really want to be here anymore! The hairs on the back of Richard's neck stood up, so he turned, in what he understood to be the direction of the entrance, and he ran.

Behind him, the screeching morphed into a low, dangerous growl. Then came the thunder of a hundred pounding feet, stampeding toward him, shaking the ground beneath his heels. All around, the walls of the maze trembled, and pebbles rattled on the ground.

Richard dared to glance over his shoulder. Through the darkness, he could just make out long, twisted horns sprouting from human-like faces. The noses were stout, the eyes milky. They ran on all fours, and they were gaining on him.

Richard gulped down something halfway between a sob and scream. His feet pounded the earth in time with his heartbeat.

He looked around wildly, frantic for an escape. All he needed was an opening, a crack in the earth, anything. But there was nothing. The walls loomed large on both sides, solid, unyielding and drawing closer by the seconds.

The sound of hooves beating the earth filled Richard's ears. The earth trembled beneath him.

His lungs burned, each laboured breath catching in his throat. Hot tears pricked his eyes, and he fought his hardest to prevent them from spilling over.

A sudden movement to his right caught attention He glanced at it without stopping. It was Father. He was still, stoic, watching Richard run.

"Father!" Richard choked.

Something caught on his foot, and he stumbled, falling heavily to the ground. The stampede was almost upon him. In a moment he would be crushed.

When Richard looked again, his father was gone.

Richard quickly scrambled against the maze wall. If he could climb, maybe he could avoid the stampede.

With a wave of relief, he remembered that as soon as he wanted to leave the world of his own mind, he just had to do one simple thing. Richard touched the sensor on his right temple with a trembling finger. Within seconds, there was a whooshing sound like a vacuum sucking up dirt and a swirling of colours. The horned creatures were almost on top of him. He flung his arms up and he was jolted back to reality. Once again, he was on the bed in Room 42A.

"You're back," Cynar said, leaning over him and checking the connections on his sensory pads. "How was it for you? Don't worry, you don't have to answer immediately."

Cynar cleared his throat, his mouth twitching at the corners, in silent recognition that mental reorientation was necessary for most after the trials.

Cynar and others who had entered the room turned around to analyse some results appearing on the screen. "But how do you know this place is real and that one was the phantom? Perhaps this place is just another form of reality." Richard must have looked worried because Cynar grinned and added, "I'm just joking, Richard, welcome back."

That Maze had certainly not been what he had expected. That noise. The groanings of the beasts. What were they? Dragons and whales? What did they even look like? He would never know, and that knowledge suited him just fine. Such places were not for him. He was meant for the higher realms, to stand among the ascended, not to mingle with filthy animals. Still, he needed to take something tangible from the experience, something real. He slipped the Cognitive Mirrors into his pocket.

That evening in bed, Richard rolled off Arora, breathing hard, while she lay inert. She kissed his cheek then rested her chin on his chest. "That was nice," she said. "But you didn't give me your all."

"Fuck off. We had great sex!"

"You were thinking about something else. I could tell."

"I've told you everything you need to know about the trial."

"A woman wants more than a man's body to know she is valued, that's all."

Richard sighed. Arora was right and that's why it annoyed him so much. He thought of the ring he'd bought for her. The one he was going to propose with. He knew she'd say yes, he just had to find the right moment to ask.

Holding back a part of the truth, he told her what she wanted to hear.

"Sorry," he said, and kissed her softly the lips. "I was thinking about my mother." He lowered his eyes with a penitent expression. That was the only response that would be acceptable to Arora, he suspected. Arora frowned.

Ooops.

She gently tugged the hairs on his chest. "Your mother? A psychiatrist would have a field day with you. What's the latest with your mother?"

He exhaled slowly. "Nothing progressive while Norman is cockblocking the new drugs. She's slipping further and further into physical decay, but he considers that natural. It's heartbreaking. I don't want her to suffer anymore. He's the one standing in the way of Mother's healing."

"Shhh," said Arora, stroking his hair from his eyes. "Sleep on it. It will seem better in the morning. Things always do."

This was such a trivial thing to say that Richard forgave her for it. She was tired. She needed rest and so did he. They kissed one last time and then rolled over, each person to their respective sides of the bed. Her shoulders gently nudged his own. He wanted to sleep, but Norman was in his mind. Norman with his knuckles and smug certainties, his glib answers and lack of doubt.

When Richard finally slept, he dreamed again of the nightmare with his mother lying under the bus singing as worms squirmed their way through her face. It shifted from Georgia to Arora. It was the fourth time he had had this nightmare.

He sprang awake, heart thudding against his ribcage as if it might implode. He clutched the duvet with a vice-like grip, twisting it anxiously. Laying next to him on the bed, Arora made a whimpering sound and curled up in a foetal-like position. In the dim light of the room, Richard realised he had pulled the duvet off her completely, yet she had slept so deeply that she had not even noticed.

It was 4am. He felt wired. He had woken up feeling like a live current was passing through him. Unable to sleep any longer, he sat up and typing letters into a phone:

Whisper alert. At Arora's, if you're home this evening—8pm—important. hope you can *ALL* make it...

*

Later, Richard, Ares and Tom sank down into the sofas. Miles walked into the room, his head bent over his phone, fingers moving with practiced ease, as if whatever was on the screen mattered more than the people around him. He sank into a chair, finally glancing up, and dryly said, "I hope we're not just here to draw up a list of useless theories. I've got other things I could be doing right now."

"Indeed," Richard said, raising one knowing eyebrow at Tom, who stifled a snort.

"Get to it then," Miles said, eyeballing the room.

Clearing his throat, Richard opened the notes he had made on his Nemdigi5000. "Fellow Whisperers, it's no secret that we're known by that name. And I've heard even in Little Jiwa.... But does anyone know who we *really* are? I'm not convinced. Over the past week, I've found out something that could enable us to maintain our mystique and go beyond."

"Speak for yourself," Ares was already rolling her eyes. "I'm not looking for mystique; I just wanna quietly knock the bottom out of the smug, entitled, punks who think they still rule this world. Mystique? I want to break things and be seen doing it."

But Miles was intrigued. "Ares, please."

Richard chucked his notes.

"I was invited to trial a drug. With a big sponsor. I signed up and participated. It was an incredible experience." They could see he meant business. Even Ares had lifted her chin. "Gone are the days of the white stuff. Nuvo 7 is White Milk on steroids."

"I've heard of the previous iterations," Miles said, touching an invisible beard as if modelling his favourite Ascended facial expression. His glowing brown skin gleamed with hues of cherry and purple under the artificial white light.

Richard told them with embellished details, of his experience of going into the holographic world of his own mind. They were spellbound. It's what the milk never was. This had a function. And he felt himself rise in their esteem. When he had finished his account, he felt more connected, a part of something that he had only ever observed before. He was dating the most beautiful girl in Nemes. He had the best friends. He had a plan to change all their lives for the better. He had a purpose now.

"Good," Miles whispered. Ares was nodding. Tom had taken a step back as though he was preparing himself. All of this, they all must have realised, was real. And that meant... Potential. Unlimited Potential.

"Order The Library perfectly, and the body will live for thousands of years. Perhaps even...forever. Death is just a symptom of psychological disarray. And by using the pill to alter and even crush the negative parts of the mind, we will reverse disease.

"Duty has called us; by honing our character we will evolve the races. We will honour Nemes by Ascending here and Ascending all others. We are not the establishment. We are the face of the new generation who are striving for an Ascended world, where there is no state, not of Nemes nor of Silany—where the Fal exists no more. We will all live forever.

The room was pulsating with excitement now. And a darkness, drawn to their excitement, seeped slowly through the cracks. It enveloped the room like a shadow and left no place for the light to hide.

"We will become the masters. This *is* what it is to Ascend. This is why the sponsor is trialling the drug. *You too can live with us*." He paused for them and delivered the context, placing his hands together and moving into prayer. "They're speeding up our Ascension. We are going to Nemes. Like they have done, we will extend our hands and help others be all that they can be. What's not to like? I mean, already I am radiant, I am pure. Next, we will join with the Gods and control the weather. We will make others become the Gods that they were born to be. We will control the stars; we will create worlds."

CHAPTER 8
Misanthropy

"I've been trying to get hold of you for days, Brother," Richard said.

"Why? What's up?" Miles was on the floor of his bedsit surrounded by scattered papers, needles, socks, a giant cube, and the arm of a doll. In a vagrant state of somnambulism, he grew a smile. He'd had too much of the White and Dream Sprinkle, evolved from the White Milk, which now came as blue goop to paste onto the wrists. Likely having just travelled around some abstract realm or far-out moon, Miles was topless and wearing tight pants that were silver. He terrified most people, but not Richard. Miles' cryptic yet academic nature was his competition, and Richard intended to use his own assets to prove his supremacy going forth as a leader—aggression, and his ability to be violent. Sometimes Richard enjoyed looking at Miles, wondering what his black skin would look like bleeding, or otherwise removed entirely. They were team-mates, and aboard the same ship sailing out of the stormy Silanese compliance and into Nemerian Paradise. The passage through was anarchy and the chaos joined the souls of Miles and Richard in a way Norman and Richard would never unite. It was for this reason, Richard enjoyed calling Miles his brother.

Miles gazed off into the distance, pursing and relaxing his lips.

Richard tilted his head. "Just tell me what's going on."

"I didn't even get past the application stage...for the job at Ipsteins." Miles picked up a letter and tossed it Richard's way. Highlighted in green: "Despite the success of your time at Ipsteins..." Richard couldn't be bothered to read one more word and threw it at the wall, smiling.

"At least you got a response. Weird though. Everything was pointing towards you getting that."

"I've been thinking. And I can only think of one reason for it. Like you. I'm still a Sub."

"If we're this side of the Fal, we're all Sub on some level. Including the ones they let in."

"Not true. Some are lower than a Sub, like your mother."

A knot twisting his stomach, Miles had been tested again. Everyone would get to re-test on their birthday and Miles came back a Three-Fourths. But if Miles couldn't get into a Nemerian institution here in Silany as a three-fourths, how would Richard? How would he become... *a man of power?* A leader? Adored by a people? "Your father was a member of the fucking Brotherhood. You're a three-fourths. What is this bullshit?"

"Still not good enough for the Halls of Power. I've been doing some research." Miles stood up, the doll's arm hitting the floor, and the air parting before him as he walked. The light through the window bounced off his silver pants. "Because my mother was half Silanese, I'm not right...In the head. Yet, if it was the other way, and she had the whole Nemerian constitution, but my father was half a bottom feeder, I'd be more bankable as a three-fourths."

Bogod, Learner and the others talked of this in their teaching, though Richard often chose to glide over those parts. They suggested exactly what Miles was saying. It was all about the mother. She had the potential to give a child love, while taking it all from him; give a child hope but screw him sideways by rendering the poor bastard a warped Sub, chained to the heel of a damned Silany. His Mother was all Silanese. It was her fault he was like this. *And she had held Father back too. No, Richard. You have met Arora, and she has guided you to Nuvo. Here you will learn, develop, and Ascend. You will save Mother, become a God over Nemes and Silany, and make Silany the new Nemes with your very own Manifesto.*

"I'm sure there are some Subs who have made it," Richard said, shaking his head. "Father's old colleague, Mani, he is the Minister of the Inferior, and they Ascended him."

"Did he test Whole?"

"I guess, I don't know."

"Was he born in Silany?"

"I don't know."

"Whether you're born in Silany, or born with any Silanese DNA whatsoever, on some level, you're still a Sub. In fact, you're a Sub-human, Subject to the Nemerians until you Ascend and become a Whole One. Right now, we are Sub-ject to them, and those under us are subject to us. Mani and men like him, from what I see, like to tout the idea that the power structures are open to people of all genetics but what if it's not true? Huh, Richard?"

Richard screwed up his face. "Fuck. It's been four months since we graduated, and others started working already. Yet, neither of us has benefitted from the promise of the University of Nemes in spite of this so-called "Ascension Acceleration Climate."

"Lara from Building Z5 is being tested next week. They say she—"

"Fuck Lara. She's the daughter of a farmer."

"Yes, but her mother..."

"I'll have her on her knees by Friday."

Richard was fuming. His skin felt like it was crawling with lice. Sweat, heat, the process of decay—the Silanese still contained within them all matter of unsafe waste materials—symptoms of Silany's general uncleanliness. Richard could almost feel what it was to be a one-fourth and hated that more than Miles' smile, which he wanted to wipe from his mouth with a razor.

Richard took a measured breath. "We need to be more cunning. Like that bastard who screwed my father over—what's his name?—Grey. We need to be like Grey."

"You've not come up with a masterplan then?"

"Not yet," Richard said, pressing his right fist into the palm, his shoulder muscles tensing into his neck and up into his eyes. He was going to have to do something. Funds for his mother's care were running dry and Norman wouldn't be able to pay for it alone. Useless Norman. The money was going to have to come from somewhere. He had a plan, though, some ideas. He just had to convince the rest of the team before they slipped into oblivion and recrimination.

As he stood there staring over Miles, he had much sympathy for his new brother, this soldier and felt a need to save them all.

Richard had Miles, Tom and Ares over at Arora's flat that night. He lived there now. It was the most discreet place to meet, especially when Arora was out with her loser friend, Meronia. The four of them were spread around the room, watching as Richard's presentation gleamed a rectangular glow on the bare wall. A 4-D image of a brain spun before their eyes with a voice-over Richard had spent all afternoon recording.

"The human brain—it enables us to think, dream, imagine, remember, hope and experience emotions. But it limits us."

The next image was of a sequence of characters—chess pieces Richard had designed earlier. The voiceover said they were: "Lust," "Fear," "Anxiety," "Insecurity," "Cowardice," and "Empathy."

"We tend to think of empathy as being a positive quality, but the flip side is that empathy can usurp our potential to make difficult choices. It can prevent us from taking the action we need, because we become overly concerned with the effect these actions may have on others. We are, therefore, bound by our own projections—mere prisoners of our own naivety and our inability to master empathy. However, the ability to temporarily switch off empathy grants us control and effectively, the power to choose and shape our lives, determining our own futures."

Having returned from the gym, Ares was sipping rehydration salts. On display was her new tattoo, the face of a ghost cloaked in a spacesuit. "It's me," she told Miles who was staring at it whilst pulling that invisible beard again dressed in a double-breasted Nate Jonzesque suit. Tom was sweating, the combination of the Nuvo myth and Arora's lingering scent was making the boy fidget and pick at a spot on his thumb until it bled.

Richard watched Tom's attention on Ares, the way his gaze roamed all over her body. From this angle, Tom could also see her tattoo and her breasts rise and fall as she breathed. Tom didn't stand a chance with her.

"This is where Nuvo 7 comes in," the voiceover continued as Richard stepped backwards. "Nuvo 7 enables us to weed out the psychological traits that hold us back physically, so we can become masters of ourselves."

He switched off the slideshow and turned on a standing light, just as Tom scanned the room. Richard wondered if maybe he thought it was his time to say a few words, but Richard dug in his heels, deciding that it was still his party.

Richard wondered how Arora would react if she were here. *Fuck. I shouldn't even care what she thinks as much as I do. I need Ares. She's good at taking the edge off.*

"We all know the sad truth: that Miles was rejected by the Bank—a *Nemerian* bank. He had the job taken from him by bloodsucking victims of a derelict system, all based on a book that doesn't know the potential of the mind. Yet, there are also believers in greater Potential. The world is evolving rapidly, and unless we lay claim to what we're owed, we're gonna lose out on any advantage we could have to Ascend. Why should we stand idly by while our opportunities for success and for progression are plucked from us? When we have studied for years to get this far? It's time to put our elite education to good use and use Nuvo to help us take back what we're owed. And we start by robbing banks."

"Located in the financial district of Silany," Richard clicked a button, and a 4-D projection of the bank's architecture began to spin. "She is the mother tree to all her children." Richard emphasised areas of the spinning network diagram, illustrating the complex Nemero-Silanese banking system, with Ipsteins positioned at its centre. "She is the nucleus of every bank in Silany, and the key connection across the Fal, into the Nemes Brain, where currency dissolves, into Nemes. I used to call it White Blood, but that was when I thought I was Silanese. The Electric Life Force that sustains Nemes and her people connects into Silany here, an ancient and derelict edifice that is but the remnants of an old way that should have already fallen. My work is to bridge the gap between the states, but my hands are tied by the Silanese man's desire to remain a slave. The type of man who wants to see heaven but is unwilling to die to see it."

"The clock is ticking and I set to embark on a mission—one that will demolish the outdated habit of Silanese acquiescence, and observe as Silany, in its desperation, reaches for its Nemerian master. I wanted to do this peacefully, but the time for that is over. Now we must bring change through chaos. I will take what is mine and you will take what is yours."

Ares' eyes brightened. "Fuck yeah!"

Miles' chin rose higher. Even Tom's glasses were removed.

"I want to rob them all."

Ares exhaled, nodding as she turned. The others were nodding too. They shared in his dream.

"And who better than Miles—who knows the layout of the building—to lead us into the bank."

"We can become the perfect criminals," Miles said and then he rose as if to assume the posture of a preacher, with Miles as the choir to Richard's ministry.

"Shame on the ancestors who made us what we are—dirty Subs with faulty genes containing contaminated traces of Silanese history.

"Let us take back from those who stole from us and made us slaves. Let us kick the faces of the dead, letting Silany fall and forcing Nemes to evolve *us*." Richard was nodding. He could see Miles was now his real brother.

"This type of work honours Nemes. It serves Nemes. It is a demonstration of our faith in Nemes. It will unify the states and go down in history. We will become legends, our names whispered for a thousand years to come. They will write our names on the Gates of Jiwa for all the lands to chant and celebrate us as their brothers. All races will become one and we will all be Nemerian. We will all evolve without hindrance, prejudice, or shame. Now who is with me!"

"I am, Richard."

"I am, Richard."

"I am, Richard."

Never again would they ever call him One-Fourth.

*

The gates to Rusty Barnfather's compound closed behind him. Richard stepped towards the glass pyramid at the top of the hill in District Seven Bungalows, a lone township in Silany that Rusty was born in and had moved back to. He always kept this spot with his work, jumping back and forth over the wall, or as he put it, "popping back and fore through the Nemes-Silany door." The Fal had many names in Silany, and it represented different things to different parts of the state. Liberty to some, order to others, and desire to many. Some even believed Nemes was just a dream, a Silanese fantasy to avoid the real truth of the condemned and the waste lands, but disassociation was a common way to deal with reality and accept one's own subservience and lesser genes. Since his father's death, Richard hadn't seen Rusty. He didn't know why. He must have been enjoying himself too much when he was still at university, fucking Ares behind Miles' and Arora's backs and shooting up the White Milk every Wednesday. He must have thought he didn't need anyone. He was, after all, soon to become a world-king. He was going places.

A sliding smoked-glass door opened to reveal Uncle Rusty.

"My favourite godson." Rusty stepped forward and bear-hugged Richard. "What brings you here? That's a large case. Planning to stay for a few weeks?"

"See how it goes," Richard said. "I might get a call from work, asking me to return." He had no intention of staying. He'd be gone tomorrow.

"You young, hectic types; I remember what it was like back in the day with your father. God, we had the girls queuing for us back then. Those *were* the days."

"How come you're back from Nemes?"

"Come in, son."

As they travelled up in the glass elevator at the heart of the pyramid, Richard was relieved that Rusty had not asked him what his job was, although he had an answer prepared just in case. Meanwhile, Richard struggled with the nagging sense of déjà vu—had he been here before? The answer seemed clear: yes. Yet, something felt different. He recognised the place, but the experience of being here was strangely unfamiliar. Rusty's penthouse was shaped like a capital T with the long ascender pointing down from the pyramid's tip. Once Richard had dropped his suitcase off in his bedroom—down the left arm of the T—Rusty took him to the open plan lounge, which stretched across the wide bar of the T. The lounge looked as though it belonged to an Old World hunter of the imperial age. A stuffed bear and lion stood like guardians, their presence unsettlingly lifelike. Above the massive plasma screen, two ivory tusks crossed like swords—remnants of a hunt long past but never forgotten. "Got rid of that shabby bungalow, replaced it with the T as you can see, the only soul left here with a love for the future. Adapt or die as they say. Do you know how old these tusks are?" Rusty asked.

Richard scratched his head, trying to answer the same question: *have I been here before?*

"A couple of hundred years?" Richard guessed.

"Four hundred years old, passed down to me from my forefathers, and this rug over here is three hundred years old Richard, preserved for longevity with the use of chemical treatments. Feel how soft it is."

Richard bent down and stroked the rug.

"Quite frankly I couldn't give two shits about it all. Every day I spend this side of the wall is just a..."

"Still...this place is pretty impressive Rusty."

"Five hundred and thirty-five days I tell you. Son of a bitches can't let me back in until my work over in the mines is up."

"Etronium?"

"Yep, Etronium," Rusty said, nodding his head to the side, spinning and walking away.

"I guess I thought you were still just cybernetics and... arms."

"Etronium, my friend. It's a faster way to get back home."

"I'm sorry it's been so long."

"Ah, what are ya gonna do, got to play my part to help shits like you I suppose, the new generation and all that crap." He turned to face Richard who was just catching up, skipping slightly to catch his godfather as he turned. "Let me look at ya." He grabbed Richard and stuck his face close to his, staring intently into his eyeballs. "You're not working for them, are you?"

Richard didn't know what to say. He had heard stories of Uncle Rusty putting folks to sleep out here and burying them in the dunes. It's why they say he built this place, to watch from a distance and play assassin free of Pano's Watch.

Richard's balls had shrunk, his penis was now the size of a bean, and his neck was tightening around a word that squeezed through and fell out of his lips.

"Who?"

Rusty gave up, released Richard and shook his head.

"Who? Exactly! That's the question your father and I used to ask each other. We used to sit right there, ya know." He pointed to the side where two unusually large purple chairs were stationed. "Talking of Nemes, the future, planning our next trip. I'd love to take you sometime soon, Richard. We ever go together? I can't remember now."

"Umm, we went once, when we went shootin'."

"Ah yes. So we did. What a trip."

Back in the day, when Richard had come here with his father, he had only ever spent time in the underground shooting gallery and not been allowed up into the upper areas of the pyramid. This was all new and fascinating to him. Richard gave Rusty a pat on the shoulder. He remembered everything now and felt at ease again in the company of his family member—the nourishment of his soul.

Rusty moved to the sideboard and began to pour whiskey into a tumbler before glancing over with a knowing smirk. "Like father, like son?"

"I'm not quite the whiskey drinker Father was. I'll just have one." Actually Richard didn't like it at all, but he didn't want to disappoint. He hoped that Rusty would get drunk. He needed him drunk and pliable. He leaned back, settling in for a long night of drinking and talking and more drinking.

"Well then, perhaps you're after something a little more, shall we say, "spiritual?" Rusty lifted a tall bottle of thick white milk. It was no doubt an old ritual his father and uncle used to indulge in. And a tempting one at that. Perhaps this could be the last time. Ah, why the hell not?

After two hours of drinking and shooting milk and recounting tedious stories about the old days and whiskey and Phillip Wise and whiskey and whiskey as the reward of Nemes and whiskey as the soul of Nemes and Nemes as the soul of whiskey, Rusty was starting to slur. "Oh, I...f...f...got to ask how y... your mother is..."

If you were high on White Milk, you didn't know it, and that was the beauty of the hallucination it generated. It saved the viewer the embarrassment of witnessing themselves by disconnecting the part of the brain that generated self-awareness. The mind was left to project only its subconscious dreams. Thus, it was easier to let go and fall in love with one's own visions, attaching to them as though they were real projections. The White Milk also allowed Ascendees to surrender their own will to the pull of Nemes, an evolved reality that was there in the future for them. The White Milk was a spoiler that was more real than any advert. If the ads on Nemes TV were educational and functional, the trip brought on by the White Milk was experiential. And everyone did it—except folks like Norman. He was a victim of an old system that feared progress, barring serums like White Milk from reaching a society that preached liberty yet failed to understand its true meaning. Ironically, it was the White Milk that revealed true freedom—a state of surrender, where one embraced their visions without judgment. The drug still served this purpose, but as he had recently told his disciples, Nuvo 7 was the way forward.

Richard drifted downward through a stream of sapphire-coloured liquid cotton and stepped onto a bank of lush green turf, clad in nothing but a simple loin cloth. Waiting to greet him was Arora and his own mother. Yet, no matter how hard he tried, he could not see his mother's face, which remained hidden by low-hanging fruit—huge, blue, and plump with juice.

"I am Nemerian," he heard Arora say to him as the shape of his mother began to shift and a tail formed where her legs had been.

"Get out of the water, Richard," Arora said to him.

"But I am out of the water," he replied. At that, the shape of the creature that had once been his mother morphed into a hard-scaled desert serpent.

"Okay, ANYTHING YOU SAY!" Richard awoke, panting and sweating.

"Fuck...Nemes." He looked over at Rusty who was out of it, head back, with dribble running down his face. He turned to Rusty's ice bath, stripped naked and climbed in.

*

Later that evening, Richard and Rusty lounged in their dressing gowns and sank into the plush comfort of Rusty's purple chairs, drinking whiskey and smoking cigars.

"Sadly, she's been in care for well over a year now. They say she has a neuro-degenerative condition. Honestly, it's tough. It's the one thing that keeps me going back to the house. Cause Norman and I, well I guess you know we never really got on."

"I had a brother once."

"Really?"

"Yeah."

*

Richard walked barefoot, having discarded his socks when they began to itch. It was as though they had been woven using live insects. At one point he visualised the feet as computers that were processing too much information and overheating. The flames rose past his thighs. Although he knew he was hallucinating—after all, the flames had turned into people—he still lowered his feet back into Rusty's ice bath. It was what they called "milk reflux," when traces of White Milk lingered in the system during a come down. It was intentionally designed to help users recognise the hallucination for what it was. It was like the end of a computer game, when the VR headset would come off and the player eventually remembered that it had just been a screen all along. He walked on as quietly as he could to the furthest end of the corridor and turned right into the storeroom. He pushed the door open; Rusty seemed to have let his guard down over the years as far as security was concerned. Maybe that was just because he knew how shit scary he could be to the vulnerable kind who lived in the bungalows nearby. The room was chilly, and the marble floor made it even colder. But the low temperature felt soothing against his feet, which had become raw and blistered with incessant scratching. Inside, there was row upon row of Skimguns, rifles and blasters.

He spent a few minutes picking up different types of weapons and weighing them in his hands, he was trying to figure out which would best suit each of The Whisperers. In the end, he just grabbed a bunch: handguns, sleek, silvery Skims with laser sighting and shark-shaped barrels. He'd left behind a noticeable gap on one of the shelves. Richard hoped Rusty wouldn't notice they were gone for a few days. At his age, and with the amount of the White he took, he should be enjoying reflux for a week. It'll have him questioning his own sanity and wondering whether he really thought that Richard took them. Although Richard didn't particularly care.

The sound of Rusty snoring reverberated around the living space as Richard passed by, sweating profusely despite wearing an open shirt, and loaded with shells and cartridges. He'd even found a grenade. He took one look at his uncle and, for a second, thought it might be a good idea to blow his brains out. Rusty was well known for his off-radar nature. Richard looked around. None of the usual suspect spy cams were lying around. Apparently, Rusty used to work for the Faj. But Rusty had stories about countless lives—all of them, apart from the time he screwed his nanny, were probably made up.

He pointed the Skimgun he was holding at Rusty's head and placed his finger on the trigger. *There's no way anyone would know*. Richard chose not to entertain the thought a second more. He had the guns he came to steal. Now he wanted to rob banks, take Nuvo 7 and save his killing spree for the Silanese who would get between him, Nemes and everlasting life. If he could save Mother along the way, that would just be swell.

"See ya soon, Uncle." Richard turned and walked away.

*

The Whisperers held their breath as Richard took out one orange and blue capsule from a metal pill container and popped it into Miles' hand. The four of them were meeting in Arora's apartment again.

"Give it to me," Tom said. He sounded like a belligerent teenager jealous of an older brother's turn.

"Not yet," Ares said. "Miles has to be first. We need to stay calm and smart here."

"Yes, there's no point in the rest of us using until Miles has mapped out his plan of the building. We don't have all the monitoring equipment, but you can press this sensor on your temple to get out."

"Once you're in, locate the book in The Library that details the layout of the bank. It could be filed in one of several places—try under Capitalism, Failures, or under Ipsteins Bank. If you want to source useful information quickly, ask the Clerk to look through the book and then place it at the front of the shelf, closest to Origin. Books closer to the front of the shelf, or the "Origin," where you'll land, are easier to remember, and those placed further back are usually dusty, and will become less vivid. Provided you do as I say, when you're back, you should be able to recall the bank's layout perfectly. Worst case scenario, you'll have to go back in. Any questions?"

"No," Miles said. He was scared but excited. Like the face of an astronaut being launched into deep space, his veins were pumping. He popped the pill and dropped to the ground.

*

Within minutes, his eyelids were fluttering. He had entered a REM sleep like state. The others paced the room. The odd question was posed, but mostly they kept glancing anxiously over at him, unable to break the silence, yet restlessly wondering what it was like to be in one's own mind.

After ten minutes had passed, Miles' eyes shot open.

The pen and notebook had already been prepared for him.

He began sketching the plan of the bank, frantically making sure to capture every detail.

"Don't forget the currency conversion point," Tom said. "Without that we're in the dark." As he had told them time and time again, this point was the key to them being able to reverse engineer the Ipsteins system. This particular point in the bank, converting Nemerian money into Silanese currency, still required older Silanese technology and was therefore highly vulnerable. None of the newer Nemerian systems for monetary transfer were hackable.

Miles nodded and carried on mapping out what he had seen. Similarly to Pano's Watch, the bank's architecture was circular, like a panopticon. The entrance to the bank and the primary hallway was on the eastern side of the building, but most business was conducted around the perimeter. Like an onion, the currency conversion point was placed at the heart of the building, protected by a series of increasingly tight circular security barriers, all based on a system of technocratic policing. Like Panoptes, the God with a thousand eyes, there was always one eye open. For this reason, like all of Nemes' banks, no one had attempted breaking into Ipsteins for over 100 years. But it wasn't just because of the security design. The Silanese had an inferior tendency to conform and presume their second-class status, their positions as interns. There was just no point in trying to jump over the Fal, rob a Nemerian bank, or do anything in this world other than comply. Comply, and study The Manifesto. It was the only way across. That was before Richard Wise took Nuvo 7.

"Okay we all need to take the pill and do the work. Empathy binding work. *But...*" He held up his palms, steady and firm, like a restraining father. Tom and Ares moved up out of their seats. "We'll save it for the daytime, before the robbery. We don't want any of us inadvertently doing anything risky that might implicate us. Everyone OK with that?"

"When do we make our move?" Tom asked.

"Saturday night." Two days away. "The banks don't open the next day."

A slow grin spread across Tom's face. It felt as if they were reliving their first night on campus—the night they had first met, the night that whispered promises had been birthed. As if that moment had never truly ended, stretching endlessly through time, forever.

*

It was 23:30 in downtown Little Jiwa, the financial district of Nexus 10. The broad boulevard flanked by conifers leading up to the largest bank in the FDS, Ipsteins, was deserted. A stray dog wandered off the pathway to mark his territory against the one artificial tree. It didn't seem to notice the four Whisperers dressed in black—two were hooded and two were in woollen beanie hats, their faces obscured by home-made masks sporting Richard's black knight logo. There were none of the AI-Pups, no Wolf Machines, no Nemerian Drones. People were going about their business, unaware of how scared they were, complying to the FDS regulations they had learnt to accept. If you wanted to bank at all in Silany, you needed to comply with Nemerian process and people in the FDS had learnt to comply.

Tom pricked Miles' finger over the screen on his phone. A few red droplets fell, activating Miles' Intern ID Card, which was required to access the bank's mainframe. Tom would wipe this record later. The doors slid open just as the security cameras were disabled and The Whisperers slid in, removing their masks. Each one had their Skim loaded and tucked into a halter slung around their hips. All of them wore the same white thin gloves.

Inside, the high ceilings were adorned with gold chandeliers that tinkled in the passing breeze and swept through this massive bank. Dim photoelectric security lighting lit the way along the wide elliptical corridor that traced the bank's perimeter.

Miles had meticulously mapped out every security door and every possible detector on his plan, each one a checkpoint where Tom would prove his mettle. The team would peel back each layer of security like an onion, infiltrating deeper and deeper until they reached the very core.

Tom, giddy with the thrill of anticipated succession, threw his head back, stamped his feet and whispered to the heavens, "Fuck you, Nemes!"

"Get to it," Miles said, giving Tom a nudge. "The CCP is just behind that door." He signalled to the Etronium door measuring two metres wide with two heavy iron bars slotted into place as a deterrent and entered a fifteen-digit code. Ares stepped in, lifting one of the bars.

Once Tom had reverse engineered the final detector, the team watched on as the door swung open, revealing the exchange point inside. It was not like an Old World kiosk, more like a box-shaped console in the middle of a room.

"Ready your digitals to receive the money, while I get this old thing reverse engineered," Tom said.

"Wait a minute, I'll take the whole amount into my digital and then work out who gets what."

"Woah," Tom said, holding up his hand. "That was not what we agreed to."

"It makes more sense to divert the money into different receiving points to cover our tracks," Miles said. "We discussed this."

"Who's in charge, here?" Richard turned his head. "If I was worried about getting caught, do you think I'd take the risk? You all have digital wallets internalised, mine is not part of my body. I'll pass the money on to you once it's safe to. Not before."

Being more than a one-fourth Tom, Ares and Miles all had digitals in an RFID chip located in the palm of their left hands, Richard was right, it just wasn't safe. Instead, Richard had purchased a quantum encrypted data-stick that he could use as a receiving point instead. Within minutes, the screen on the conversion point was flashing sequences of numbers.

"Ready to receive? I'm just going to get it rolling," Tom said.

"Do it," Richard said, licking his lips eagerly. The face on his watch glowed green. He watched as the numbers rolled, starting in the 100s, then rolling into the 1000s, then the 10,000s. There was nothing in their way. It was a clean operation, and Nuvo was a sure failsafe. The numbers were confirming that. "How far do you reckon we can go?"

"That's enough," Richard said. Tom released his grip on the dial, and the number on Richard's watch stopped at 74,556 strata.

"That was easy," Miles said.

*

Richard's head was throbbing.

His phone vibrated. It was Rusty on a video call.

"Rusty, I'll call you back."

Rusty went to speak but Richard cut the call.

Within minutes, Richard had finished his final transfer, this time via the National Bank of Fallorin. With that weight now off his shoulders, he picked up his phone again and began to dial Rusty's number. He didn't want to deal with Rusty, he just wanted to be home with Arora. Besides, he already knew what Rusty would say. But he called him back anyway, *because he was family*.

"Rich, my boy."

"How are you doing, Uncle?"

"Richard, I've got more fingers in more pies than your mama ever served Silany. You took my guns. I want 'em back." Rusty winked and continued in a low voice, "I know about Ipsteins."

"You know nothing."

"I know everything and nothing. I have the power to crush every bone in your maggot body by nightfall, but that wasn't part of the promise I made to your coward of a father—your father who I used and disrespected and in whose image you are made...I knew you had it in you." Rusty smiled through his beard, and his eyes glinted at Richard.

With a sudden pang, Richard realised that Rusty was proud of him.

"You've got to make it easy for me to keep quiet about this, it could cost me my livelihood." He shook his head. "I'm not joking."

"I know. I'll make it worth your while, Uncle."

*

Norman met up with Theo in a diner not far from the Red Sea. It was early in the evening and all of Silany seemed to stink of mildew and rain. They played Blackjack while drinking coffee. After some time, Theo laid his cards down on the table. "Final year of my apprenticeship as a human rights lawyer, the funds got pulled."

"Why pulled?"

"A memo arrived at the office one day in January last year that said: "Theo Wantou will no longer be able to continue his training, the Department of Home Affairs has decreed it is no longer an economically viable option for him." I was so close to finishing, Norm. All that work and now it's gone to waste. And you know what they wanted me to do? Train to be a mortgage advisor. I couldn't think of anything more soulless."

"What did you do?"

Theo shook his head. "Had to take it."

A week later, Norman approached a single storey whitewashed warehouse on the outskirts of Nexus-10. A dim glow from inside the building was the only indication that anyone was inside.

He banged hard on the door and gave whoever was inside two minutes to respond. Norman used the butt end of his rifle to loosen the hinge and then leaned all his weight against it. Nothing. So, he kicked the door down and ploughed his way through. Norman was squatting heavy these days. Down the corridor to the right, two harmless men sat in an office surrounded by piles of papers and white bags. The younger one looked up at him with a face that was resigned and held up his hands. The older man rolled his eyes upwards as if beseeching divine intervention, then pushed himself up from the table limply in a half-hearted attempt to run. He couldn't run from Norman.

Lunging forward, he took hold of the upper arm of the older man. "Mark Ganopolos, Tobias Tramp?" He didn't wait for a reply. "On behalf of the state of Silany, I'm arresting you for the illegal distribution of drugs in Nexus-10."

At the same time, three miles away on the other side of the city, Officer Ant Atherton was arresting a far less respectable man. He didn't attempt to knock on the door of this seedy establishment in the heart of the city's red-light district. He battered it down and dragged out a shifty looking man with protruding ears. It was the man known by the moniker of Red Fish. "Arthur

Stanage, you are under arrest for supplying illegal drugs to the people of Silany."

Lashing out with all four limbs, Red Fish didn't give up as easily as the others. "You're not going to get away with this! People need me. They'll come knocking down your smug door begging you for mercy! YOU NEED ME! Don't you want to know who is *really* behind this? Don't you?" One of the police officers used all his strength to hold Red Fish back, while the other handcuffed him. Knowing there was no longer any point in resisting, Red Fish's twitching body stilled. Ant later told Norman that he reckoned the Fish had worked himself up so much that he might have had his last swim.

*

In the early hours of the morning, Norman trudged up the metal steps of his apartment in the favela. Three of the key players were down. This should have been the best day of his career, but instead he only felt a numbing exhaustion. He had stuck to his moral guns the whole way and the effort of doing the right thing had snagged every fibre in him. He should have been on the biggest high of his life, but instead, Norman took off his shoes and crept into bed. Wracking sobs shook his body.

Not only was he sure that there was more that he'd not been able to uncover, but in using every scrap of his strength to crack this assignment, he had allowed his own needs to fall by the wayside. It had been over six months since Norman had had more than three hours sleep. Thankfully, it was Friday night.

The trilling of the phone woke him the next morning. Normally he was able to jump out of bed, but this morning was different. It was 10:04 am and he'd already slept for nine hours, though could have gone longer. His movements were sluggish, and by the time he got to the phone, the ringing had stopped.

*

It was one of those blustery spring days when everything seemed clear and fresh. Norman walked along the lane towards Medway Care Home and allowed the budding of the crocuses along the side of the road to feed fresh hope to his soul.

Entering the care home, he was stopped short by the crestfallen expression of a receptionist. "Norman, we tried to call you...to tell you, but there was no reply... I'm so sorry for your loss, Norman."

*

Norman watched the way Richard clung to Arora under a huge black umbrella. He seemed unstable. Rain fell—swallowed up by the thirsty, hard red earth near the grave. Arora seemed mesmerised by the rain, as if in a trance. Richard's elbow interlinked with hers. He muttered something in her ear that Norman was sure he had heard correctly: *"Just when I was about to bring her back."*

Norman moved away from the two of them to the other side of the grave. Blinking at Norman for permission to proceed, the celebrant began the service of remembrance.

"Out of dust and into dust, this precious light has gently gone out." These were the only words that stuck with Norman that day. Neither he, nor Richard, had prepared any personal words to say about their mother's life.

At the end of the ceremony, a tall, grey-haired lady came forward to shake Norman's hand. Her eyes glistened with tears that threatened to spill.

"I'm Lilliana—an old friend of your mother's. I regret I didn't visit her more. I wish I could make amends. But it's too late for that now." She leaned forward to whisper in his ear, "I know that you must be Norman," and pulled away.

Richard threw Norman a cold, hard stare but kept his eyes fixed firmly on the coffin in the grave as four people standing on each corner began throwing spades of dirt. All the guests left, including Lilliana who had tossed yellow flowers on top of the grave before she sank into the background. Along with her, Richard had followed suit, placing on the coffin The Manifesto in between a bouquet of fresh roses and lilies.

Even in death this guy just won't let up, will he? Norman stayed behind for hours, and grabbed The Manifesto from Georgia's grave when he was sure he was alone. In it, paperclipped to the first page, he found a poem:

Solace for a Savage Soul

Something in the fall of the rain.
Something in the shadow of the moon.
The new moon rising, in an autumn sky.
Strangers passing by,
Strangers passing by.
Who can trace the pieces of a broken heart?
Who can redeem me from the dark?
Rainbows in your eyes,
Rainbows in my eyes,
And the moon in my heart.

Fractured reflections in a broken mirror glass
Reflections of life,

Reflections of love,
A broken past,
Like an ending…

Sounds of time,
Fuzzy memories,
Spirits in the wind,
Spirits on the wing,
Like the ghost of the morning,
Searching for solace for a savage soul.
Beasts on the wing,
Wild in the autumn sky,
Solace for a savage soul.

The sound of children in the muffling of the day,
Like an ending, and the turning away,

Tell me the sound of one hand clapping,
Time tears down all empires,
Time takes all heroes.

I dance on moon beams
I shape shift in shadows,
I turn, lured by a bright eye,
I turn, and join the creatures of the dark,
All at the precipice of history.
Solace for a savage soul.

Norman shed a tear. He thanked his mother and said, "I won't part with it again. There's work to do now. See you again someday, Mum."

CHAPTER 9
Trait Theory

It had been five months since the funeral. Richard had not shaved or cut his hair. He had started wearing darker colours. Part of him wanted the time before she had passed to stand still, so he could rescue her as planned. *One day I will create time.*

Running his fingers through greasy black hair, he finished the paragraph he was writing. He got up, stretched, and carried his stiff body over to the corner of the office to grab the whiskey. Rusty had delivered a truckload after Richard paid him for the guns. The trade was fair, but Richard had won. Two months earlier, Richard had found and rented this disused ninth-floor office-come-flat-come-pad in downtown Little Jiwa, a short ride from the FDS. Great fronds and ferns sat near the front glass wall and others were dotted around the inside to oxygenate the flat. It was a clean flat, with wind blowing off the coast, up a bank, over a long and perfect artificial lawn and up nine stories into his apartment. It then passed through the flat into the backroom and out the bedroom's balcony into the FDS. Richard had the best of both worlds: he'd stand naked facing the wind and the water in the mornings, and at night he'd lean over his bedroom balcony in a dressing gown with the wind on his back watching the city lights. It was part of his routine. In the middle of the day, he'd sit at a glass table, with his mind, the plants and, whiskey for company. If anyone saw him this way, he'd look pretty strange, but many were suspicious these days. This was the nature of Pano's Watch. And the new, more subtle surveillance wasn't helping. Nemes had introduced a report system, a social benefit programme in an attempt to root out more crime. Everything was being reported now using Nemerian data mining systems and stored in giant data banks made from etronium. Such artificially intelligent systems were deciding what to do with the Silanese, how to evolve them, how to re-educate them and bring them out of their condition. Countless new ideas were tested, but none to the maxims of The Manifesto. Its principles were now the bedrock of Silanese institutions—at least, what was left of them. The old was systematically uprooted and replaced with the Nemerian new. At the same time, The Whisperers hovered on the fringes of Nemes—half in, half out. Their rituals of fire, goat's blood, mantra, and White Milk bound them to Nemerian ideology, yet they were still exiles, left standing outside the wall. Georgia's death had complicated their Ascension, as Richard was still in mourning. On one occasion, he had Ares dress as her and wear a mask of her face. But it didn't work. Nothing was working—except the wind, the thinking, and the steady rhythm of his writing. But that was enough. Richard's manifesto was finally taking form.

Miles lay spread-eagled on one sofa and Tom on the other, their eyelids flickering. They'd both popped a Nuvo pill not too long ago. It had to be done. Development was key if they were to succeed, bring the system to its knees and cross over the Fal. So much had been learnt since Ipsteins. Not through discussion or planning, but by spending time in their own minds, re-orienting their own psycho-architecture. These days, Tom no longer perspired, Miles was no longer 'black' but, simply, 'was what he was', and he no longer laughed. Ares no longer cared for things—all traces of empathy and femininity having been purged from within her. She now considered herself sexless and had her breasts removed. She used her vagina to move energy, not in the way the Silanese considered natural, but transactionally, to procure power. There were few emotions left to express. The heart was now nothing more than a functional pump supplying the organs and the tissues with key nutrients. Meditation, ritual, and time spent in the Mind, holographically portrayed as the Nuvo world. These were the ways of living these days. Clean, focused and united, they were Ascending. They were just waiting for Richard to play catch-up. Tensions did surface. Ares had told him that he walked arrogantly at times, when he chose to walk in the nude with only an open gown to mimic an air of modesty. But Arrogance was a trait, a symptom of Judgement. All of this was being combed through. Slowly but inevitably, the other Whisperers were transcending human form. Being was their direction, post-humanness the assignment.

Looking at his watch, Richard tapped them all on the soles of their feet. Here, trigger points connected him to the inside of their minds, so he could remind them of the outside world. Miles' body shook, his chest expanding, and he awoke. He sat up with his head in his hands and Richard handed him a small paper cup of water.

"How was that?"

"Good. I no longer have a childhood."

"Any closer to figuring out how to manage empathy more effectively?"

"The more I try to bind my Empathy trait, the more Guilt tries to mess with me. I had him literally jump on my back when I was in there just now, punching me. I had to think on my feet about what memories I could lead Guilt to, to stop him getting in my way."

"Guilt is a pig."

"Guilt is a thief. That's how I got him. Used that line from the great book. *Guilt is the thief of life. Don't waste your time on guilt, which is designed to hijack your power and replace it with feeling.* That got him off eventually."

Tom sat up with a grunt and a heavy sigh.

"Two hours, 15 minutes this time," Richard said. "You know the rules."

"Fuck the rules," Tom said. No longer a geek with ginger hair and spots, Tom was well groomed, well suited up, and confident.

Richard crouched down in front of him. "Addiction is the pathway to destruction."

Closing his eyes, Tom stiffened. "You're a killjoy, Wise, always pissing on the gates of revelation. I'm not addicted. I'm in training. Anxiety and Inferiority just kicked the bucket."

Changing tactics, Richard walked over to the drinks machine. "I'm going to the gym."

"She's not there."

Ares was always there around this time, the only one of them to have gotten an official job, but she didn't do it for the money. There were men there she could use, while working as a kickboxing instructor on the surface. Richard would head down there most evenings, and they'd screw each other in the changing rooms, after closing time, without speaking. There was no emotion, just pleasure—sensations to experience, observe, archive, and improve on. "Hit me with this," "hit me with that," all was tried and tested, sex with Love was atypical and now a long-since forgotten ideology.

"Maybe she is, maybe she isn't. Don't pop another Nuvo. There are rabbit holes, and there are *rabbit holes*."

That night, she wasn't there. Ten nights passed, and still, she had not returned. Walking, drifting, he thought only of Mother, and Arora too. At times he'd stand on the side of the road looking over Silany the entire night, like a lonesome vampire surveilling the landscape in the dark. Few things, in fact, crossed his mind. He saw from the Nuvo how many of his thoughts were not even his, and so didn't even need to be re-ordered, but burned. These days, he entertained his thoughts less, instead, letting them simply pass by. These days, Richard chose to trade wisdom for resources after he visited his mind. White Milk, grub, the ass of a whore and things of that nature. And there she was again in his mind. Arora—the only angel. The others in his clang were always succubi, demon wraiths draining his own Potential, vampiric insects feasting on his wisdom, taking everything, and providing nothing. But not Arora, she had given him Nuvo, she brought hope to those who had none. She was the other light in the night sky, and, one day, he would take her hand in marriage. And *Norman will watch me, and he will beg to know how and what I do.* He stood at the bottom of the Fal, and he screamed a word louder than any man from Silany had done since the time of the war, when Adam John called the Silanese "To Arms." Richard called, "Father" and he called, and he called, and he called.

*

Ares walked into Richard's flat. "Hive of activity, I see?"

"In some corners of the room," Richard said, turning around from his desk. He was working on his version of The Manifesto. He only had to complete a few more chapters. Then he would reveal it to the people. Ares walked past Richard, scanning him and his book. She looked over to Miles and Tom, and then quick as a flash, brought her right arm up, and forcefully dropped it, straight into Richard's jaw. She followed through, almost falling herself, and sent Richard spinning until he landed face down on the glass table.

"Prick," she said. He must have promised her a quick lay and not delivered. Richard had started seeing other girls openly, and he wasn't shy about it. If he had kept his promise to Ares, there wouldn't have been time to get ready for Arora. He preferred making Ares beg.

Richard stood up and pulled a knife. Ares pulled a gun.

"Sit down and write your book. I'm faster than you, I'm high on the Sprinkles and I couldn't give a fuck about Nemes. How's that for kicking Fear into the next dimension?"

Richard had begun rotating his jaw around in his face. It didn't hurt as much as it should have, but that might be because he seldom felt pain these days. Pain was muscular tension that tended to form when the mind feared the truth, a defence mechanism to protect a person. Richard had done a lot of work on himself so tended to see injuries as an inconvenience. Physical pain was extremely rare.

"How so?"

"I could see it in there. This place we call real is all dead. The Nuvo Mind is the only real thing. Kick the idea of Nemes, of Silany, and neither exist. All that exists is the mind. With that, I don't care if you die now, or if I do, cause I don't need what you need, Messiah Man."

Richard threw his knife onto the glass table and sat back down to his book, sad that the knife hadn't broken the table. "So, what's the point? Why are you still here?"

"Because you promised me you would help make things burn."

They smiled at one another, and she holstered her gun in the back of her leather pants. Richard exhaled and carried on writing.

The original version belonged in the pre-Nuvo past. Not that he'd been there since Uncle Rusty took him shooting, but he'd seen the papers, he'd watched enough Nemes TV this last moon and had decided for himself that Nemes was decadent, but weak. It needed reforming. Apart from robbing more banks, bringing Silany to its knees, and Ascending, he needed something else. Some form of insurance, some place to channel his doctrine. If Father had been alive, he would have been proud of the new saviour of Nemes. It was titled, *A Society of Mind: The Cognitive Pathway to Nemerian Ascension.*

Ares raised her eyebrows at Tom and Miles as they both came out of their trance. Tom spoke first.

"Subs are only here to provide Silany with the illusion of inclusivity, of social mobility. We're Subs to the Ascended, but they are lesser than Subs to us because they are choosing not to choose. We must cut them off. Demolition and destruction and flames is the only way they will learn. It is the only way we can help them choose. Let's rob more banks and watch our people burn their statues."

Miles turned to Richard. "You heard the man."

*

Richard followed as Tom pushed open the swinging doorway into Spektraskope, Gauthier's house, art studio and gallery.

"Now, this is something," Richard said looking around at the entrance lobby with its ten-metre-high ceiling. At the back of the room in the centre of the wall ran a constantly moving paternoster lift with flashing green and red lights that indicated when it was safe to get on and get off.

Located just outside of Little Jiwa, Gauthier had been selling obelisks, glass pigs and sculptures of Bogod to the rich elite, the invisible Nemerian Ascended who basically ran Silany out of Little Jiwa and through the FDS. Think tank projects like "Sustaining Silany" and state agencies like the Nemerian Health Organisers. Now they had moved back in, and they needed art to host their dinners. Gauthier made art as well as guns. So, men like Gauthier were good to know when it came to the inside. Though when it came to payday, the elite would send one of their henchmen here, and even then, Gauthier had to receive an envelope wearing a blindfold. Perhaps then, the elite were as invisible to Gauthier as anyone else. *Who knows*?

On either side of the approach to the lift, metallic sculptures depicted circuitry, motherboards, vast machines comprising cogs and wheels, gears and chutes with no apparent purpose, and huge men with their hands on their hips and antenna protruding from their heads. There were horses with cybernetic whiskers, dogs with cubes of circuitry for heads and...a portrait of Dr Cynar smirking insidiously. *Strange*. This last year, the FDS had received more funds from Nemes, so Little Jiwa was turning into a kind of mini-Nemes. This was also their long-term plan, to turn Silany into Nemes. The idea was that its people would then become Members, unable to function within its own society unless they, as members, followed Nemerian rules. It should have been renamed Little Nemes, but the Financial District of Silany was still the preferred epithet for this future of futures. This was the war that was really playing out, and it was happening in dark rooms, hidden coves involving some of the shadiest figures. The old Silanese council was still clinging to days long-gone. Nemes let them cling but replaced the names gradually. Nemerian design, the money, the culture, all of it was trickling into Silany. And nowhere was more obvious than in the arts. When Tom first met him, he was sketching root vegetables with lead pencils. Those days were gone. Once Gauthier named his price, the elite had their pictures framed, monuments built, and gemstones carved into the shapes of human nipples. He was now working on a new piano, built only from Silanese excrement.

"These were all built by Gauthier," Tom whispered.

"Impressive." Richard was gazing to the right at a silver eagle sculpture with wings of liquid metal that moved in fluid, wavelike motions. "In Miles' words, we can do with a mind like Gauthier's on our side."

Upstairs, Tom knocked on a door, then turned to Richard.

"Miles told me Gauthier is a two-thirds."

Richard was silent. He had no idea. Tom was nodding as if to confirm what Miles told him. This was his idea, and Gauthier was his friend. Richard was just going with it.

"With Ipsteins, we were lucky the first time," Tom said, "but they will know we're coming now. The sewer system works for me. It's complex enough to evade others, but simple enough to navigate with Nuvo. We'll memorise the checkpoint on the other side to a fast Skim or SkimBike, whichever we prefer. Our getaway points will be nowhere near each bank, that will be our key strategy."

"Tom, we've been through it all. Plus, we have plenty of guns to use as a starting point for weapons design if this works..."

But there was still something Tom wasn't clear on. As they waited for Gauthier, he kept running through the hatched plan.

"And the scramblers, they won't be able to trace and track us but if they suspect something, those sewers are going to be filled with lash-vortex-trap-boxes, Skimsniffers, and the infra-SWAT guys. Our Sub heads are going to end up on virtual pikes, and all the Subs from here to Nexus 10 will be under suspicion."

Gauthier opened the door.

"Are we going to war?!"

He was an interesting man, indeed. His springy light brown hair was shaped into a flattop Afro with short sides. His silver silk robe was tied loosely at the waist, exposing his bare chest. Every bounce of his feet uncovered the cock ring between his legs. He flashed a predatory smile with closed, green lips.

"No, we're slinking back to Silany like sorry Sub cowards, licking our wounds and settling for cheap toilets. Of course we're going to fucking war," Richard snapped.

Gauthier draped himself against the doorframe, shifting into a suggestive pose that appeared to have been for Richard's benefit.

"Why don't we just hack the bank and work it like you did Ipsteins?"

"Because those firewalls burn your retinas off."

"Hmm," Gauthier said. "Walk with me." He turned his cape billowing behind him, and the men followed.

Passing all manner of slaves, Gauthier tossed one his scarf and pulled another close to lick her nose. Richard stepped past a small topless, olive-skinned black-haired woman who was holding cherries on a golden tray and followed the artist into his studio.

"Gentlemen, welcome to Spektraskope."

Richard didn't quite know how things had escalated to a war footing, but he felt fate surging behind him, all of history standing up like an angry mob at his rear. He turned and found the topless woman beside him. He ate one of her cherries. Her lips didn't move, and her eyes stared down to let him look at breasts that pointed up. Gauthier, untangled from his slave, reached across with speed and slapped the slave hard across the face. She stood, still as a statue, the tray unmoving in her hands. Her nipples began to erect. Richard held his breath. Gauthier watched the slave. Satisfied with her response, he plucked a cherry from the tray and spat the pip out.

Tom must be part of some secret sex cult. Where the hell has brought me?

In his studio there were a couple of three-metre-high printing machines on either side of the room, white cubes, one with an orange-tinted glass door, and another turquoise—both with robotic arms and instruments crouched inside like rooting birds.

"What's this?"

"A new laptop for my new client. Completely agentic."

Richard crouched down to examine the Etronium-plated laptop on the surface of one of the printers. It was flawlessly designed—sleek—and there was a pulsating warmth emanating from the machine. He avoided touching it directly.

"You can make stuff this complicated?"

Gauthier shrugged languidly. "It's easy to me. Like shelling peas." He had a smooth voice that belied his true character.

"What's your limit?"

"I don't have one. I push it further every day."

"I like you," Richard said.

"Careful. He's going to make you prove it." Tom smirked.

"I'm undoubtedly too expensive for some out-of-work chump—Tom, you're a decent guy. Miles? Already shagged him. This one?" His eyes flicked over Richard. "Hmm. I did my research. I know all about you."

He clicked his fingers, and a petite slave girl appeared with a folder in hand. Gauthier passed it to Richard. Inside, there were photos of his parents, of Norman, transcripts from school, and their old address. He really had done his research.

He closed the folder and handed it back to Gauthier. "Good to see you're thorough."

Gauthier's expression seemed to say *duh.*

Richard turned and started reviewing Gauthier's artwork, a sculpture of a black angel holding a blade to the sun, an ivy plant that seemed real but was an artificial projection. Richard moved his hand through it. And Nemes itself, a mini model of the future, with the title: The Future Now.

"Nemes," he said. "Where—"

Gauthier appeared next to him and whispered in his ear. "Where the air is so clean you can smell the water spring a mile away. A mile away."

Richard turned to him.

"It's just a dream, you know," Gauthier said, "we are the animators, we are the creators, they make us build what they want because we have what they don't. They need us, you see." He pirouetted away, practising his ballet. Richard was losing patience, he wanted to rob things, steal his way into Nemes if he had to. Anything to avoid another day, here with these degenerate freaks.

"We just robbed the Ipsteins Bank, and to do that we used a little more ingenuity than it takes to make a metal dog with a square head or a poxy laptop." A smile twitched at the corners of his mouth as he watched Gauthier's mouth fall open.

"Riighht," Gauthier said. "That was unexpected—'

"We used a doorway drug to rewire our brains, it makes us unbeatable," Richard said, relishing the shift in power. "We'd like you to print us doorway guns, magic guns, so that we—The Whisperers—can win the gunfights."

Gauthier leant back into the couch. "Okay, it sounds like fun. Just... What exactly does this involve?"

"Taking Nuvo 7. Levelling up your tiny mind. Robbing the banks. You'd—"

"Woah! Stop right there," Gauthier said. "I'm a two-thirds, you little shit. I can have you polishing my boots with your tongue tonight." He calmed down. "Look, I can supply you with guns, but I'm not sure about this whole junkie shit. My ex was an addict, the White messed up his whole mind. Couldn't even get an erection..."

"We use it in a very controlled way," Tom said. "It's more like a medicine than a drug."

"Gauthier, I need you to be in, so you're in."

Gauthier sat down again putting his head in his hands. He began to cry. After some time, he raised his head. "Look, the money is tempting, seriously, but you're...I am going to get caught. You're going to get caught. We're all doomed. I had the whole thing ready, with my clients. And now you've shown up here."

"We're not going to get caught," Richard cut in, "because of this." He found the purple Nuvo 7 pill he'd stashed in his jacket pocket and held it next to his eye.

"No," Gauthier said, "that could be horse poison for all I know. Two-thirds don't wallow in the gutter."

Richard reached around and pulled from his waistband one of his godfather's Skimguns. "When I first used one of these, I used to imagine my brother's head to focus, to win. I don't even know who you are, and you know my darkest secret." He raised the Skim and aimed the barrel right where Gauthier's eyebrows met in the middle of his forehead.

"What the hell are you doing?" Tom said.

Richard held up a Nuvo pill. "Open his mouth and put this in it."

*

An hour later, Gauthier peeled himself off the leather chaise longue and began shuffling in erratic little triangles. He flexed his fingers, rubbed his cheekbones, then slapped his own face—twice—before letting out a strange, breathy "awhoo... awooo."

"What my mother wanted for me; it was only one thing. Not to pass as my father did, an addict of the Lucky-Lukey-Fives. They were his thing. Awhoo. It was not dissimilar to the White Milk of today, but it was a lot less safe and absorbed through the eyes. Awhoo. Awhoo. Growing up, "Gauthier" would walk in on many a *Sunbathing Session*...Swingers Sunbathing happened on every full moon. My father would recline, naked, as the potion-soaked cucumbers did their work on his eyes."

Gauthier was putting Richard on edge now he had just left his mind and the triangles he was forming were ones he was also drawing with his fingers.

"Even my mother, Julianne, did not find the ritual suspicious, but this is the nature of the Silanese. Escapism, ritual, hallucination, addiction. My father, Walter, hung himself on a Wednesday with the cucumbers taped to his face." Gauthier was speaking faster too.

"Gauthier could never eat a green vegetable again. Julianne wasn't wrong to cast that rule over young Franc—my original name—but the sword you fear will always find you in the end. I want more, Richard."

"Finish the story, I haven't heard a good story in a while."

Gauthier smacked himself, the sound sharp in the quiet.

"Her one rule, turned into a single binding spell. Isn't it always the way? Nobody loses themselves quite like the Silanese? Take Marco Alakija the 3rd, Count of Herne and keeper of the Mongadillo Honeybee." He made slow swimming motions, rubbing his ears as if adjusting to deep water. "He used to swim in LL-5, mixing it into his own lakes. For years, he stayed so high on the stuff that he lived entirely in Nemes—though only in his mind of, course. And because he was a Count, he formed a religion with a thousand followers, all devoted to the same grand delusion. To self-vanishing. They all killed themselves together. Something happened that night, something awful. They all saw the real Silany. It was a shared, bad trip. And to make matters worse, Dog Scanners and Cyborg wolves were deployed that day, fresh from testing. It was bad timing."

"I should say."

Gauthier calmed himself and began drinking something from a glass on the side.

"Naturally, they all shat themselves. God knows how the wolves appeared to them on their trip, but the Count ran headfirst into his own hive of Mongadillo. Apparently, it took him eleven hours to die from the bee stings. The howling fell over the rolling hills that night and Julianne moved our family to Cax 15. But she couldn't escape the Silanese gene. The men liked their drugs. Walter liked to sunbathe with cucumbers and after he died, I—young Franc—left my mother, became Gauthier and carried her one rule. "Never take them," she said to me. She didn't want her boy to become what Father was. I tried. I really have. First art..." He exhaled, running a hand through his hair, as if brushing off old ghosts.

Richard looked around the room: drawings of vaginas eating insects, statues of phallic vegetables being ejaculated over by swarms of faceless demons.

"But now you Richard have shown me Nuvo, nothing will stop me. Nothing will stop my reunion with Walter."

"So...you're in?"

"I need unlimited access." Gauthier poured the remainder of whatever it was he was drinking at his own face.

"I'm not sure that's a good idea" Richard said.

"You have no idea what power is in your hands."

"Oh, yes we do," Richard told him.

Gauthier began rubbing the inside of his thighs and squatting up and down. "I just don't want to be dependent on you for getting the drug every time. Allow me unlimited access then I can use it when I want. Please?"

"No," Richard said.

"What Richard wants to say," Tom cut in, drawing closer and putting his arm over Richard's shoulder, "is that he's not sure of the exact amount to give you access to."

Richard squeezed his eyes tight for a moment then released them "I'll liaise with my supplier, see how much Nuvo she can get hold of in one go. Let me do that first."

"It'd better be good," Gauthier told them. "Or I'm out."

"You're never out now, Gauthier." Richard was tapping the handle of his Skim and sliding it back into his waistband.

*

The evening light cast a purplish hue on the curve of the Etronium apartment blocks on the perimeter of Little Jiwa Central Park. Hand in hand, Arora and Richard meandered along one of several paved pathways that crisscrossed the lawns.

"Do you know how long it's been since we've done anything together?"

"Not really," Richard told her, his mind on the elaborate and fantastical guns he would get if he could only pump Gauthier full of Nuvo 7. Better, more powerful and discrete than anything he'd had from Rusty.

"Exactly, my point." She dragged him to a stop and stood in front of him, forcing him to look her in the eyes. This was all right. He liked her eyes. "What's the point of it all—of us—if we can't even make the time to enjoy life together? Seriously. It's been five months."

"But we're here now, aren't we?" he said. Her disquiet a hulking hairy thing ever-present, germinating, and annoying. On his next Nuvo mission he'd see if he could at least downgrade Guilt. Lock Guilt out of The Library.

"Either you're in or you're out. There's no in-between."

A sudden panic took hold of Richard, and he forced himself to be in that moment with Arora, right then and there. The warmth of her, her eyes, thighs, chest and fingertips, her vibrancy, and her generous supply of the

Nuvo 7 pill, all could be whisked away, leaving him bereft and exposed and without his super guns.

"You're right. You deserve more of me," Richard said. There was so much that he'd kept from her over the months, the bank robbery, his intentions, all of it. This wasn't normal in a love match. He needed to "Nuvo" out the bits of his mind that made this not seem normal. It didn't matter if it was normal or not. It was normal for him. Maybe he should tell her all of this.

They sat down on the grass chair and watched the sun sink in the pink sky, their hands fondling one another. Manoeuvring Arora into position in front of him, Richard held her against his chest and felt her heart beating through her ribcage. He remembered guiding Lust towards the "Arora" book in his mind the last time he had Nuvo-ed. Lust knew a lot about Arora, and he hardened against her soft body. Now was not the time for sex, however, and he goaded his mind into the purpose at hand.

He breathed softly against the back of her neck. "I'm sorry if I've not been all there for you."

"That tickles," she said. "You can't have it both ways: intimacy and distance."

Turning around, Arora gave him a sharp look. He smirked.

"You know what?" he continued, running a hand through her hair. "You might find it hard to believe but I've become a better man since Nuvo 7. It's not just about spending my time exploring the mind, the possibilities, it's about me trimming off the less productive parts of me."

"Like what?"

"Well, I've become more focused when I work. I'm less likely to procrastinate."

"Mmhmm." Arora nodded and shifted her position slightly so that she could look at Richard's face. That was true at least.

"We're thinking of adding one more person to our little team dedicated to exploring Nuvo's possibilities, and it'd be good to have a few more pills to share out. Could you help us out?"

"Richard, please. I'm taking enough of a risk already."

"I am doing all this for you baby."

"You won't be able to do any of it if I get caught."

"How many more a month can you get?"

"Five per month, maybe, without setting off any alarms with security."

"You won't, you're amazing, all pretty looking and clever. You can do it."

"For you, I can love."

While it wasn't an "unlimited supply" by any means, it should be enough to win Gauthier over. Five meant at least one per week for Gauthier alone, and he could throw in some further incentives. If he couldn't be convinced, he would either force Gauthier to manufacture the guns or just shoot the pretentious twat.

"Let's head back," he said. "It's getting dark."

"I'd prefer to stay here a bit longer," Arora said. "I'm enjoying being us for the first time in ages. It won't get that dark, anyway."

Richard bit his lip knowing he couldn't wiggle out of the big reveal any longer. There was more that he needed to do to make things right with Arora today: tell her the truth. She had been accepting of the fact that he had once taken money from the university, so why not this?

He snuggled closer to her. "Do you remember when I took money from the university to support my Mother, and you called me a hero?"

"Of course," Arora said, running her fingers lightly over his knee.

"How would you feel if you knew we, as in...we're behind the Ipsteins Bank raid?"

She flinched, stood up, turned away, turned back, and punched him in the stomach. His hands held her, half winded.

Her face was red and contorted. "And you're going to tell me that you're planning more, aren't you?"

"Ah...er...yes."

"Shit," she said. She picked up her handbag and began to walk away.

Richard slumped back, his head spinning. He still had things to say. She couldn't run off like this. He jumped up, caught up with her and grabbed her by the elbow and spun her around to face him.

"I want you to know how special you are to me. I've neglected things recently, and I don't want you to have the impression that I don't care, because I do..." He swallowed hard. "The thought of losing you makes me terrified, and I'd understand if you wanted to give up on me." His eyes filled with tears and again, strangely, he found that he'd not forced them.

Arora was holding her breath. A strange tingling sensation ran over the surface of his face, and the backs of his hand.

Fumbling in his jean's pocket, Richard pulled out something small and sparkling and held it in his open palm. It was a slender silver ring encrusted with a single gem of pure Etronium.

*

"This is not just pleasure, is it?" Gauthier asked, raising one eyebrow at Richard. They were on a video call as Richard fingered the face of Gauthier that was floating ten inches in front of his *Series-9 Nemescreen*.

Richard laughed. "Always a pleasure to speak to you, though!"

"Huh?" Gauthier said.

"My contact will provide you with a monthly supply."

"What happened to unlimited? A monthly supply? I don't like "monthly supplies"? Gauthier wants unlimited."

"That desire for everything is something you'll be able to correct on your first entrance. It's normally to do with a lack of milk."

"I don't use that shit, that stuff's for the scum bottom two-fourths, and your lot n' all."

"I meant real milk. Your mother's liquid."

"Oh, I say."

"My contact, she works for a pharmaceutical company—she is only a junior, but she'll come through."

"She's your girl?"

"My fiancé," Richard said, almost giddily, then switched back into an angry man. "Listen. The five will be enough."

Gauthier's eyes lowered. "So, when do you want to come over and start creating your weapons?"

"You're in then?"

"Like I have a choice," Gauthier said. "I can't exactly dig the old hag up and find a nipple to suckle."

"I have some ideas. Maximum and specialised firepower. I'm sure you can build on them. In fact, let's rewire your head so you *can*."

*

The vast hall in the Mansa building—the very same hall where Richard gave his inaugural speech was adorned with fairy lights, ribbons and bunting. Yes, it was nostalgia that had led to Richard and Arora choosing this place as their wedding venue. It was the place where they had first noticed each other and the location that had inspired Richard's vision for a more inclusive and generous world. Only three months had passed since he had asked her to marry him, but with ready money available for the ceremony, there was no reason to wait a moment more. It was a registration wedding only.

There were no guests and the happy couple didn't even need a witness. It was all recorded on Nemes' Nine Eyes. Contracts were signed and they were in and out. One of three that day.

Richard felt good, it was the right way to deal with it, to deal with her and set an example—the trajectory—for the new phase of their lives. He had control of himself. Now it was about gaining control over others, and that meant to first gain distance and maintain what little control he already had. That night he typed a message to Norman*: Richard Wise is a married man.* He received no reply.

CHAPTER 10
The Hoard

The service tunnel rose in a near-vertical climb. It contained sixty metres of rusted-metal rungs. Richard moved carefully, each pull straining his already burning muscles. Weighed down by his kit and weapons, he breathed fast and shallow, his head heavy with exhaustion. They'd been climbing in almost perfect coordination for miles through what may well have been the *Maze of South Bend.* But on the Ascent, everything was different. If Richard faltered now, if exhaustion stole his grip—he wouldn't fall alone, he'd take Miles and Ares with him. It was a hell of a drop towards nothing but concrete. But more importantly, it would be a hell of a shame to have achieved so much and to have come this far, only for it be undone by a misstep and bad boots.

He emerged into some sort of sub-basement that stank of copper-sulphate and dust. Flashing his torch three times into the tunnel aperture, he signalled to the others that he had reached the surface. When they arrived, he gestured for them to keep quiet as he crept towards a slither of glimmering light, which, on closer inspection, appeared to be a door. They were supposed to come up 100 metres south-west of Ishin Conduit, in the tangle of yards and warehouses behind the HQ of Armiger-Choo Dev. He unholstered the smaller of his firearms, the Double-Penetrator Blastaar—at least that's what he called it. Shouldering open the door, there was no one there, just smashed crates and clumps of weed. The night air was refreshingly welcome after several hours in the sewers.

Their hoods up, they feigned nonchalance to appear like nothing more than three people walking home from the gym. They kept their conversation casual, even throwing in the occasional talk of crunches and bench presses for any surveillance bugs or cloaked drones that might be eavesdropping. They made their way to Ishin Conduit, following it to its end, until they came to the intersection where PHO Technology Consolidated faced Gulsig Heavy Aerospace. Here, the Skimatik they had rented was waiting for them. It was a sleek, low, emerald green vehicle, with pewter-grey race stripes, that they had hired in Arora's name in the Jelleny District only the day before. It was only as he climbed in the back and nodded at Tom and Gauthier in the front that he allowed himself the luxury of congratulating himself. They had done it: entered, overcome, and emptied the Hyland-Hara Banks.

He pulled down his hood and let his head loll on the rest of the back seat. High-rises and neon streamed overhead as Miles and Ares whooped and screamed beside him, celebrating their latest victory.

Everything had gone to plan, the sewer map, the practice drills in the Mind Maze, the guns had fired beautifully, and all of Hyland's defences and kit had been scrambled and disabled before anyone knew what was happening. A massive money pit drained and captured. Hyland-Hara was the first. It would be one of ten. They would hit ten banks then retire. So far, all Richard's strategising had paid off and everyone had kept to the script. They would use a rota system: three in the raid, two in the getaway Skimatik and mix this up so no one would be at risk of capture on any raid. The guns, pre-designed and printed in Gauthier's gallery, were to be customised to address each bank's security set-up. Tonight, they'd used the Double-Penetrator and the Bunker Chunker RPG launcher because Hyland used cybernetic droids; along with Ares' Living Lazer Lance because they'd needed to cut through a steel wall six inches thick to infiltrate the bank's basement from the sub-basement, and the sub-basement they'd accessed by using Richard's Funnelweb Eight-Legged Cerebral Limpet Mine. All these guns, they agreed, would be passed on to Uncle Rusty—or U-R as he was now known—and stashed at his compound so they couldn't be traced. No one in Nemes would suspect Rusty of being involved in the heists, and all of Silany were basically shit scared of him, now that he had a T-Castle on a hill. Allowing him to customise the designs himself ensured he'd never snitch. And if anyone was ever apprehended or separated, they would pop a Nuvo 7 and wipe their memories of anything to do with the scheme or each other.

Half the money they stole was going to good causes in Silany. This had been Arora's idea. Richard didn't particularly like it, but he liked that she liked it. It would keep Arora sweet and on their side, make her think this wasn't just about getting rich quick and screwing over Silany. It had a positive, almost loving aspect.

Richard, now almost deaf to the noise the others were making, hardly noticed when Tom opened the sun hatch and Ares, having removed her boiler suit, was dancing on the roof in her underwear. His mind on more important matters, Richard started to worry. They had taken much more money from Hyland than Ipsteins. He was going to have to find an expert launderer or risk getting caught, by a forensic accountancy tracker app, or worse, a Mortalizer's laser shotgun. Still, he'd knocked over a big bad bank with high walls and fearsome defences. He missed the rush of this already. He needed another challenge and fast. Something bigger like pulling off a coup that no one else could achieve.

Across the street, Richard noticed a neon sign that read *Cosmicomics*. It shimmered ruby-pink in the misty drizzle and Richard couldn't tell if the weather had turned or if this was the effect of the Nuvo 7 pill.

Moments later, he was spread-eagled on the hotel bed. The Mimesse Hotel was one of Little Jiwa's cheaper accommodations, though none of its hotels were truly cheap. He'd made an excuse to leave the Niteflight Bar where the others were celebrating the raid on Hyland. He'd said he was tired when, in actuality, his mind was on fire. Hyland had been like squashing a bug when only a hunt for the big game would quench the fire in his mind. He was alone now and he was not supposed to take Nuvo 7 alone, but he had.

The glittery-pink sign pulsed and expanded until it was a floating lozenge-shaped balloon hanging over the bed. Richard laughed, delighted, and held up a limp fist to it, like a baby swiping at a mobile—mesmerised. When he shut his eyes, they slammed shut and soon he was drifting downward through a cone of darkness. The pink balloon was a tiny speck a million miles above that grew smaller and smaller still, until Richard landed with a heavy thud on the floor of The Library.

Under different circumstances, the books on the shelves that held all his memories—memories of his dead *Mother* and dead *Father* and idiot brother and the seeds of his own greatness and grandeur, would have been too alluring for him to resist. He would have lay sprawled on the floor rummaging through the volumes, reliving and reordering the past. The idea of that bored him now.

In The Courtyard, the Traits, his mooching and shifting doubles bored him, too. But the opening to the Maze glowed when he turned towards it. Its off-brown colour now looked more like pale gold; that it still wanted him was a relief. Excited, he allowed himself to be swallowed up by the entrance and enjoyed the way that the brambles now swirled to let him pass. It was only when his feet met the ground that he realised he'd been levitating. Or had he? It was hard to be sure. The passageway curved ahead and continued on into a distant raucous burble.

He followed the bend. It was the first part of an S-bend that fed into a dogleg, and then a T-junction. He was further than he had ever come before, proving to himself that he was evolving the more he dominated Little Jiwa and mastered Nuvo 7. There was a loud yap-yap-yap coming from above his head, a yap-yap-yap that sounded more like a pneumatic drill. He imagined a giant dog covered in scales that he could kill with his Double-Penetrator Blastaar. Whatever it was, it scrabbled overhead. When it finally stopped, it let out a long, guttural shriek—like it was vomiting up its own insides, ripping itself apart from the core. Richard quickened his pace, following the new bends and turns in the maze much more closely, but whatever was above him was howling like a famished werewolf ready to devour its prey.

The passageway opened onto a jutting platform, where a stark white bridge stretched ahead of him. Something dark lurked on the other side, waiting for him. It wanted Richard to stand there, to bask in his false triumph over the creature in the Maze. The very creature he had run from screaming last time.

Above him, loomed a huge expanse of darkness. Beneath the bridge was the same thing. Richard felt that he had grown two or three inches since he'd entered the Maze and hoped this was his reward, one that he could take back to his own reality. He strode headlong towards the bridge.

As he quickened his stride, the screeching and clicking sound grew louder and closer. The louder the sound, the more the bridge called to him—seductive in its promise of safety. It wasn't until he'd crossed the bridge that the illusion cracked. Richard stopped cold, a sudden stillness overtaking him, as if some part of him had realised too late that the danger hadn't been left behind. As he looked up, those hard-won two inches of height dissolved just as quickly—as if the awareness alone was sufficient to press him down into something smaller, something easily crushed.

The bridge was vast and not altogether solid. It had a goo-like texture that clung to him and 'metachrosed' into shades of purple and scarlet each time Richard moved. It formed a hole in its centre, which Richard took to be a mouth, exposing several rows of fangs, each the length of Richard's thumb. A large dollop of brown goo dripped from near its head and fell at Richard's feet.

He turned and ran for the entranceway. There was only a wall there now where the passage had been, and the smell of wood rot was even stronger. Desperate to breathe, he forcefully gulped down the toxic air and turned towards the bridge again, only to find that the rotting, stinking thing had come down the path to block his way.

Though its hand had shrunk in size, it towered over him, the size of two elephants stacked on two more, shifting and pulsating in impossible ways. Its now violet and lemon-coloured leathery skin was cracked and hairy. Tentacles spilled out endlessly from its hind quarters, pooling in a writhing mass around its lower half.

And then the head—turnip-shaped and grotesque, surged upward from the tangled mass like it had just remembered it needed one.

The head convulsed like it was choking on itself. Then, like a striking cobra, it snapped back and lunged forward. Not once, but twice. Each thrust sent him stumbling. But Richard was running out of space and feared the creature would be on top of him soon. It gurgled and thrust one last time then spat out a silver cocoon onto the floor.

The mass tore itself apart, peeling away in thick, quivering layers. Chunks of flesh hit the ground with a wet, final thud. And in the space left behind, where there should have been nothing, a man stood—tall, silent, regal, as if sculpted from the celestial winds themselves. He was as noble as a stag in an ancient wood.

"Dad," Richard whispered. "Daddy."

Daddy put a shotgun in his mouth. And then he was gone, his brains painting the earth around him.

With a jolt, Richard snapped out of the reverie and ran to empty the contents of his stomach, which gushed out into the bathroom sink of his ensuite hotel room. His clothes had vanished, his strength drained, and he was back to being plain old Richard, although he should have achieved his god-like form by now. The world below was too real, too deadly. Up here, he was in control. He wasn't leaving it again.

*

The following night, sometime past midnight, Richard found himself wedged between the two vast periscope-like vents on the moon-white tiled roof of the Ju Cybernetics Building in the Kova District. His head was clear now and his stomach settled. He was armed, though he'd promised his new wife he wouldn't be. A mini-Penetrator he'd printed off before his evening nap lay snuggled in a sling hidden in his swirling rainbow coat. A muscular woman in her early thirties stepped towards him, slower than she needed to, obviously trying to show caution, or fear, or both. Her skin was so black it seemed blue, alluring. Her dreads hung loose around her shoulders, framing a face he couldn't quite read. She had on black motorcycle boots, black leather trousers, black leather jerkin, and revealed a bare midriff. He hoped this was Kemi, the one Gauthier had said knew how to shuffle a pack.

"Ah, at last the face that broke a thousand banks," she said.

"Only two," Richard said. He was already dead in the water if she was an undercover Mortalizer.

"Two is more than anyone else has ever knocked over."

"Two times five is a legend," he said.

"Ten? Ambitious. I like it. Though you'll need to be ballsy *and* lucky."

"You let me worry about luck. Our mutual machine artist friend says you're the best cleaner in Silany."

"I can remove the stains from your whites, sure. How much you gonna take, assuming they don't cut your crackers off?"

"Your point?"

"My point is my fee will depend on my risk and my risk depends on yours."

"Eight per cent," Richard said. "And you agree to a little procedure we have if you get caught and we don't..."

"Ten, and twelve and a half if you want me to agree to some brain-death-gene shit to protect your asses."

Richard agreed. He'd been prepared to go to twenty for the right cleaner. That she'd settled low meant to him that she had confidence in him that he was going to kick high and consistently so.

Kemi nodded. "Did you launder all of it last time?"

"No, just what we didn't take as part of our cut."

"Ooh, that was a shitty risk," she said. "You need to launder the whole lot before taking your cut. The bots of Nemes are crawling around town, and in every glitch and system-pocket the state is looking for any trace of that code."

"Are they?"

"Yes, they are, and suspicions about your source of funds, these first two payments, are dangerous."

A cold feeling passed through Richard, right down his guts and to his groin. His legs were beginning to freeze. "That's why I'm hiring you, Kemi. You right the whites."

"Moonboy, I am your totally underhanded lawyer-accountant-realtor combo."

"We all get the fuck-off funds, and no one needs to die. You get your half of the cut, and the other half of the cash is to go to the Silanese state."

"Your call, of course," Kemi said with a shrug. "But if I were you, I'd spend it on something worthwhile or decadent, not waste it on this shithole."

"It is a shithole, but it's my shithole. Over time, I want to invest in some businesses here. Sentimental shit connected to my father. He passed away a few years ago now. And of course, I'd like to buy a property of my own. You can work out those sorts of deals, too," Richard said.

"Oh, I'm sorry to hear that," she said, lowering her eyes. "But the dead bore me. I intend to send the money via clearing houses in the outer semi-rogue districts like Fallarin, Tawa and Little Jaffar—but only towns I have dealings with, then after some time, that money will come back through different channels. The money you want to gift to the Silanese state, we'll have to send via a "benefactor" so that it looks bona fide. I have people in mind who can do the transfer. The money that you want to keep for you and your guys would best come from a business partner so that it looks like money you have earned for a one-off job. I currently have dealings with a micro-financier in Little Mito and an Etronium merchant working in both states, who would be able to help you out there. It's best that the funds come from more than one place. Making sense?"

"I think we should drink," Richard said.

"I think we should knock-boots." She took a step towards him. "I've always fancied it against one of these sloping triangular roofs."

"The idea of money gets you going like that?"

She smirked. "What do you think?"

Behind her, the city glittered ruby-red and azure-blue. The great spiked spire atop the mighty central tower of Nera Nana Industrial split the full moon in two.

*

Richard turned away from the screen and focused on the polished teak desk in front of him, the documents there and the silly little promises they represented. On the TV, a newsreader who looked too big and buff for the frame explained that it had been six months since the day the Bankers Five started their campaign to rob some of the most prestigious banks in Silany. And last night, the Makaria Bank in Little Mito became the fourth target. Despite heightened security in all the Nemerian banks, the robbers stole over 250,000 strata. No one, including Nemerian security services, had a clue who these dangerous fanatics were or where they were.

"You can't help admiring these fuckers," said Kino Yakin. Richard didn't give a shit what Kino thought. A thrill was still coursing through his spine. He had blown a cybernetic security guard's head off last night with a gun called The Pincer and collected a cool quarter of a mill while he'd been at it.

Yakin was the business manager of Nate Jonz—the bespoke men's tailor where Father had bought his Nemerian suits. Kemi had transferred the funds, and Richard had signed the contract.

"Mr Wise, you are now the owner of Nate Jonz," said Yakin. "I'm sure you will make us immensely proud to be associated with you." Beaming, he stood up to shake Richard's hand.

Richard grasped the sweaty palm. "I hope to make you proud, indeed." He could hardly believe it. Nate Jonz—the shop was his. He might rename it Phillip's. Or perhaps, Richard's. He might rename it Rich Phil's. He might just pull it down altogether. He might forget about it now like he used to forget the girls he had in Pollen X. He'd already purchased the SOLO whisky distillery in Little Mito, another business his father had adored. He'd kind of forgotten about that.

"Listen," said Yakin. "You're clearly flush with cash. I don't suppose you'd be interested in buying a property in Little Mito? These days, they basically mirror Nemes Mito. So much so, it's like you don't have to leave. I know it's not as close to the heart of things...the real N, but what do you say?"

"I might be."

"My brother, Taneesh, is something of a property broker. Last year, he decided to buy up and convert a derelict church building on the outskirts of Mito."

"Little Mito?"

"People don't add the 'Little' these days, so much, generally."

"Don't they?"

"It's beautifully developed. Palatial. You'd be the envy of Silany. You'd be seen as you truly are. Nemerian. Would you like to see it? I could show you around."

"I'll speak to my wife."

Only 3 months later, Richard and Arora moved into what they affectionately named "The Castle." Richard's whole being pulsed with the potential of the place. He left the flat in Little Jiwa with the keys on the glass table, silk gown on the floor and plants dead. The Castle had new plants, and it came with a slave to tend to them. Entering the huge central grand hall was like walking into a showroom. There were storeys on storeys, a wine cellar, a library, eight bedrooms, four bathrooms, two kitchens, a roof terrace and a cavernous garage. An apiary. A surveillance array. Indoor fountains.

A mummer's gallery. Richard visualised his three cars stashed here, and his growing arsenal of guns and swords on display in the trophy room. It had been a long day of watching people shifting boxes, moving furniture into place, and sourcing additional bits of decoration to fill their new home. It wasn't enough. Only Nemes would be enough. But this was what he wanted, right here: confirmation that he was on the right track. He got it now, finally. It was because he'd aimed for Nemes, that he had the most toys. He was Ascending. For as it was stated, one must "Judge a Tree by its Fruit." And Richard had borne fruit. A half hour earlier, Arora had crashed in their new king size bed in the master bedroom. So, Richard took a shot of SOLO whiskey alone and went to stand on the roof terrace. All of Silany was laid before him, glittering like a million campfires or candles. He was physically exhausted, but his body pulsed with energy and excitement.

His mother had been wrong. There was no divine force guiding and shaping their lives. One made their own way in life. The life force was in them and through the disciplined use of Nuvo 7, he was shaping himself into the person he wanted, chose, and needed to be—all by himself. He was becoming the individual's individual.

"*Father,* look," he whispered into the godless void of the night. He had managed to buy this fantastic complex, as incredible in its old-world scale as Rusty's glass pyramid, and with his own money. He was sorry that his father wasn't here to see or share it. That he wasn't here to see these sights, the whole of Silany lit up, and all of Nemes in the distance, beyond the Fal. A light rain fell but he didn't move. He watched the city's labyrinth, and its neon lights reflected off his polished shoes. *Sorry, Dad. I am more. I am developed.*

*

"Thanks for seeing me at such short notice," Superintendent Shepard was leaning backwards in his seat and bouncing in it. His eyes were rimmed with dark shadows. His office smelled of cigars and sweat and seemed even more grey than usual. Even the light that drifted in from outside was grey.

What other choice did I have? Norman stared at Shepard, hoping that despite the gulf in rank, he could still make the old soak uncomfortable.

"You've been working with us for two years, you've done an excellent job, bringing down two of the key players in the Party X ring, gathering vital information related to Party Z..."

"Thank you, sir."

"It's time to move you onto another assignment. Utilise your detective skills elsewhere." He gave Norman a slow smile.

Norman's first instinct was to try and contradict this, to ask Shepard to reconsider. Cases were still open. Cases were getting more complicated, bigger. It was short-sighted, foolish even, to redeploy him now, when he was so close to nailing the heart of the cartel's organisation. Then it struck him. It wasn't foolish. It was smart. Whoever was making the moves was seeing his opponents moves ahead. Norman kept up his stare and knew Shepard was the pin that held the grenade intact.

He's trying to get me away from uncovering him. For a moment, Norman was worried that he had expressed this thought aloud, and when he spoke his voice came out with a choking sound. "And to what project are you assigning me?"

Shepard leaned forward and pushed a new file across his desk. He raised his eyes towards Norman. "The Banker's Five. I thought you might fancy a new challenge."

"That's a big case, sir. Would it not be something for the Mortalizers?"

Shepard waved away the remark. "They have their hands full."

"Downtown, then? The Financial District."

"They're our banks, too." Shepard tapped the file, forcing Norman to look at him. "Our banks...banks that are in our jurisdiction."

"No problem."

What have you done now, Richard? Under the desk, Norman clenched his hand around his pen until his knuckles strained.

"How's the Makaria bank?" Norman asked once the drinks had been ordered. That evening, for the first time in several months, he'd met up with Theo at The Red Sea Cafe. A picture of Georgia and June in their heyday was still up on the wall.

"Great, actually," Theo said. "But, you know, after the hit in Mito, they've cracked down in a big way. We're having to work longer hours so that there's always at least two on site at night."

"Can't they just hire extra staff?"

"They probably could in the long run, but as a cheaper short-term solution, they're just increasing our hours."

"And paying you more, I hope?"

"You heard how much those guys got away with?"

"Yes," Norman said curtly, knowing that this was his way in, but not wanting to jump in, in case Theo joined up the dots too quickly. "You enjoying life in Little Jiwa?"

"Sometimes," Theo said, sipping his latte. "It's more relaxed. People are so efficient, and you haven't got the incessant traffic problems, of course, or the smell and the crime. But I miss the sense of community here—my family, you, friends. How's your own work?"

Norman wriggled his shoulders to ease the tension in them. "Good," he said almost automatically. The real truth sat heavy on the tip of his tongue, teetering between the urge to reveal all and restraint. He needed to say it—had to—no matter what it meant for Richard. His stomach roiled and twisted in knots. He couldn't remember the last time he'd even spoken to his brother. It had been 3 months now and he still hadn't congratulated him on his engagement. He regretted that. "But it's been weird, you know?"

"Weird how?"

"My boss has just reassigned me. I wouldn't mind so much if this new one didn't have some areas that were somewhat...personal to me. Look. You need to swear to secrecy. Can you do that? You must swear to never repeat any of this to anyone. Especially at Makaria. And especially to anyone connected to Nemes."

"But Nemes isn't real"

"Of course, you're right." Norman offered a sad smile. Enough people believed it was. They didn't *know* it didn't.

Theo stuck his tongue in his cheek, levelled his eyes with Norman's and mimed slicing his palm with a butter knife.

Norman leaned in. "I'm not 100% confident, but I'm fairly certain that Rich is at least one of the Bankers Five, if not the brains."

"You think?" Theo put his hand over his mouth in astonishment.

"You don't think he's capable?"

"He's capable alright, but is it credible?"

"Look, a while back I found out he'd been stealing money from the University. It was on record, so obviously, someone in the higher ranks didn't care much about it. I mean, petty theft by the only Silanese kid to win the Basil Black Scholarship. Who would want to take that up and erode the hope of Silany? He was paying for Mum's care too. So, I also turned a blind eye to it. But you know what I can't figure out, is that since then, he's not gotten a job. He says he's working for Uncle Rusty, but I made some calls, and it turns out he's not. It's all a front. And get this, you ready? He's just bought himself a castle."

"A castle?"

"Literally, a castle."

"Bit conspicuous, if he's been robbing banks, isn't it? What are you going to do?"

"I feel like I'm a spider caught in a drainpipe. I can't go up as I'll get squashed, and I can't go down cos I'll drown."

Theo nodded to himself. He held Norman's gaze with a concern Norman had never seen before. "If you ever need to talk," Theo offered.

Norman acknowledged the offer with a slight nod and then quickly changed the subject. Theo was chasing a woman who was out of his league, mostly Nemerian, apparently, a three-fourths, obviously, and that was the real reason he'd wanted Norman to come out tonight. It was a boring problem, and Norman didn't know what to say. When the waitress lit the candles on the Red Sea's table and a different, low mood took hold of Norman, who was reminded of Mum and her long shifts here. He turned to her photograph and silently wished all his problems were also boring.

"Theo, you know that day, you remember, when I shot the hare?"

"That was a long time ago."

"Seems like yesterday to me. I remember the next day, I went over to Uncle Rusty's. Richard had been going on about a shooting range, and now that I could shoot, I just thought…anyway, I saw..." Norman stopped himself. Didn't want to go there.

"Yeah..."

"I mean...listen, forget it. I don't really know what I saw. Change of subject. Just a thought, you might be better off with a Silanese girl."

CHAPTER 11
Pursuits of Perfection

Gauthier was in the office when Richard arrived. It was not yet 8 am. Richard had taken the loop-train across the river to Sate-voa, then walked from there to the centre. Despite walking in the soft morning drizzle, coffee in hand, Richard was groggy. Gauthier had collapsed against the aubergine-black leather divan. His arms were splayed on either side, his head tucked into his chest at an awkward angle, all while the tightness of his thin pants drew much desired attention to his manhood. Some silvery, spindly object hung from the longest fingers of his left hand like a cigarette.

As quietly as he could, Richard shrugged off his waterproof jacket and removed his shoes. He slinked towards Gauthier and gently plucked the silvery spindle from his grip. It was another Lazeleton UnPicka, a lock-picking needle laser and universal key they'd designed and printed for when they'd negotiated the holographic maze installed in the Fou-Kader Bank. Richard scanned around for the strongbox. The strongbox lay overturned on the floor at the other end of the divan. Gauthier had pulled a late one and crashed here. He had his own premises where he could do whatever he liked. No one was watching him there. But no, the man who once feared addiction was looking for something he knew they kept here.

Richard crept into his capsule office and checked the CCTV playback. Gauthier had let himself in at 3am. As suspected, he used the Lazeleton to flip the lock on the strongbox. He'd swallowed a Nuvo 7 so quickly you'd have thought it was an antidote for the plague.

Gauthier had gone down quickly, deep into his mind. He'd been under for nearly four hours. Damn it.

Richard patted his pockets for Cynar's Cognitive Mirrors. He always kept a set on hand in case anyone ever took it dangerously far. *What could he be doing in there?* He placed one of the beads on his temple and the other on Gauthier's before ingesting one of the Nuvo 7's left in the strongbox.

Within minutes, Richard began to tumble through a familiar tunnel of black emptiness. As he sailed down, his neck tingled with anticipation. He was thinking about Mother and Father—what they could have been, what they should have been, what they never were—before his nostalgia was interrupted by an abrupt landing at the Origin of Gauthier's Library. Unscathed, he stood up quickly and scanned the room. It personified the beauty of ugliness. It was larger and more labyrinthine than he had expected. There were study tables nestled throughout red-carpeted rooms, criss-crossed and walled with full bookshelves which were engraved with text: *"If evolution is outlawed, only outlaws will evolve."* Richard noticed a particular shelf: *Gun Assembly*, just as a cold draft intruded, tickling the back of his neck. And from the seeming stillness of The Library, screams began to sound against a background music of tintinnabula symphonies and melodies.

Richard followed the screams through windy corridors and out into the courtyard. It was snowing. Blood made its way through the whiteness of the ground to Richard's foot, where it began to pool. Its metallic scent filled his nostrils until he could taste the metallic tang on his tongue. Shocked, he raised his head. Gauthier was hacking the clerk—his father Phillip—to death in a bloody rage as other traits ran for their lives. Severed limbs lay on the concourse of the courtyard square amidst a stampede of lizard-monsters and demented bull-like creatures, which charged right at Richard. All while the Maze of South Bend went up in smoke. *Chaos.* This was how, in the pursuit of perfection, the depth of Gauthier's own self-destruction was revealed.

Richard pressed the sensor on his right temple.

He jolted awake. He had the sudden idea to piss on the crown of Gauthier's head. And so, he did, until Gauthier broke through his mind's surface and came too—mouth spluttering, hands flailing and eyes still clenched. But Richard's anger was so visceral that all he could do was spring forward and punch him in the jaw.

"What the fuck, Gauthier!"

Gauthier, head dripping with sweat, raised his two fists at the ceiling and shouted, "Perfecter, purger, iron-mind, I eat weak things and grind them with my head, teeth and guts, I am evil and evil is good, I am the overcomer, I am the water, the purebred, the night, the superman unshakeable, untameable and damn near unbreakable—I am Franc Gauthier."

"Take this break," Richard said, and punched Gauthier in the face again. The babbling man collapsed onto the divan, toppling it over backwards so his legs were splayed in the air in an unsightly V-shape. His head cracked against the floor.

"You degenerate asshole," Richard said, lifting him up by the lapels and shaking him vigorously. His eyes would not stop flitting from one side to the other like a hyperactive toddler.

"Richie baby, how are you? Ouch! Ouch! Shit. Must've pissed myself."

"Yes, superman pissed on his own head, he's that super. You stealing from me now, eh? Getting high on my supply? You can print your own, you know that."

"It's not as good," Gauthier said. "Her supply is best. It's just more... chewy."

Richard dropped the man, whose legs buckled once more and collapsed onto the floor.

"Stop doing that."

"You've been under for four hours. Something's gone very wrong."

"Why, what? Because I pissed myself?"

"What the fuck have you done?"

"Nothing."

"Gauthier?" Richard reached for the Lazeleton, switched it on and started to glide the searing crimson laser lance towards Gauthier's left eyeball.

"I am superman. You can burn my eyes out, but I'll still see clearer than you. I strangled Fear and Conscience."

"Fuck me, you're properly incomplete."

"It wasn't enough. Restraint and Empathy were bugging me, so I lit them up."

"You're not even human anymore."

"Yeah—it's great."

"You fucking idiot!"

"Idiot? You're the encumbered one."

"Your Traits are to be *managed*, with reason and logic, *not* removed! I have no idea what's going to happen to you now."

"I do. I'm going to rule this world."

"You have a bit of a rival there, one who isn't a jumped-up scrap-fiddler with half his brain in his trash file."

This could be interesting, Richard thought. He was trying to breathe, to filter his anger, bring it down a notch. He could already envisage this situation getting out of hand. He could imagine blood on the carpet and the bother of moving a body from densely populated central Little Jiwa.

"I have robbed seven banks," said Gauthier.

"*We* have robbed seven banks," Richard retorted.

"You couldn't have done it without me."

"We did one without you."

"You won't be able to do anymore without me."

"I think you've said enough, pisspants. I think I'll have to reconsider your access to Nuvo 7."

"You said an unlimited supply."

"Not I didn't. And that was before you started to walk in your junkie uncle's footsteps. Or was it your father?"

"I've committed seven robberies for you, and I have not been paid fairly. I demand a bigger slice, or you can't use my place, my machines, my knowledge, my strength."

Richard glared at Gauthier so hard the junkie-joker's outline started to look like it was burning up. He almost admired his nerve. Instead, he thought about his options—*Options: 1. Tell him to screw himself and risk him snitching in a Nuvo 7 withdrawal-induced, cold-turkey-chicken-shit, fever; 2. Kill the snitch and risk being caught and executed for the sake of his sorry ass; 3. Tell him you'll think about it to buy time for a better plan.*

"I'll think about it," Richard said, "Clean yourself up. You stink of piss." He picked up the strongbox and left the office, slamming the door behind him. No way was he keeping the Nuvo 7 stash in the office anymore. He was going to have to take it to The Castle. He had enough safes there, one of which was in a very secret position in the wine cellar. He'd work from home today. Most of that work would be devising a strategy to cope with the new Uber Gauthier. He couldn't believe that he'd just had to literally piss on a friend. But he now had a working example of what could go wrong with Nuvo 7, and where it could lead. He would have to be careful himself. He would have to be prudent. But maybe it wasn't the same for everyone. Maybe it would affect the strong differently to the weak, like Gauthier. Maybe he, Richard Wise, would prove exempt.

*

Later that afternoon, the sound of rain pattering on Richard's roof terrace's retractable geodesic shield caused him to surface. He rolled from the lounger onto the AstroTurf. He'd been under a long time and wasn't sure now what he'd intended to achieve by going under for what felt like days. The Library was misty in his head. He might have been dreaming, but in the dream, he'd hung his Shame. He couldn't shake the image of one of his doubles kicking and struggling, hoisted in the air, and surrounded by chaotic spectators, who shared the same face. Maybe he could delete that later.

He slouched his shoulders as he made his way down two flights of stairs to one of his kitchens and grabbed a bottle of mineral water from one of his fridges. He used to like drinking that, 'cause Norman drank spring water, like a dog, directly from the source. On a divan in his library, he now felt like he'd just risen from a hundred-year long sleep. He took out his phone to check that he was still in the right time period and noticed a headline in his newsfeed: *Dinova takes a Gamble on Gamble: Pharma Giant brings on a Bright Young Thing.* There was a picture of Arora, smiling, demi-goddess-like. Hera Moon, her crabby boss, had made her a partner. He should feel happy for Arora. But he wanted to smash Gauthier's face in. He knew now he had been merciful earlier. He should have been rock-hard. *And where am I in all of this? Where the fuck am I? Aren't I supposed to be the first one to know when my wife gets a promotion?*

He was sitting in the dark when Arora returned from work. The dark was best. He was able to bloom in the dark. His thoughts could take up as much space as they wanted. He heard her shoes tap-tap on the floor somewhere down below. He heard her call his name, unsure, it would seem, which of The Castle's many chambers he was hiding in. There was silence and then her soft footfalls appeared outside the library. She turned on the light. She was radiant, too radiant, swirling in the sudden glare.

"Oh," she said, approaching. "Are you OK, darling? You've not got a migraine or anything?"

She leaned over and kissed him on the cheek. Her skin smelt of musk and work. Richard flinched. He wiped off her kiss.

"What was that for?" Arora asked. Her voice was clear, perky. She didn't even care.

"You know what for," he said.

"No, I don't."

"Are you going to tell me what the fuck is going on?"

"What is going on?"

"You're supposed to be my wife."

"I am your wife."

"Then why do I have to find out from the public fucking news?"

"Oh. My partnership. I was keeping it a surprise. I've booked a table at G'Pai's at ten. I was going to tell you then."

He could tell she was telling the truth, but he didn't believe her.

Arora frowned. "I thought you'd be happy for me," she said. "But, seeing as you're clearly not happy, I think I'll go out and eat on my own."

Huffing, she began walking away.

Richard bristled. He remembered Norman in the ring and how it could be like punching at a waterfall. He was going to have to silence her, keep her here for good, *maybe in the wine cellar, chain her up down there. Or bury her and move on.* Just step sideways.

Richard sprung up, grabbed her arm and yanked her back down.

"You fucking stay where you are. I've not finished with you." This was big. He could feel the magnitude of it, the scale of the wrong she had done to him.

"Get off, Richard." She wrenched her arm free. "My God. Have you been under today?"

"Don't make this about me."

"How long were you under for?"

"I deserve to know these things first. You're not better than me."

Arora flinched. "So much for the wonder of Nuvo 7," she said under her breath.

"Fuck you," he said, looming over her. "Look at this place. Look what I built. We used to live in a hovel."

"Hardly."

Richard loosened his belt. He needed it whipped across her ass or wrapped round her neck; he wasn't sure. He reached for her.

"Hey, get off me!"

He cracked the belt across her arm like a whip. She cried out, tears springing in her eyes. The sight of them made him hard. It was easy to shove her to the ground, to use his weight to stop her kicking him off.

She pushed against his chest, fists pummelling him with no effect. She was grunting, sobbing now. Sitting with his full weight on her hips, he grabbed her wrists and looped the belt around them. From this view, she looked like a blood sacrifice, bound and ready to join the creatures of the dark. She winced when he yanked the belt tight enough to pinch the skin.

"Richard..." The tears were flowing freely.

He unfastened her trousers with desperation. She bucked beneath him, legs kicking wildly like she was *an animal destined for slaughter.*

"Richard, stop!" The strength had come back to her voice.

He paused and struck her sharply across the cheek, the sound of it so clear in the small space. She cried out and buried her head in her shoulder.

"I won't be denied what I own," Richard spat.

He yanked the white corduroy trousers free of her hips, her thighs, her knees. He heard her crying now and felt her body tremble.

Heat pulsed through him, lust and anger mingling.

He bunched the silk of her blouse and shoved it over her head. The bra followed, torn and ripped up over her shoulders, her perfect breasts falling free. She flinched.

"Richard...please don't do this."

He grabbed her jaw and pushed his thumb deep into her mouth with vindication, then wiped it around her cheeks and under eyes. "You did this to yourself."

He worked his trousers down to his knees. Forcing her legs apart, he settled in between them. Her breath hitched. She was tight, unyielding.

He thrust once. Hard enough to make her groan. She was enjoying it. *She wanted it.*

She twisted beneath him, but he kept her legs spread, palms on her hips. She was his. She would always be his.

He drove into her again, harder, faster. Beneath him, her body softened. She relented, giving herself to him completely. He squeezed her breasts hard enough to leave fingerprint marks. He watched them bounce in time to his thrusts. He enjoyed every moment of her surrender.

He'd built this castle, this empire. He had given Arora everything. She owed him for what he had done for her.

He pinched her nipples, and she winced sharply. *She liked it*. She knew she deserved it.

When he finished, he screamed. It was guttural, animalistic, far away as though it wasn't his own.

He stopped and caught his breath. Beneath him, Arora was shivering. Goosebumps covered her flesh.

He came out of her and leant forward; his body lowering onto hers.

Arora turned her face from her shoulder. The tears were drying. Her jaw was locked. She stared at him. And then she spat into his eye.

He recoiled with a hiss.

There was scrambling beneath him and then something hard connected with the back of his head. He fell to the side, dazed. A knee caught his stomach.

He blinked, wiping the spit from his eye, fumbling with the other hand for his boxers.

When he looked up, Arora was gone.

Heat coiled through his chest. "*Fuck!*" He picked up the hardback beside him—the one Arora must have hit him with—and hurled it at the opposite wall.

He found his phone in his trouser pocket. He didn't know who to call, who to offer her to. Instead, he used the app to turn the lights off. First in the library, then in the rest of The Castle. It was better in the dark.

*

He was unsure how long he had been lying there, on his side, with his hands wedged between his thighs. He wasn't even sure what library he was in. For a while he thought that perhaps he was in some stub of the last Nuvo 7 dive. If he could rearrange the books that related to Arora and maybe check that Shame was OK. As long as he he hadn't lynched Shame, things would be OK. They could be reassembled. Eventually he got up and limped to the main kitchen, where he took a long swig of water from the dispenser and hobbled to the master bedroom. He expected Arora to be in the en-suite shower room or reading in bed.

"Arora?" Richard asked, looking around and seeing nothing amiss other than a dent in the bedding on her side of the bed. The room was empty and there was no sign that she had even had a shower. *Oh well, I'm sure she'll be around somewhere.*

Stretching his shoulders until they cracked, Richard paced the room. Having Arora out of the way for a bit would give him the headspace he needed to finish off the final chapter of his manifesto, working title: *Society of the Mind: The Cognitive Pathway Beyond Nemerian Ascension.* This is what he would do. Leaders don't stop working, carrying on long into the night. He cleared the desk in his study and sat down for the next couple of hours to finish dictating his tract.

It was 1am by the time he finished. All of the neuro-linguistic science and cognitive map space now spread out before him like the strands of a spider's web as seen from its hub. Time was a hanging disc. The strings of his mind jittered. He needed to tell someone about this. He phoned Arora. She wasn't answering and she hadn't contacted him at all while he was in the zone. He wouldn't have minded. She was allowed. He needed to talk to someone who might get it. Tom—nah, too mathsy. Miles—nah, he'd just sneer. Ares—nah, she was likely high on kickboxing-roids—she'd become a proper roid head of late now. She didn't even have any tits. Gauthier—he was as good as dead. Ah, not spoken to him since university, but Adonis Andirack, The

Highmind, otherwise known as The Brainbox, was his man. Adonis was now working for Nigera Pharma, one of the two big global pharmaceutical companies. Richard phoned him.

"Adonis, Wise here. I've just rewired The Manifesto. Want to help me change the world?"

"Hi Richard."

"I can eradicate all diseases."

"I thought that's what Ascension was all about."

"I think it's a scam, a system to mediate our own potential. So, fuck Nemes."

"But your new route isn't a scam?"

"No. It is the pure way."

"The way for what?"

"For others to be pure."

"Ambitious! I'd like to find out more. If it's good, I can pass it on to my superiors. Chase me up later and we'll talk strategies. Speak soon." The tone beeped and the line died.

Richard lay flat on his back and sighed. Nigera would fall. He could take that over, just as easily as he could rob a bank. He could then use its facilities to mass-manufacture Nuvo 7. He was going to be a greater social engineer than Bogod himself. He would beat those smug, decadent elites that run Nemes, simply by existing, not that he was sure who they were, but they were there. Somewhere. But there was no time for them now. There were family issues to tend to. This bitch needed to be tracked down. He'd have to sweet talk and play the apologetic possum for a bit, get her back on his side until a new supply system could be secured. In the meantime, he would pay kids to burn the statues of Bogod.

His phone rang. It wasn't Adonis with a list of queries. It wasn't Arora for phone sex. It was Norman.

"Arora's here. Stay away from her. She's frightened of you. But remember, I'm not."

Click.

CHAPTER 12
The Maze of South Bend

"We have now achieved the state of mental perfection. We no longer need to rely on Nuvo 7." After two months without Arora, Richard had finally found the perfect way to spin the missing Nuvo 7. He'd decided it was more effective to let his team believe that they had reached the height of their intellectual evolution than to let them believe even for a second that they couldn't execute the final bank robbery without further brain enhancements. The Whisperers were assembled in the offices of the Spektrascope. Gauthier hated leaving his space, so meeting at his place had become the norm.

"So, if you have any left," Richard said. "I'm giving you the option of handing them over to me for disposal."

Tom, Miles and Ares all nodded, sombre and solemn.

"You've all used up your stash?" Richard asked them.

They continued to nod. Not a peep. Gauthier's eyes, however, were so bloodshot they appeared pure red. He cackled and nearly fell off his chair.

"You're not using, are you, G?" Richard asked, well aware that only Gauthier had the ability to print his own Nuvo. Sure, maybe it wasn't as pure as Arora's, but he'd had two months to refine the process. Perhaps he'd finally worked out the kinks.

"What do you think I am?" Gauthier asked. "A time-traveller?"

A degenerate asshole, who is the loudest mouth in Silany. He'll get us all killed before we burn down Bogod and blast the Fal.

"OK, let's go over the plan again." Richard held up his hand and pointed to his temple. "Phase one ends on Skastis, our family-friendly Festival of the Dead. Tomorrow night, we knock over the Makaria Bank on Theta Square. Then we vanish like bats at sun's-up."

And after the vanishing, he could resume his search to find and recover Arora, pry her away from the clutches of his white-bread brother and once the supply was secured again, resume his own experiments with Nuvo 7.

"Listen, there can be no fucking this one up. This is our legacy. We pull this off, and that's ten out of ten successful robberies—a perfect record. We'll be set for life with the money we take, and not (many) a living soul will have been hurt in all this. But I reckon, because we robbed another branch of Makaria, they won't think we'll hit another one, at least, not so soon. So, we can do this unarmed."

"Bollocks," said Gauthier, "I want toys, and I want to play with the toys."

"Gauthier, stick with me. We don't need violence to take this stash."

"Excuse me." Ares held her hand up casually. She appeared relaxed and nonchalant, like a student criticising a teacher just enough to make a point—but not enough to get in trouble. Richard could already tell what she was going to say, and in all fairness, she'd have a point. Gauthier currently went on every raid even though his greatest strength was designing the weapons, not field work. And while they were all now excellent at unarmed combat, she was still by far the strongest, swiftest and the deadliest fighter on the team. If Richard was serious about going in without any metal—not even a simple Stub-Jak gun or a Jak-Pin pistol—then it only made sense to bring their best non-metal weapon. That was her.

"I know," Richard responded out loud to her unvoiced question, "but I think the current team make-up is working well, no point changing it now." What Ares didn't know was that Gauthier had not only demanded to be included in the strike team, but he had threatened to snitch to the Mortalizers if he wasn't given his way. It was better to keep him inside the tent where Richard could keep an eye on him. "Listen, we're not going to hurt people—"

"Why?" Miles asked.

"PR." Richard shuffled around his table and ripped a cloth from a tray he'd prepared earlier, revealing tumblers, an ice bucket and a bottle of 100-year-old SOLO whiskey he'd stolen last time he'd been at the plant. Stolen? He thought about the absurdity of the idea. He owned the show. It was all his to thieve.

"Cheers," he said. "Tomorrow we are legend. Tomorrow, Nemes will become Little Nemes. Old Nemes. It will be a myth. We will build our own Nemes; a better Nemes. And we will lead the people. Into the New Nemes. Our own Future of Futures. And we will say to the people: You too can live with us. That is why we are not going to hurt them."

*

On the Night of Skastis, Richard was first to arrive at Spektrascope. He hoped to double-check all the kit and costumes and assess Gauthier's mood before the final raid. He was a little disturbed to find the building unlit when, usually, the downstairs gallery was lit all night. He let himself in and prowled among the artworks Gauthier's machines. When he didn't find Gauthier in the office, he crept up the stairs into the upper floor apartment where

Gauthier lived. The door was open. The lights were all off. When he turned on the bathroom lights, he found Gauthier passed out alongside the shower cubicle in a pool of vomit. Luckily, he was slumped on his side. Otherwise, he would have choked to death. This could possibly have been the best thing that could have happened to the group, Richard thought, and he realised that a year ago he would have felt a pang of guilt at such a thought—even though he hardly counted Gauthier as a friend.

He kicked the sole of Gauthier's boot and kept kicking it until Gauthier's head started to shake and incapacitated man rolled over onto his back and spluttered awake.

He eased himself up off the hard floor, smiling broadly. "Let me get myself a drink," he said. "Before you start ranting on about getting ready for the robbery of the century."

"How long have you been under?" Richard held up his hand.

"It was wild," he said, shrugging as he tried to sidle past Richard, no doubt looking for water.

Richard grabbed him by the throat. "How long?"

"Fuck you."

"How long?"

"Since you guys left."

"Twenty-four hours?"

"Oh, fuck me, you should have been there, Rich. I canned them all. It was like, no, it wasn't *like*, no—it *was* a bloodbath. Even my mother. I saw them all."

Richard let go of him. "You killed...*all of* your traits?"

"Nearly! And in the bloodiest ways possible. I am not just a giant; I am not just a god. I am a giant god. Now, let's steal, Pussywillow."

"I think you should stay in the Skim with Miles. I'll get Ares to work the bank." At least *she has some element of self-restraint.*

"Don't relegate me, Twattica. I'll tell them everything I know before I take them down in my next series of masterstrokes."

Somewhere below them, a door slammed shut, followed by silent footfall. The others were down in the office.

"C'mon," Gauthier said. "Let's crash it."

*

It was midnight in Theta Square, and a blood moon hung over Little Jiwa. Tonight marked the Festival of Skastis—a night when the unearthly and the restless were said to walk among the living. In Silany, no one took chances. Doors were locked, lights dimmed, and people hid beneath their bedsheets, hoping morning would come untouched.

They chose the intersection of Kawa and Tinova. Richard, Tom and Gauthier, all in red pumpkin masks specially designed for the occasion, infiltrated a party trail that swept along the Boulevard of Metallurgy and finally into Theta. No one paid them any attention beyond the odd student type who professed an admiration for the masks. As for Tom, if you knew him well enough, you could tell it was him beneath the mask simply by his jerky, lopsided saunter. And as for Gauthier, Richard wasn't sure there was much of him left at all beneath the mask. The Makaria Bank loomed over the square; it was a dome strafed by ebon flutes and studded with black plate glass windows for effect. It was easy to lose the crowd and disappear into the line of ornamental trees alongside the bank. By now, the foyer was completely dark. But plenty of lights on the upper storeys were still lit.

Crouching down behind a bollard, Richard urged Tom to scuttle into position by the bank's main doors, where he would attach one of the scarab-beetle-shaped limpet mines called The Smotherer. It had been designed with AI to pick this particular bank's lock and conceal the breach from its

AI security, sending the CCTV cameras into a loop that made them report the moments before Tom arrived forever. Tom twirled his finger, the signal that it was all OK, that it was now safer to be in the bank than in the square.

*

Richard made everyone stand still in the darkness of the foyer for a good 30 seconds, the agreed length of time. It was just long enough for them to know if they had tripped any systems and alerted any guards. The first thing to do was for Tom to hack into the mainframe and kill the lights in the upper levels. By the time they knew what was going on upstairs, Richard and Gauthier would have already made it to the top of the data banks. Tom ducked down and sat with his back to the desk. He took his tablet out and started to prod and press the keypad.

"Look at the state of him," Gauthier cackled, pointing at the mask. "The vegetable technician."

"Shhh," Richard said. "You'll have every Mortalizer from here to the Fal down on us in seconds."

"C'mon," Gauthier was rolling his shoulder and jogging towards the elevators.

"What the fuck are you doing?"

"Taking the fire to the fuckers."

An elevator door slid open. Gauthier sashayed inside and spun around, twirling his ring finger like a gunslinger with an invisible gun. He cocked his pumpkin head, and the doors closed just before Richard reached out to haul him up.

Fuck fuck fuck. The Makaria had fifteen floors. How was he supposed to know which one Gauthier was headed for? Intentionally, he'd not told Gauthier where the money was so he couldn't go rogue. His job was to cover

Richard's back. *Fuck.* He looked up and watched as the digital white numerals above the doors climbed to twelve. Then they stopped. He frantically summoned the lift, stabbing the button repeatedly, even though he knew it wouldn't make the crate arrive any quicker. It took forever...

When the doors opened on the twelfth, he entered a long corridor hung with abstract art and stark white lights. The scent of burning, like overcooked bacon, conjured up the memory of a stench like a shit barbecue in Old Silany. He could smell something else he didn't like, too, something metallic. He knew what it was. Six or seven men in lightweight suits were sprawled dead along the corridor, all lying in their blood. *Shit-Fuck.* This job was supposed to be clean, yet some considerable firepower had been deployed. And someone would have seen this freak show. Someone would have called the authorities, the police, Mortalizers. Tom was still in the foyer, a sitting duck. There was no point killing the lights now.

Richard spoke into his earpiece, "Get up here, now." And where the fuck was Gauthier?

Richard took out his gun—there was no way he was going unarmed—and crept along the corridor, careful not to step on the dead. Halfway along, he noticed an open door. What drew his eye was that the corpse sprawled out on the floor had no burn marks. There was no blood. The neck was at a weird, dislodged angle, like the man had been ambushed from behind and had his neck broken before he could react. Gauthier in his hyped-up, maniacal state was easily capable of snapping someone's neck. But why? Did he just have a primitive desire to get his hands dirty? To feel the life snuffed out of someone as the ultimate hit, the last unrepeatable thrill? Then he noticed it—the item on the plinth.

It was a 3-D printer—silver in colour, square in shape, and still warm to the touch—its upper-case memory still intact. The last two products it had generated were The Owl, which was some sort of gun, and The Rutting Stag, which was some sort of knife.

Fucking Gauthier. Designed his own set of weapons, printed and assembled them here.

He must have been desperate to kill, hungry for the taste of real blood.

Back outside at the intersection, Richard paused. Somewhere to his right he could hear a scuffle and some sort of hollow bang, like someone had kicked a metal cabinet or something. He didn't wait for Tom, and instead, followed his nose. Offices on either side were empty now save for the corpses. The hallways were littered with the carcasses of surveillance drones, shot down by Gauthier on his rampage. The ruckus was coming from what seemed to be a larger hub office, some sort of nerve centre.

Gauthier had his back to the door. He was holding a man down on the desk, gripping him by the hand and pinning him in place with his knee.

"Fuck off. I've called the police," the man screamed.

"The pass code, prick, or I'll have your balls."

"I don't know the pass code."

"You do."

"This is a fucking bank, not a kid's social hook-up site!"

Richard realised that he recognised that voice, that voice from his childhood. His blood froze. He took a step forward, only to lock eyes with Theo's fear-filled ones.

Gauthier reached into his coat and took out what looked like a short sword, which he drew from the scabbard with his teeth. The blade was black. Red smoke wafted from the blade. He let it smoke at his side for a second. It even scared Richard to see what must be the *Rutting Stag,* unleashed.

Gauthier dropped his *printed* gun, raised the blade and sliced off the man's hand.

The man screamed as blood gushed from the stump that was once an arm, bawling in Gauthier's face. Richard sprinted to them and sternly cautioned Gauthier to put it down, slowly.

"You don't know the code," Gauthier said. "You're no fucking use then."

He flicked the blade.

Theo's head rolled along the floor.

Tom appeared, almost like he'd materialised there out of thin air.

"Who the fuck did that?" he shouted as soon as he caught sight of the headless and handless body on the floor.

Gauthier lifted his mask, licked his lips and began howling like a wolf. He climbed on the table and raised his fists in the air.

"I am the Blade of God, Rapier of Heaven."

Richard waited for Gauthier to finish this proclamation. He then raised his Stub-Jak and using the sight, sent three old-school lead slugs through the bridge of Gauthier's nose.

Gauthier fell to the ground with a quiet thud, lifeless now, only a few metres away from where Theo was slumped.

"Shit, shit," Richard said. "I can't feel relief any more..."

"He's not your fault," Tom said, "I brought him in."

"Well, of course it's your fault..." Richard grimaced, then looked down at Theo's body. "This guy. The one without the head. He was my brother's friend."

"Your brother?" Tom asked. "The White-Blooded Paladin of Silany."

Richard took a sharp breath. "We've got to abort. Get out of here..."

There was some strange rumble in Richard's head that at first, he thought was the blood pulsing in his temples. Yet, the sound only grew louder. To his horror, he slowly realised it was the rampage of boots. He needed to move. Quickly.

Two uniformed officers in tactical gear and helmets swung into the room. Richard raised his Stub-Jak and let the sight find the head of the nearest officer, come into focus, and with it, facial clarity. He squinted at the eyes of the officer. Richard's eyes. *Norman's eyes. No way, is that Norman?*

But it was, and in a moment of hesitation, he found himself surrounded by armoured SWAT Mortalizers.

Richard knew that it would only take one false move, one cocky quip, one gesture, and he'd be smoked.

"Drop your weapons," Norman told them. He sounded serious. He sounded butch and authoritative. He sounded real.

Richard choked up, his throat sticky and his temples buzzing. For now, he kept silent.

"Lose the party masks," the second police officer—a middle-aged Silanese with a raspy voice demanded, glancing over at the two bodies on the floor. "Two corpses on arrival. One of them—it's hard to tell who—their head is missing."

"One moment, Blake," Norman said quietly, putting a steadying hand on his colleague's forearm.

A chill ran from Richard's face down to his feet. He put his Stub-Jak gently on the floor. So did Tom. They both pulled off their masks.

Norman's gaze was cold, so cold that he could have had Empathy removed by Nuvo 7. He didn't even seem surprised. It was like he had known all along and what he'd arrived at here was just the eventual unfolding of a plot that had been set twenty moves ago.

"Checkmate," Norman said, but Richard couldn't respond. He could barely breathe. "You've got blood on your hands, Rich," Norman said. "Cuff 'em, Blake."

Richard glared at Norman, trying to goad him into saying more, something to make this seem solvable. He was rich, after all. Surely, things could still be rectified. His actions today were simply a demonstration of what he could do—it was a show about the elite of Nemes. It then struck him that he had no idea who these hierarchies were—these people—were. He had no idea who he was trying to overthrow. Where was the audience in the opera of Richard's life? The very people he had worked to help were now gone. They'd abandoned him. He was on his own.

Blake clamped his wrists together behind his back and Norman felt his Adam's apple bob. He wasn't quite the stone-cold king he wanted to be. Richard wondered whether he should warn him about the head, but before he could utter a sound, Blake dragged him and Tom over to the door and lined them up against the wall.

"Stand still," he ordered. "One false move and we'll blow your foot off."

Norman walked over towards the two corpses. First, he pulled the mask off Gauthier, then nodded. "Gauthier DuPont."

"You know him?" Blake said.

"He's been on our radar for a while."

Theo lay flat on his back with a dark red stain across his torso, no head and his missing hand still on the desk. Richard knew the head had ended up under the table. His stomach tightened as Norman, who had already crouched down—and having reached under the table, brought out the head, horrid. He stood in the middle of the room with the expressionless mass dangling from his fingers by strands of blood-slicked hair.

He whipped around to Richard, eyes watering, barely able to restrain himself. "*You* did this?"

"It was Gauthier. But I'm sorry to disappoint you, Brother," Richard said, a muscle twitching near his eye. He didn't want to give Norman the satisfaction of thinking he cared.

He was my brother, Norman's eyes seemed to say, but he kept the words to himself. Richard's heart ached deeply, knowing how much his brother was hurting.

CHAPTER 13
En Passant

The wide skirt of Arora's otherwise tight white dress shone in the darkness as she sashayed across the Great Room of The Castle, searching for the remote control to activate the overhead lights. The app on her phone wasn't working. Neither were her agentic home systems when she called for them to "turn the lights on". In the entrance hallway, she had muttered that Richard must have found a way to lock her out of the house's systems. As a result, Norman had been forced to shoot the front door lock open—although he'd assured her he would call police support workers to replace it. The house was all that remained of her possessions now. Now that word was sure to spread across Silany that it had been the lair of a psycho-killer and master thief, she couldn't risk drawing thieves to it. She finally found a remote control tucked between the cushions of a plush, pink sofa in the corner of the room to her right and activated the overhead lights. The room was a vision of opulent grandeur, adorned with elaborate fixtures, heavy tapestries, and antique chairs and sofas. It exuded an air of baronial wealth—stately and commanding. To Norman, however, it felt less like luxury and more like something decadent, almost diseased.

"And this is all you think you've got?" Norman asked her. He'd brought Arora back here so she could collect some of her things quietly while Richard was locked away in the Fal. He also hoped she might be able to help him sift through Richard's kit for evidence—preferably a paper trail that could lead them to the missing money.

"The sole remaining asset from the marriage from hell," she murmured sadly, shifting her eyes around The Great Room. "I'm so embarrassed of it."

Norman looked around the room, thinking carefully before responding. "I don't like it either," he said, eventually.

Feeling reassured, she gave a small smile. "I suppose that's to be expected since you come from the favelas. There are no Great Castles in the Favelas. It's a good thing too. They're great, big, ugly things, really"

"You're right," he admitted. "I don't know much about Great Castles, but I learned a lot growing up in the favelas. And as my biggest lesson, I learned that getting too involved with the Manifesto can get you killed—like my dad, and now like Richard."

"But Richard's not dead."

"For now. But, Arora, he was caught in a Nemerian bank in the middle of a robbery. What's more, he was holding a discharged weapon while two corpses, one of which had been violently mutilated, lay on the floor right where he stood. At worst, he's facing the death penalty."

"You need to help him, Norman."

Norman was first stunned and then dismayed. "You want me to help him? He raped you..."

Without skipping a beat, she fired back "It was the effect of the Nuvo 7. He wasn't thinking straight. Surely, with so much of that stuff in his system, he can plead diminished responsibility?"

Norman's stare hardened. "He's between worlds in the Fal. He belongs to neither Nemes, nor Silany; there's *nothing* I can do for him now. Besides, he took the Nuvo knowing what it can do—the harm it could cause. And with the Silanese government cracking down on drug usage, it's highly unlikely that pleading diminished responsibility will help him now."

"Perhaps, but sometimes, you just need to escape. Surely you can relate with that longing" she said, catching his eyes as if to say, *we'll likely die in Silany, and Silany is no paradise, Silany is hell–there's no escape from this hell.*

Norman's frustration showed in the tightness of his jaw. "He killed my friend. The only thing to do is plead guilty. Maybe that'll reduce his sentence to life in prison, maybe it won't. But you need to understand that time in prison is hell. These prisons are overcrowded with angry, violent, men and women who want others to pay for their crimes. Living quarters are rife with TB, cholera, and Riggs' Disease. Rats as large as female cats swarm the cells. They can devour an entire man, leaving behind his polished bones stood up in his boxers for his cellmates to find."

Holding a steady gaze, she simply replied, "Maybe it'll change him for the better."

Norman didn't respond immediately, just gave a slow nod and said, "Where's his office?"

He followed her up several flights of broad winding stairs, admiring her slender form in spite of himself, as she led him to a room in which she believed Richard used to lock himself away. She was beautiful—much more than Richard deserved. Norman couldn't help but feel a bubble of anger rise in his chest at the thought of how his brother had hurt her.

In the office, there was a large oak desk littered with the sort of accoutrements of success that would appeal to Richard: a bottle of SOLO, tumblers, an empty decanter, cigar cutters, watch winders, candles in candlesticks, and an Etronium-plated laptop.

Norman dropped himself into the swivel chair and flipped open the laptop.

"Did you know if he had another one of these?" he asked.

Arora shook her head. "He wouldn't have had a work *and* a play laptop. He didn't have a job."

"It's locked. Any idea what the password might be?"

"No idea."

"You think I'll be able to guess it?"

"If I know Richard, it's likely an eighty-eight-character password containing mirrored letters and a song about drinking that has been written backwards."

"You're right. I'll take this back to the police station. Our Computer Forensic Analyst, Blake, will be able to hack into this thing in five minutes."

Norman rifled through the drawers in the desk. In the bottom one, under a stack of vintage SOLO distillery brochures was a pale violet plastic sheath containing a document. Across the cover was written in block marker: "*Hard Copy Cognition: A New Manifesto–For the Sake of Nemes.*"

He pulled out a printed paper bound document. It was 100 pages long—much shorter than The Manifesto Norman's dad used to read. It was entitled: "*Society of Mind: The Cognitive Pathway to Beyond and Above Nemerian Ascension.*" The stated publication date printed on the front was only five days from now. Was Richard supposed to announce something once the bank jobs were done? Though the language was terse and typically *Nemerian*, it was considerably more readable than The Manifesto. Norman had never been able to finish that thing.

A few sentences jumped out to Norman:

The mind is a playing field that needs to be re-ordered and maintained thereafter.

Nuvo 7 and its future iterations will provide the most effective non-invasive pathway to managing disorders of the mind and raising humanity's standard for achieving its highest potential.
Axiom-X is a state of purity, producing the same level of innocence as a child, yet it is more powerful than the Nemes Mystic.
The world will only benefit from this evolutionary advancement. Our human capabilities will extend beyond intellectual prowess. As a race, we will accomplish greater achievements than the world has ever known. We will control the weather and give life to creatures of all types. Even the lowest class of the Silanese-born will evolve.
The higher self needs no one—nothing—but itself to succeed.

Norman put the manuscript down.

"Any good?" Arora asked him.

"Not really."

The text was yet more evidence to use in the case against Richard. Norman had to hand it over back at the station, though part of him wanted to burn it. To stop this self-hatred from getting out and tearing down the last remaining fragments of their society. But one way or the other, it was going to get out. And a market of young, dumb, fools would be waiting to swallow this crap and see this as an invitation to topple over more statues. He stuffed the manuscript in the pocket of his raincoat. Maybe he could get Richard to denounce it. Maybe Richard should be the one to burn it. But the *Hard Copy* note, which was mark*ed* on the file, made him think there must be one, if not more, back-up copies somewhere. He had a few hours to make up his mind: bin, burn, bury—or be a good cop. For now, he focused on his next task—Arora's protection. He planned to take her to the police station, where the team would devise a plan to relocate her somewhere safe. With Richard's accomplices still at large, she had become a target.

*

At 3 am, the rain lashing down on New Jiwa had finally driven the last of the hardiest Skastis revellers back into their dens. Norman, still so wired from shock and adrenaline that sleep felt impossible, arrived at Spektraskope to find the gallery bathed in a harsh white light. The strange contraptions inside cast jagged, shifting shadows in the shapes of monsters across puddles on the floor. Detectives combed through the building with methodical precision, while four Nemerian Mortalizers—brutal enforcers no sane person would dare cross—stood guard, their presence a silent and stout warning. He found Blake in the upstairs office taking fingerprints from the control panel of a 3-D printer. "There Is No State" was written sloppily on the upper right-hand side of the panel in red marker.

"Anything to report?" Norman asked.

"Upstairs apartment is a state—filthy, to be honest. There's vomit everywhere. We found what looks like Nuvo 7 in the bedroom. There are two different sets of prints here, which could belong to your brother and Gauthier—but we won't know more until we analyse the footwear and tire track."

"Alright, good work. I found some rambling notes and his laptop at my brother's place—I need you to break into it."

"I will. After I've had, like, a year's sleep."

"We've got enough already to send them down forever."

"So..."

"What's your question?"

"Same as yours."

"Where's the money? Because someone is still getting away with a ton of stolen money."

*

Outside, they huddled deeper into their coats against the rain while Blake took advantage of the building's meagre cover for a cigarette break. He smoked Silanese Heaven 11s for the raw, earthy hit. They were thicker than the 10s but loose enough to stain his thumbs yellow with stray tobacco. Not that Blake seemed to care.

"If they're as smart at laundering the money as they are at robbing banks," Blake said, "we might never trace it."

"You mean, *really* smart like spending it on castles and distilleries. No, my brother thought he was going to get away with it and still flaunt it all in our faces."

"That doesn't mean we'll find the rest. We're not white-collar investigators. We're street drug enforcement detectives."

A commotion stirred just beyond the gallery's corner, where a narrow street met one of Little Jiwa's dense, rain-drenched city-squares. Under the harsh cone of sodium light spilling from the façade—its glow fractured by the heavy rain—the Mortalizers were forcing a soaked, dishevelled man up against the square's iron railings, their movements sharp and unyielding.

"What are those thugs up to?" Blake whispered through a cloud of white smoke.

"I think we have a rare sighting."

"A rare sighting of what?"

"A vagrant. And luckily for him, they don't know what to do with him. C'mon."

As Norman jogged over, he could see that the man was now on his ass on the wet paving and the Mortalizers had their rifles trained on him, ready to eliminate him, as though he were...

"Woah, woah," Norman said, waving his arms. "Leave him alone."

The Mortalizers backed off. Norman reached out his hand to pull the vagrant up. He was heavily bearded, gaunt, and draped in what was surely the oldest coat in Silany. He stared up at Norman and didn't take his hand. He was wearing a disposable face mask. He must have been sick. Norman's hand hung mid-air until the man started to scream and scrabble backwards until he rammed himself hard into the railings. The Mortalizers laughed.

"Not this time, not this time, I'm not well!" the man shouted.

"What the fuck is he going on about?" Blake said. He was coughing hard, out of breath from catching up with Norman. Goddamn those 11s.

"I don't know. Have we met before?"

"You tried to set fire to me, you bastard. All I wanted was some money for my treatment and you kicked me in the head!"

"Listen, friend," Blake said, "we've not been here before—'

"No," Norman said. "He thinks I'm Richard, my twin."

They took the drenched man into the gallery and threw him a blanket to wrap up in. They made him coffee and gave him an energy bar. His name was Atto Nett. He used to be some sort of programmer before he caught a strain of MTv-88 and his boss fired him, causing him to end up on the street. He'd assumed the Mortalizers were either going to deport him or shoot him.

"So, you hang out here a lot?"

"Sleep in the park. It's gated at night. No one bothers me, and I don't, them."

"Yet, my brother assaulted you?"

Atto scrunched his face up. "Look, the guy who owns this place, we used to be all right. He'd give me change. Sometimes a grilled cheese or some noodles in a pot."

"Gauthier?"

"That's the one."

"He's dead as well."

"Fuck me. Who killed him?"

"My brother, most likely."

"Your brother is evil, man."

"So, it would seem. Why'd he kick your ass?"

"It was on a night like tonight. The door was open, so I crept in. He didn't usually mind. I called out and all. They were upstairs. Four of them, and Mr G.—Gauthier. You, I mean, your bro was reeling off some instructions. Then he saw me and before I could process what was happening, he pounced on me—Mr G. had to pull him off me. He had a flask and a lighter and everything. He was all right like that, Mr G."

"You remember what they were talking about?"

"Not sure."

"What was my brother saying? Think."

"It's all a blur, just some words that sounded strange at the time. "Booo ah Trifellows"."

"Trifellows?"

"Think so."

"You seen these folks?" Norman flicked through a fan of photos from inside his coat and took out two.

"They were all there, and they've been here a lot. Mr G was all right before then. And that black guy looks at you like he's scared of how bad you look compared to him, and the girl looks like she'll kill you for a shot of tequila."

"You prepared to say all this in court?"

"Doesn't all this high-tech spy stuff capture all the...people? Why do you need my statement?"

"Most of that stuff isn't operational. It's just "there.""

"Shit. That shit makes you scared. Wait—is that why they put it there?"

Norman turned to Blake then back on his new friend. "You prepared to say it all in court?"

"What's in it for me?"

"A hostel bed."

"Done."

Norman walked back into the rain to call for a Skimatik to take all three of them back to the station in Nexus 10. Blake followed him out again to light up another cigarette.

"Trifellows?" he said.

"Third biggest Nemerian financial services outfit in Silany."

"And obviously rotten."

"When we get back, you take Atto's statement. I'm going hunting."

As the red lights of the Skimatik approached, widening in the gauzy rain, Norman could smell the money coming back. He thought of Theo and how he was supposed to tell Theo's parents. His fingers tightened around the pistol in his pocket—then he caught himself, remembering who he was. Right then, his phone buzzed twice. Arora. Her message read:

Booo = Bou = Kemi

*

At 5.25 am it was still neither dry nor dawn in Little Jiwa. Norman had changed into a civilian shirt, a clean, whitish one. He'd gone to The Castle to "requisition" some formal slacks and a tan business raincoat he'd found in Richard's dressing room. He now stood outside an eight-story apartment above the intersection of Simril and Grippen Borse. He was hammering the door with his fist. He had been for some minutes when a woman opened the door: frizzy-haired, groggy, barefoot and in a pale orange negligee.

"Richard? Do you know what the time is?" Norman stayed silent. "You know, Richard, we agreed to meet only on the roof…I suppose it must be urgent. So, what do you want? Say something. Is everything okay with the cash flow? It should be squeaky clean now. Untraceable."

"Have you heard the news tonight?"

"I crashed at ten. Unlike some, I work for a living."

"I got caught, Kemi."

"What do you mean, you got caught? You OK, Bou?"

"Bou at Trifellows."

Norman tried not to smile and reached into both pockets of his coat, retrieving his pistol with one hand and with the other his badge.

"I'm not Rich. I'm Norman, Officer of the Law of the Nexus 10 Precinct. I just lost my best friend tonight and if you, Kemi, don't tell me everything you know about where you laundered my brother's filthy money, you'll spend the rest of your life in the Fal."

Kemi rested on the back of her bare feet and pressed a finger to her cheek. She looked Norman up and down, slowly. "Can I get you a drink, Officer?"

*

The polished marble floors squeaked beneath Norman's feet. He felt the hot breath of his father's shame on his neck as he paced the corridors of the Fal, accompanied by a silent Mortalizer. He tried to be less like his mother and not blame his drunken father for what Richard had done, especially to Theo. He was pretty content with holding Richard to account. He was pretty happy blaming Richard for Richard's acts. The difference between Nemes and Silany is that in Silany you are what you do. For the sake of his parents, and for the sake of Arora he would try to keep Richard alive. At the very least he'd try to stop him becoming a martyr for the rapacious void he and his ilk called a philosophy.

The holding cell was a grey cube on the western side of the inner octangular. Richard was sitting bolt upright on a metal chair shackled to a metal table. As soon as Norman was ushered into the room by the Mortalizer, Richard began tapping his heels against the table leg. Norman knew Richard was doing this only to irritate him. It was irritating but he refrained from asking the Mortalizer to discipline Richard with his taser and knuckleduster even though it would have been within his rights to ask for such assistance.

He sat down opposite Richard, ignored the incessant tapping, and placed a file on the table. He checked his watch. 9.15 am. He opened the file and started to sift through a number of documents and photographs.

"Neglecting your paperwork, Officer Wise?" Richard said, forcing Norman to face him. "Am I going to get off on a technicality?"

"You can call me Norman."

"Okay *Normal*. Are you sure you're safe being left alone with me?"

"You're not usually a violent man," Norman told him. "Then again, that was before you rewired your brain to remove the bits of you that made you a human."

"It's a shame you think so. I tend to think that bits of me have now become almost godlike."

"That's why you're in here, and I'm over here. That's why I am the law, and you are chained to a table."

"Details," Richard retorted, with a bored look "Are the last resort of the peasant."

"Your divine majesty, let me remind you, that you are even according to yourself, a Sub. And a Sub in Nemes' most feared jail. Someone who has been caught red-handed after a series of heists that embarrassed the state and brought shame to Silany."

"Well, it's your word against mine."

"I'm here to tell you to plead guilty."

"Norman, come on. I was in the wrong place at the wrong time. Gauthier went berserk. He was the one holding Tom and I hostage. He had us in his grip all day. I shot him to *defend* Theo, but I was too late."

Fine," Norman said. "I have the testimony of Officer Blake and a team of Mortalizers to confirm that that isn't what you said in the room. I also have the blueprints of the unique guns and the swords you used in the Makaria job. These were loaded into the 3-D printer in one of the bank's offices. The schemes for all the other firearms, scanners and explosives you used in the previous jobs, are on Gauthier's machine, and your fingerprints are all over the frame and the keyboards of both printers. The vagrant you doused with petrol puts you in the gallery multiple times. Heard you give up your cleaner, who is at this moment testifying against you in exchange for immunity. You told your wife and your wife told me what you were up to. Like Kemi, she's also been granted immunity."

"Kemi," Richard said, his lips curling. His feet had stopped tapping. "I should have fucked her when I had the chance."

"The police in Silany know you started stealing pretty much as soon as you arrived at the university, which doesn't do the reputation of our family name much good. My colleague, Blake, cracked your laptop three hours ago and we found detailed plans for each of your jobs. We've located your four associates, all who are now wanted felons, one of whom is now deceased." He slapped down photos of Tom, Miles, Ares and Gauthier on the table. "And, finally, in The Castle I find this." He flipped the new manifesto over his shoulder and waited until it thudded onto the floor. "Murder. Rape. Theft. Conspiring to defraud the state. Misuse of funds. Use of illegal weapons. Narcotic violations. It's not a case of where to start, but where to stop. You plead not guilty, you'll get the death penalty."

Leaning forward in his seat, Richard traced a figure of eight with his forefinger on the table.

"You missed out the sweetest one of all, brother. Remember when I worked for Jonas the Fish?"

"The fishmonger who was..."

"Murdered by the fourteen-year-old angel-eyed me. See, he said shitty things about Nemes that shamed our father, so I followed him home and set him straight with one of his own knives."

Norman froze, horrified. Richard smirked, no doubt enjoying the silence that had descended in the cell, how the atmosphere grew colder and colder the longer no one spoke.

"Why did you even tell me that?" Norman said.

"We need things to bring us closer together now that we're orphans, we need things to share."

"You need to confess on the record."

"Need? I need? Norman, if you beat me at a final game of chess right now, I will provide you with a full testimony."

"On what condition?

"Nothing, other than that we play a game, you and I, to win. A final hurrah, if you will. Come on, Brother. For old time's sake. What have you really got to lose?"

Richard's dark brown eyes blinked hard and for a second Norman could almost believe he was innocent, that there was some unseen side to all of this that could exonerate him, and they could go back to playing chess and boxing again.

"Rich, it's a stupid idea. If I lose, which I usually do, you die. Even if you give a full testimony, you're a Sub to them. You need to confess now to have half a chance."

Richard shrugged. "It's your loss. You'll be forever wondering what I was going to say. You'll have passed up the chance to find the final piece of the puzzle to the robberies."

Norman shook his head. "Don't worry about me, Rich. I've got all the evidence I need."

"I suppose you're feeling a bit sore about Theo."

"Don't you dare speak his name. You should have lost the right to breathe the day you killed him! But today, you've lost the right to speak his name," Norman spat out, his heart racing.

"Or what? You're going to kill me?" Richard shook his head slowly. "But I'm your brother, Norman, and you want to kill me. Theo should mean nothing to you compared to me, especially, *especially* now that Mother and Father are dead. There is only one way to erase the hate you feel in your heart."

Norman's shoulders slumped over, and he felt a great weight pushing down on his shoulders. There was nothing left in the world for him to look forward to anymore, nothing beyond this grey cube of a prison floating in an endless ocean of hate.

"Theo meant everything to me," he finally said. Lowering his voice to a whisper, he continued, "you deserve to hang for what you did to him, and I would love nothing more than to be the one to pull the world from under you. You are no brother of mine."

"Look, let's both calm down a second."

"He was more of a brother to me than you could ever hope to be, Richard. You're nothing more than a walking tsunami; chaos and destruction lie in your wake. Everything your hands touch turn to dust. You have nothing to offer anyone, least of all me."

Richard didn't respond. The chains clanged suddenly as he reached a manacled hand to stroke his chin as though to measure the weight of Norman's words; the edge of his heel continued silently tapping against the table leg. He composed himself and filled the silence once more.

"You've come here for information, haven't you? I'll help you, brother. I'll tell you about the drug. You can use a Nuvo 7 pill to enter your mind virtually and remove both the memory and the associated emotion."

"You're drowning in the poison inside. I don't understand why you've chosen this path. I've never believed in any of this, and neither did Mum. You know she wanted us to have and stick to a moral code—real values like hope, truth, *justice*. These were the things that mattered to her. Look, your fate is now out of my hands. But if, somehow, you manage to weasel your way out of this, it would do you good to remember her. You know, Richard, sometimes I think that if you hadn't forgotten her, maybe you wouldn't be heading down the same path Dad did—dead, just like him. And all for the same pitiful reasons."

Richard's eyes filled with tears. He put a hand to his face in mock grief. "I did all of this for the good of society."

"A blatant lie," Norman fired back.

"For Nemes."

"Nemes?" Norman's voice erupted from his chest, fierce and unrestrained, like the roar of a lion. The question that had been simmering inside him—the one he had never asked, never understood—finally broke free... *"WHY DO YOU CARE ABOUT NEMES?"*

His voice echoed and Richard smiled, waiting for the silence to return.

"Do you love me, Norman?"

"Oh Jeez. I love the truth, Richard. And I detest lies."

Richard sank into himself, his chin resting on his chest, barely breathing. "How does a man know what is true? What is right?"

"She told us how."

"When?"

Norman said nothing. He sighed, stretched, and stood up. Richard was now slumped in his seat, looking around him warily. He was tempted to go and give Richard a hug, but he held back. It was too late for Richard. Maybe some time in isolation would wise him up, convince him to cooperate.

"Last chance Rich, or I'm gone," Norman told him. "Confess."

"Fuck you, Norman."

*

The following morning at 5 am, Norman was awoken from a necessary sleep by some droning, nagging noise that seemed to come from the end of a long earthen tunnel that he eventually realised was his phone ringing on his nightstand. He sat up in the dark and saw from the number it was Tamara from the station. He felt the need to prepare himself. Richard was easily capable of killing himself in prison in an act of defiance or provoking the Mortalizers or other inmates. He couldn't ignore the call.

"Wise," he said.

"Sorry it's early," she said.

"Is he dead?"

"No...he's escaped."

"What the...?"

"It seems the remaining members of the gang we failed to apprehend have employed some rather extraordinary technology to break your brother and Tom Trommel out of the Fal just an hour ago."

"They've made a queen pawn."

"Pardon?"

A cold, gaping emptiness opened within Norman, as though a vast chasm had suddenly torn through him. Richard—free, out there—out on the loose. *I know Silany, Richard, and I am coming for you.*

"I'll be with you soon."

CHAPTER 14
Angels are Brutes

Her phone rang twice.

"Arora, you okay? Got everything you need?"

"I'm fine, really."

"You sure?"

"Yeah. Just...resting. Not missing at all. I am making fire—with real wood—if you can believe it."

In the end, Arora had chosen the wilderness as her escape—a way to recentre, to find herself again after losing so much in the chaotic wake of her estranged husband. She had settled in the forests of Silany, making a home on their far edge in an old, hard-to-find cabin. It was the perfect place to disappear.

The forests of Silany. Norman used to walk them nearly every day—back when life was simpler. When he had the dogs and the world still made sense. He wouldn't mind that life again—the wild streams, the hares to hunt. Back then, it was the only thing that felt real. Everything else? Just an illusion.

"Any news on Richard?" Norman asked.

"Yes." There was a pause on the line. "He's planning a robbery."

"How would you know that?"

"It's how his mind works." He could hear her breathing. "He's lost all his money. Kemi gave up his accounts. He needs money and now he has nothing to lose. He'll likely think he'll lie low and change his ID, his appearance and then disappear. But his arrogance won't allow him to disappear quickly. He'll want one last chance at victory before he vanishes forever."

"They're going to need Nuvo 7."

"Right."

"From what I hear, only one department of one firm in Nemes actually makes Nuvo 7. You should talk to my partner, Hera Moon."

"Got it, thanks," Norman said. Then after a brief pause, "I'll be coming your way soon to bring you a few supplies. Also, do you like dogs?"

*

The air in Sub-Basement 23 of the Bukhova Sugar Company was thick with mould, stagnant water, and the stench of sewage. A place built to be forgotten, it swallowed both time and light. Richard had long stopped counting the days since he and Tom went into hiding, but he could see time weighing down on Tom. Months without sunlight had drained the colour from his skin, leaving it waxy and yellow. He was the only Whisperer who bore any resemblance to Richard, making his own reflection feel like a ghost of himself. His beard had grown unruly, his once-kept appearance slipping, but tending to it felt meaningless now. If he could just get his hands on Nuvo 7, he could erase his Vanity entirely. They had been down here since they broke-out of the Fal's not-so-maximum security prison. They had come across this nexus of rooms deep under Liao and Ichin on one of their earlier expeditions through the sewers of Little Jiwa, trying to find entry points into sundry banks. As the rooms seemed abandoned, they'd made a good hiding place for The Whisperers' special weapons cache. It had been a neat move of Miles to choose this as a bolt hole and use the wall-busting radio-blasters and holographic smog machines to bring down the Fal. A lot of Mortalizers had died that day. It felt good to have been the cause of so much death and chaos.

Richard reclined on one of the two-hundred thirty-year old office swivel chairs stored in Sub-Basement 23. Tom was still hunched over his laptop. Richard thought when the money came back, he would buy a spa hotel, out in the desert somewhere, and shower for days. Ares and Miles had put on disguises to leave for the day to buy food and supplies. They were getting showers up there, in health clubs and hotels that rented rooms by the hour. Why couldn't Richard rent a room by the hour up there? Why was he the most wanted man in Silany, and probably Nemes too, when he was the Vessel of Truth and the Man of the Future of Futures. Fucking Gauthier, and fucking Theo for getting in the fucking way.

"Yowza," Tom said, spinning around on his chair. "Think I've cracked Arora's Zazuma file."

Richard peeled himself from his seat and slapped Tom on the back. "So, what have you got?"

"Give me a chance, I've only just got in." Tom opened a file. A 3-D version of Nuvo 7's chemical compound appeared, looking like some angular cosmic octopus that sucked numbers and equations to it like a singularity. "Gold-dust," Richard said. "You can see why Gauthier's moonshine version was pure rot. This is perfection."

"Look at her, she's beautiful," Tom said.

"OK, let's bust one final batch of Nuvo 7 from Zazuma Pharma, and replicate the ingredients using a printer."

"We haven't got a printer."

"Miles needs something to do."

"You say that so lightly. Are you planning to do the Zazuma job then?"

"Ares," Richard said, smiling down at Tom with raised eyebrows. "You're our master hacker. You need to help her get in.

"She might say no."

"Ares and Miles did a pretty stand-up job of breaking us out of prison. Look, crack open that last bottle of SOLO. Take a break. I'll fill them in as soon as they get back. Here, let me look at the rest of her files?"

Four hours later he had sifted through all of Arora's data, including her personnel records, assessments, references and footnotes in all of the business plans and grant applications she had devised for her scientific projections and sales forecasts for Nuvo 7. He had rifled through all her notes and speculative punting about Nuvo 7, alongside numerous other drugs. He felt a compulsion to know everything there was to know about Nuvo 7. He had to know. He knew he'd lost her. He had trained himself not to miss her, because if he missed her, he wouldn't be able to execute the next part of his plan—to enslave her. He'd intended to use Nuvo 7 and some nifty cognitive mirroring to crank up her Subservience and switch off Rebellion, Righteousness and Self Preservation, moulding her into his personal, round-the-clock mule. The plan had been simple—embed her inside Zazuma as his mole. That was until he realised that if he wanted Nuvo 7 now, he'd have to steal it from Zazuma himself. And a raid like that? It would only work if he had the element of surprise.

He had owned Arora's body once. Its memory was mapped and internalised in his mind. But that wasn't enough. He wanted all of her. As he scanned her data, absorbing every detail, he was building a blueprint of her mind. If he could have also plucked her consciousness from her skull while in possession of her body, extracted her thoughts, and turned it into a rose bowl for his mantelpiece, something he could display and admire as *his,* he would have.

The last document in the file had triple password protection and needed Tom's Supra-Hakshank X46 Decrypter to open it. Even then, it took a record 45 minutes to crack, and then a further 20 to decode the text: *a contract for services drawn up by the Faj Department of Medical Science and authorised on behalf of Zazuma by Hera Moon and Arora Wise.* He read it once and unpacked the turgid, technocratic language in his head. Then it hit him.

"What is it?" Tom asked. "You look like you just ate some of Miles' cooking."

"She lied to me," he whispered, his lungs quickly filling with rage with every breath. "Nuvo 7, it's not what she said it is." Richard's mouth wouldn't work, he felt like he was hearing himself from far away. "It's not designed to create a society of mind. That's a smokescreen. It's not even going to be used in Nemes. It's going to be used in Silany, to keep them all—*docile*—limited so they just all keep...digging for ore and tending to the people *who dig for ore. It's all about Etronium.*" He couldn't quite believe it. It was a scam, another ploy to not only separate them from Nemes, but to also push them down further into their base Silanese condition, condemning them to remain in abject poverty—abandoned and alone—under the guise of Nemerian Ascension. It was a perfect distraction. *Nuvo 7 is White Milk on steroids.*

"It's to replace something called Kova 3 that they've been putting in the water for decades, centuries maybe, because the Silanese are starting to become resistant to it."

Shit. Is that why Norman used to drink the water from the spring? How the fuck did he know?!

"You mean, we didn't get to be educated because we're smart enough to be Nemerian. We're just tolerant to some dope?"

"That's the crux of it."

A heavy weight settled on Richard's shoulders, and he hunched his shoulders. Arora had never said a word.

Somewhere nearby, metal clanked in the pipes. It was followed by the slow slosh of water echoing from the open manhole leading down into the sewer. A flashlight beam swept across the opening—Miles and Ares were right on time. Tom met Richard's gaze. Richard met his.

"Let's bring the state down," They cried in unison.

*

Whether Arora had spoken or stayed silent no longer seemed to matter; betrayal, she knew, wasn't always in the act. Sometimes it was simply in leaving. Yet, she was fearful. Because a love like hers and Richard's didn't end—it curdled. It waited in the quiet spaces between what had been done and what might still be forgiven.

She should have felt nothing. After everything he'd done—the monster he'd become—Arora told herself that he deserved everything he got and more. That in fact, she ought to rejoice the day they finally caught and executed him for the pain he had brought to the people of Silany. But when Norman and his team rehoused her and told her they were closing in on him, something inside her broke. It was sharp and sudden, like a muscle remembering pain. She thought back to the first time she laid eyes on Richard, standing on the stage of the Great School Hall of the University of Nemes, delivering his acceptance speech for the Basil Black Foundation Scholarship. He was dashing, yes—but it was his charm that caught her eye. The bold confidence that might have unsettled other women had, for her, signalled safety—assurance that he carried enough strength and ambition for both of them. And as time passed, so did the love that quietly bloomed between them. It had come gently, but it had been real. Even now, her heart still reached for him in ways she couldn't comprehend. But Richard was no longer the man she'd fallen for. The charm had curdled into arrogance, then cruelty.

He is a bully, she thought to herself, wincing at the recollection of the night he stopped being Richard—when his love turned violent, his heart twisted beyond recognition, and she fled with what little of herself remained.

*

Back at Nexus 10 Station, Norman skipped the coffee, the small talk, and the usual updates. Instead, he dialled Hera Moon again. Yesterday, he had warned her to expect a security breach that night, but he hadn't asked for reinforcements. He had told her to hold back the plant's elite security detail, to let the intruder believe he'd slipped through unnoticed, because this wasn't just a break-in. It was part of a trap."Oh," she said breezily. "I was just about to call *you*. There *was* a break-in last night."

So, they *had* managed to crack Arora's ID. It was to be expected. That Tom was good, well in advance of the skillset of the average greedy hacker.

"Nothing was damaged or destroyed," she continued. "Stealthy job, a whole consignment box of Nuvo 7 was taken."

"How many pills were in the box?"

"Two-hundred and twenty."

"Film?"

"We set up an additional loop. Our usual video glitched at 11.45 pm Obviously, they didn't think we'd wear a coat *and* a scarf."

"Clever cat," Norman said. "Describe the perp to me? It may be that I don't even need to come and inspect the video myself."

"She was wearing a mask, a gas mask, old style, the sort of thing you'd need to find not buy. She's lithe, sinewy, slight, but looks tough. Long brown hair."

"Thanks," Norman said. "Let me know if she comes back."

He didn't need to see that film to know it was Ares, Richard's champion and proxy in the ring. She'd had black hair, so the brown must be a half-hearted attempt at a disguise. Norman remembered that day in the ring—the sharp snap of her kicks, the way she scrambled onto his back. She could have killed him. But she was all force, no power. Force was immediate, but it was fleeting, burning out quickly. Power, on the other hand, was self-sustaining, feeding off itself, without the constant need for fuel. He knew how to beat her now, how to beat them all—with power over force. And all it required from him was to completely let go of fear. He closed his eyes and heard his mother's voice clear as day: *my boy, let go of the fear, only then will you realise your true power.* No sooner had his mother's words left him, than his father's sharp rebuke rang out: *Angels are Brutes, Norman.*

It was as though the ghosts of his parents had resumed their endless quarrelling in the halls of his memory. His mother's gentle righteousness had always clashed with his father's hardened realism, and the mental strain of holding both truths at once pressed against the walls of his mind.

But this time, Norman didn't hide from it. He listened. Really listened. And for the first time he understood that they had both been right—his mother with her unwavering belief in always obeying the two rules, and his father, who had long understood that the world rarely afforded the luxury of clean hands. Perhaps morality wasn't absolute. Perhaps it was contextual, shifting with intention, circumstance, and heart posture. If a bad act was done for the right reason…was it still bad? Maybe sometimes the right thing required becoming someone you never thought you'd be. Maybe there were no good or bad people at all—just choices you made, and the consequences lived with.

But this wasn't about what his mother nor his father had died believing. It was no longer even about Theo, though his death carved its own unhealed place inside Norman's chest. It was about him—who he was becoming, and what he would choose to stand for when it mattered.

Just then he recalled the Super's words, the quiet warning that one day he'd have to choose—between one path and another, between himself and his brother, between life and death. And now, Norman felt the weight of that moment pressing down on him. The choice was coming. He would count the cost, and it would be true. And for the first time, he found himself wavering—uncertain whether he could still honour his mother's rule: *always obey the rules.* He opened his eyes again, his mind now clearer than it had ever been.

*

The track leading up to Silbak Hill was so muddy that even Norman felt a twinge of anxiety—one wrong move, and he could lose control of the van. At the top of the hill stood the hut where Arora was hiding, the only occupied building among a cluster of flint cabins. Once home to Etronium surveyors who had found no ore, the hill remained steep—a real bastard to climb. In the back of the van his dogs, Juny, Ram and Tan, barked and barked, their gums dark, teeth flashing, and droplets of drool spraying everywhere. He had picked them up en route from Mr. Johnson's place, deep in the hills of the forest of Silany. He had then sat with the old man for a minute and a half, exchanging only a few words.

"How's yar father?" Mr. Johnson asked him.

"Dead," Norman said.

The dogs needed to come home. With the feud between him and his brother, he needed the closeness of family. At ninety, Mr. Johnson was at death's door. With his eyes clouded with cataracts, he had no vision left. He had no leg either—just a wooden club in its place. But Norman wasn't worried. Sally, his missus, was still around and keeping things together. She and the old man had other dogs, a goat, bats to eat the bugs so their crop would survive. He had enough company and all the help he would need in his final days. What Norman wanted was his dogs back. His dogs and some weapons. As a gesture of gratitude for a decade-long favour and a tribute to the centuries-old bond between their families, Norman left them some money—after all, the Johnsons and Wises had been tied together since long before Georgia's father. Then he gathered the weapons he had lodged there for safe keeping. His boss had suggested he take them from the armoury at their unit as a backup. Norman had his window down, the cold wind stinging his eyes as it howled over mound and stone. Norman's mind flickered back to his brother and the wake of destruction he'd wrought, all in the name of some grand illusion over the last decade. His jaw tightened into a scowl. His brother had taken so much from him and Theo's murder had been the final crushing blow. No one—not even his brother, would take anything from him again. It was time to settle things once and for all.

On the small gravel concourse outside the hut, he lifted the cardboard box off the floor of the van and took it to the front door. The dogs had quietened down and there was a stillness in the air.

Arora opened the door, the steam from her bath still swirling around her. She was carefully wrapped in a white towel that barely covered her torso, her hair wrapped in a towel just as carefully. Her smile was radiant, and the usual tension around her eyes had melted away. She looked beautiful standing there in the doorway. Norman wished he didn't see her that way; she was his brother's wife. But then again, she knew he was coming—she could've covered up more but had chosen not to. He plonked the box down on the small wooden kitchen table. She removed and stored everything from the box: paper packages of barley, oats and other things. Norman looked around him. He hadn't been here for years.

"It used to be just a single wood cabin. Theo's Grandpapa called it The Outpost. Men used to sleep in it when travelling to the summit." A Hunter's Paradise was its actual name. "God, there must have been a thousand men that passed through here."

From his tote bag, he pulled out a selection of fruit and vegetables.

"Arora, I'm close to figuring out which bank they're going to go for next. Can you just go through the list again for me?"

Bringing two glasses of fresh spring water to drink, Arora handed one to Norman and sat down at the table with hers.

"You found the spring okay, then?"

"Yeah, it was just like you said; follow the path down, then up when turning left."

"Do you want to get dressed?"

She pulled around her a giant shawl. The fire burned in the corner that the dogs were resting in.

"You don't need an excuse to come up here, you know. I thought I'd given you what I know about banks anyway?"

"New patterns are emerging."

"Richard was hardly telling me all the details."

"I know," he said. "Bear with me. This is going somewhere. And maybe I just need to talk this through with someone. Richard is going to take down Ipsteins."

"What? He's already done Ipsteins."

"That's exactly why he'd do it again. No one thinks he'd be that brash. It gives him the pay-off he needs and the chance to go down in history. He can hit the bank much harder too because he's already killed. He doesn't have a reputation or a set of morals to protect anymore. If I were Richard, it's exactly what I'd do."

"Would you?"

"...Yes."

"How do you know?"

"Because I know my Richard—my inner Richard, I mean. And I know how to tame it. I don't need to rid myself of it. I understand and accept that it is a part of who I am, but that I also have enough control to understand when to use it. That had always been the problem with him...and my father. They didn't know what it was, that animalistic instinct inside them and what it could achieve, nor that it could also be tamed…" He didn't need to explain it, she must know what it was, the wild part in her that made her Silanese. She glanced down at his forearms, noticing for the first time, his large, reddened hands. Her nose flaring slightly, she nervously bit her dark, full lips. Her cheeks warmed and the warmth spread through her chest to the rest of her body, causing her feet to tingle.

"Wild horses," she said.

"What?"

"What you're talking about—my mother used to call it, wild horses."

"So, what are you going to do? Camp out the bank?"

Before she could grab his arms, he pulled away, scraping his chair back. He stood, pacing and gesticulating as he pulled words from his mouth with his hands. Arora used this time to gather herself, pulling the shawl around her shoulders even tighter to distract herself from her quickening heartbeat.

"That is trickier, but I'm fairly sure I've figured it out. The length of time between each robbery matches a pattern. It's not that obvious when you first look at it, but it's there and it lines up with Richard's thinking."

She stood up and walked into the back room. He followed, keen to tell her more. He let the door swing close behind her.

"The second robbery took place exactly a month after the first one. Then, if you look at the third one, it's two months plus an additional week. The fourth one took place three months and two weeks afterwards...and so on. That's it. It's an extra month and extra week each time." He found himself out of breath as he waited for her. In an effort to catch his breath, he turned to face the pups. pleading with them to "go" with his eyes. They each gave a low snarl and turned away from him. Soon after, Arora walked back out in jeans and a small, black top. Parading barefoot, she rubbed her hair down with a towel before heading back to her chair next to her boots that had hikers' socks in. Norman walked over to the dogs and knelt to rub the dogs' ears while Arora laced up.

"Without fail, they always took place on a Saturday night. I don't know why I didn't see this pattern before!" Norman stood and slammed one fist against an open palm. "I just didn't have enough evidence to connect Richard to all of the cases, but now here it is, plain as day. Stupid, really"

"Norman, you are far from stupid."

"Based on what I've figured out, it is obvious when the final heist is being planned. Three days from now."

Arora stood up and walked to the window and looked out. She pulled her hair back into a ponytail and Norman, not for the first time, noticed the curve of her waist. The way her jeans hugged her wide hips. He couldn't tell which was sexier on the woman—the gun in her waistband, or the curve of her hips. He could tell she was agitated; the back of her shoulders were tense. *Maybe she wanted to pull her gun and shoot something. Or someone.* But she couldn't do a thing apart from wait it out and staying hidden in the cabin.

Turning from the window, Arora smiled at Norman with sad eyes. "You know... you're everything Richard should have been."

Norman's breath hitched. They were words he wanted to hear, but he couldn't help the guilt that settled in the pit of his stomach whenever he allowed his mind drift to their shared history. Though Richard had been wrong to have hurt Arora all those weeks ago, it hadn't justified Norman taking something that wasn't his to take. Not when that something was as rare and precious as Arora. She deserved the moon. Not a single night of passion where she lay vulnerable in the arms of an inlaw because she wanted to forget her husband who'd just hurt her. As for Richard, his ambition was his downfall. Norman had tried only to live by their mother's rules.

"I feel useless," Arora went on, turning back to the window and wrapping her arms around herself—blissfully unaware of his thoughts. "Just stuck out here in the boondocks."

"You can't get involved in this," Norman said. "We need to prioritise keeping you and your baby safe."

*

In Sub-Basement 23, The Whisperers sat in a circle surrounded by lit candles that were laid out ceremoniously in the shape off an arc. Richard had decided that if the final heist was to go down in history and for that, a sacrifice was required. They'd performed rituals many times over and the blood of the mountain goat was often their sacrifice of choice. This time, they drained the blood of two mountain goats. During the Nemes Sky Moon, they made Tom's thigh bleed with a pocket blade while chanting part of the chorus to *Ghosts of Silany* by Muchndt. Richard now wanted them to feel they were on a mission to a higher plane. They had morals and values to absolve or attain. They were going to strike a righteous blow using all the cunning, guile and rogue tech in their possession and in their hearts.

He explained they were going to enter Ipsteins by the Jezper 11 sewer overspill tunnel. This ran beneath an exposed cavern, which, if you climbed up to it, has a crevice known as the Bunny Hole. It led to a deeper cavern that once served as a vault for bullion back when banks still reserved gold—about two-hundred and fifty years ago. This in turn led to a tunnel that ended at a blast-proof door, which opened into Ipstein's version of Sub-B 23. Then again, the term blast-proof meant only blast proof to everyone but the famous Whisperers. Once in the basement, Tom was to feed the camera array with an A.I molly feed that would make it look like it was last week in the building. Then, they would destroy security systems and staff using radio-blasters, putting to use the 3-D printer Miles had stolen from Cycom along with the newly printed Owls, Stags, and the new Prog-Rock shock grenades that could be fitted into the new, improved Sonic Boom Boy launchers. They were going to go in as a foursome this time, as it was likely that Ipsteins would be heavily guarded by Mortalizer-equivalent security guards, Cyberzoids, mobile-mini-turrets and bank clerk fodder. Staircases from the sub-basement led to storerooms that connected to the staff restaurant that itself opened onto the main foyer. They all knew where they were going after that. Get in, get out, vanish with a million each downloaded onto devices.

Tom, Ares and Miles, were wide-eyed and up for it. They each sat there, fists balled at their sides as if they couldn't wait for the shooting and the stealing to start. They had been with him from the start. They were his people. His kin. If he hadn't downgraded his sense of Honour via the transcendental scalpel of Nuvo 7, instructing the clerk to limit Honour's access to The Library, he would have died for each and every one of them. It was a problem that his memory of doing this came with some twinge of regret.

"Obviously, we need something for courage and something for luck," he said, "and as we've polished off the last of the SOLO, I think it's time to chomp on these babies." He handed out five pills to each of them. "Do whatever you need to do to prepare. Get behind the vision. If it's easier, get the clerk to do the heavy lifting, tell him to keep fear and any other hindrances out of The Library. They must not interfere."

He himself wanted to take on Fear by introducing Fear to Resignation. He had not told any of the others, but the fear of the possibility of death was slowly creeping up on him, threatening to break his resolve. He had stood in a corridor of corpses on the last job. He had seen Death come for Theo. He had been Death to Gauthier. His brother had turned down his game of Chess-or-Death, so he no longer feared Death. As for Richard, Fear would be downgraded, it would be suppressed. He wanted to fear nothing but himself.

Everyone took their Nuvo 7 pills and shuffled off into whichever dark corner they could find to tap into their own ruthless and sinister perfection.

*

The door that led into the Ipsteins restaurant was of no comparison to the blast door, which had needed Tom to deploy the F8 Muskrat limpet mine to give way. There was some whispering in the dark corridor before it was decided that Ares should go first as she was the warrior. She used her Rutting Stag hot knife to cut around the lock on the door. There was a disturbing smell of molten steel as the handle fell off and it clattered on the floor on the other side. Here, Richard knew he'd done right by himself on his last Nuvo dive because he felt no trepidation. He knew he was about to enter a hail of Mortalizer fire as soon as they pushed that door open. He felt nothing.

Ares raised her knee, bumped the door with her heel, and hurried in, radio-blaster raised. Richard followed. The room was empty. The room was quiet. Light from the square outside glimmered on plastic table tops and a marbled-tiled floor. Last time they had come in from the front. Maybe Ipsteins was not expecting an attack from below. The foyer was the crucial area, the zone of contest. Shhh. Don't take anything for granted.

The foyer was deserted, too. Tom held his arms out wide and spun around, like you might when you first enter a palatial hotel room and realise you are staying there. Richard flicked his eyes upward, drawing his attention to the chandeliers above. They were magnificent—gold and vast.

"Don't get distracted," Richard said.

"There's no one here," Miles said.

"Yet."

"You're the smartest guy in Silany," Ares said. "They probably thought lightning wouldn't strike twice."

"They probably knew we'd never rob a bank again," Tom said.

"Shhh. Don't be complacent." Richard wasn't feeling the usual buzz of terror, nor did his heart fill with dread at the thought of what they would do with him if they found him armed in a bank for the second time. He felt about as apprehensive as when he'd walked into the Pollen-X club in Nexus 10 for the second or third time. "Remember, Currency Conversion is beyond the Fourth Skin—the bank's defence barriers," he said. "Weapons at the ready. Formation Mantis when the doors open." Formation Mantis meant he and Miles, the tallest at the back with RPGs, Ares and Tom at the front with guns.

Tom used a scrambler called the Vignette Piknik to open the first door. Inside, in the first of the elliptical corridors that created the bank's central core, the coast was clear. A line of strip lights to the left. A line of strip lights to the right. Pale powdery light.

"Next door is on the left," Tom said.

"Reverse Mantis," Richard called, meaning he and Tom would lead, while Ares and Miles walked backwards behind them, so that anything approaching from the rear would be liquidated before it could strike.

Tom cracked open the second door in an instant. In the second corridor, as they strode forwards looking for another door in the left wing. Richard remembered going up in the elevator during the last job and the remnants of Gauthier's pillage waiting for him. He felt nothing for those men now. He recalled Gauthier's Stag covered in blood when it sliced through Theo's wrist. The blood had gushed onto the desktop, still warm on the blade—how speedy that kill had been. Richard hated that Gauthier fucked this up for them. Richard regretted that Theo chose the wrong side. But this operation was going far more smoothly than he had dared hope. While Tom was cracking the third door open, Richard glanced at Ares and her pursed, plump lips and wondered if maybe he should take her to bed for a celebratory fuck after this. He was lonely. He had no wife. He had no brother.

The third door opened, and they walked casually into the next room, which was empty.

It seemed to take them longer to find the fourth door, the door that led to Currency Conversion. It was almost as if they had traversed the entire ellipse at least once before they found it. Richard was sure they were going to have to blast it, because if he were Tony Ipstein, he'd have reinforced it with a booby-trap, and had it under 24/7 armed, manned security, a well-armed guard. On the other hand, it really was beginning to seem that Ares' single strike of lighting theory might well be true. Sure, the door was a big one, but so was Tom's TikTokAtak mine.

Inside, the octagonal room, with its indigo steel walls and dodecanedioic data bank, was flecked with bits of door and gear systems. Ares and Miles took the door apart, with Ares grabbing onto the left door and Miles, the right door.

Tom crouched down to the data bank and flicked open a panel with a screwdriver and inserted his Virus-V scrambler that in five minutes' time would disable all of the firewalls, fail-safes and lockdown apps in the system.

"I reckon," he said. "If they were going to hit us, they would have hit us by now."

"The noise?" Richard asked.

"Yeah. I can fool AI. The human ear, though, that's different."

"We're nearly done," Richard said. "Miles, Ares, we're nearly done."

"We're done," Tom said, meaning the panels protecting the USBXZ5 portals could be removed and all the bank's credits downloaded onto remote devices. Tom flipped the panel and plugged in his stick.

Richard noticed him frown and then press the stick harder.

"Rich," he said. "There's no money in the bank. I think this is a trap."

A great rumble shuddered through the building. Richard looked up, feeling as if doing so would buy him time to think. The floor shook beneath the weight of whatever charged at them. His skin flushed with a prickly heat as images of the stampede he'd barely escaped alive flashed endlessly in his mind. Was this some sort of joke by the bank to best him. He cursed loudly and at no one particular as it dawned on him that Fear had not been neutralised. And then the lights went out.

*

The world suddenly inverted. It had become a green-tinted film negative of a world as Norman secured the night-vision goggles led his team—three Ipstein security guards in Kevlar vests and anti-flash visors, two Mortalizers—to the last point of the curve before the Fourth Door. Debris littered the floor. Blast damage and striations marred the walls. But the corridors stood empty, there was no one in the corridor. Heads of the other team commanded by Blake, soft shadows on the other side of the doorway. A pink glow flickered inside the room, sending pale rosy flashes against the opposing wall. A flare, thought Norman. They've thrown some sort of slow-burning flare at us. He blinked. Maybe it was time to throw a stun grenade in there in return. He whispered this to Blake over the interlink: "cover me, then withdraw your men to the bend as I withdraw. Got it? "

They were like two hearts beating as one.

Something flipped in the doorway. Steel balls bounded from both sides of the door.

"Grenade!" Norman shouted and urged his men back, the six of them running and then leaping onto their stomachs.

BANG. Norman rolled over onto his back, coughing, covered in bits of rubble and dust. He must have lost consciousness, though he couldn't be sure for how long. Struggling to his feet, he raised his gun and pointed into the cloud of smoke. One of the bank tellers next to him had had his arm torn clean off. With an exposed bone jutting from the shoulder, he was pressed flat against the wall, frozen in stunned silence. Norman urged the other men up and shuffled along the wall, gun raised, towards the door as the smoke cleared.

"Blake...do you copy?

"Copy, Wise."

"Update?"

"Two dead."

"Theirs or ours?"

"Ours."

"They still in there."

"Far as I know."

Something with spikes flew out of the door aperture followed by a whipping sound. It sunk into the wall and released four short cables that attached themselves at all four points of the compass about ten centimetres out.

The entire contraption quivered, once and then twice. A corona of flash, as orange as a July twilight blinded deafened them. It was so loud you didn't even hear it, but it hurt just the same. Blew a dirty great hole in the wall. Cough, splutter, hack.

"Pull the men back."

"Lead the men out."

As Norman rounded the corner of the bend, he noticed the sooty outlines of black figures were hurrying across the breach. The big one was last, the one he'd not seen before. Could *this* be Miles? As the smoke lifted, Blake stood behind Miles, his feet planted firmly, knees locked, and arms extended straight. He gripped a modest Silanese standard-issue revolver, and with a single pull of the trigger, the bullet tore through the back of Miles' head.

As Miles collapsed, his form was hidden by the light of a second orange gun flash. They'd blown the second skin.

Norman stepped over Miles and into the blast-hole just as Blake met him. Ahead, smoke coiled and crept up and across the ceiling like a cresting wave, mixing with the stink of sulphur and human shit. Striding forwards blindly into the cloud of specks and smuts, he caught for an instant the smudged figure of Ares holding a brutal-looking blaster. Something detonated above their heads. The Mortalizers coming up behind returned fire. Norman dived one way, Blake the other as the Mortalizers piled through the gap and fired. Chaos followed. Another orange flash and another crack in the world that sounded like it could bring the city down on them. The first layer of skin was down and Norman was now sure that they had reached the foyer.

Even though Blake was standing next to him, with so much gunfire and shouting, Norman still used the interlink to instruct him to bring the second SWAT to create the Ring of Iron around the entire building. "And Blake, get the lights back on."

Blake turned, cupping one hand around his headset. Norman rushed into the smoke. One of the Mortalizers ahead of him flashed red and burst into flames, falling over backwards, writhing in agony. Ares fell back, disappearing into the murky darkness. By the time Norman reached the last breach, where the bank's Skins fed into the foyer, the remaining Mortalizer was crouched at the side, firing repeatedly at someone who was returning heavy fire. Norman squeezed in beside him. The light overhead and in the foyer came on, a wave that came over their heads and flickered across the ceiling to the great glass entrance doors.

"Status update?"

"She's behind that first pillar, Officer. Another player's behind the pillar to her right. If we advance while she's loading, he'll hit us. If we deal with him first, *she'll hit* us."

"The one behind the right pillar," Norman said, "what does he look like?"

"It's not the little one. I think he got away."

"You relay that to the other group?"

"I'm fighting a fucking war here!" A thud against the other side of the wall, a flash. Some sort of acid-squirting shell must have landed, as something viscous and disgusting to smell spilt across the floor in front of the breach.

"The one behind the pillar? He looks like me?"

"Yes. Not one of ours."

"Keep her pinned down."

Norman waited for the latest round of heavy fire from the foyer to stop, before leaping across the breach and taking up a position where he had a clear view of the pillars. If this were chess, Ares would be at position C3 and Richard at F5. Ares was angled against the far-side of the pillar, firing now into the space above the "arch" of the breach. He'd never get a shot at her and not at this range with his type of gun. Ares stopped. She must've needed to change her clip. And here, as the Mortalizer fired in Ares' direction, Richard bobbed behind pillar F5 and his fire drove the Mortalizer back.

There was no time to overthink it, to take calculated risks or precautions. He thought back to the first time he fired a gun, when he shot the hare, and he dug deep to hone his instinct. That's what Mum always wanted him to do, follow the gut. Of course, he could now order the second SWAT group to take the foyer and back Richard into a corner, but he and Ares would take many men with families down with them as they fell. He had to do this himself.

He took his grenade out of his pocket, pulled the pin and held it rigid. He could angle it so it would explode against the pillar positioned at C3 and semi-circle behind Richard at F5.

The Mortalizer was firing at Ares and Ares was firing back. The acid spill on the floor stank and making Norman's eyes water. Blake and two other guards piled in alongside the Mortalizer. Norman pulled the pin, counted one, two, and released the grenade. It flew over the acid spill and the debris close to the breach, from which it could have ping-ponged anywhere. Instead, it rolled across the smooth marble floor, glittering against the lights. It struck the base of pillar C3 and then on the rebound picked up speed. It curled across the floor in an arc that reminded Norman of the shape of a scorpion's tail. Ares stopped firing and retreated behind C3.

Richard swung around F5 and let off a round in Norman's direction. *Did he know I was coming?*

The grenade exploded with a hollow bang. Part of the pillar shattered. Shards and fragments flew everywhere, and screams could be heard all around Richard was thrown forwards. His foot, which must have been closest to the blast, flew in the other direction.

Norman, keeping one eye on the unknown figure spread-eagled on the floor, used his finger to point at Ares. "Priority target is the girl!" He got in ahead of the line of fighters behind him, and made a beeline for the suspect, who he now realised was Richard. Norman decided that Richard would have to do, even though he'd have liked to settle his score with Ares. Once he was on top of Richard, a newly released smoke bomb nearly knocked him off his feet. By the time the vapour had cleared enough to see, Blake and the sundry Mortalizers and guards were standing around looking perplexed.

Norman waved his gun in the direction of the restaurant.

"She's gone through there," he shouted. Shit. The little tech-goblin, Tom, had probably escaped that way too. With any luck, the army stationed outside would catch them.Richard rolled over onto his back and tried to sit up. He flailed about awkwardly, trying to manoeuvre his way to freedom, until he suddenly let out a terrified scream as he reached for the stump at the end of his left leg. Blood flowed profusely. In a flash, both Norman and Richard were reminded of f that day when Father blew his brains out.

Norman prodded his gun into Richard's forehead, who fell back flat on the floor, banging his head.

"Ow."

"The foot's worse than your head."

"I thought you only loved Truth more than me?" Richard gasped. "Don't kill me. I need to tell you something."

"I had something to tell you once. What I saw at the Pyramid while you had gone to visit Uncle Rusty. You didn't want to listen to me then, so I won't listen to you now. Besides, if you really had something to tell me, you would have done it before you caused all this death."

"I brought liberty to Silany."

"Yeah, I read your book. Your plan didn't work."

"No, you don't get it." He was desperately trying to keep a level eye with Norman. His right hand, though, was creeping over to his left side and some sort of pouch or holder strapped there. Could there be anything dangerous lurking in there? Perhaps a pocket laser, a dagger. Or even a suicide mine?

"Remember what Mother told us," Richard pleaded. "Remember, Norman. Because it's you that forgets. It's you that always hurts me—Mother said...to...never to "hurt" one another, Norman." Richard's hand was getting dangerously close to the holster. "Never hurt one another. Play nice. Like when we were kids. Listen, I need to tell you. I've worked out why we are the way we are..." Richard flicked open the popper on the holster and tried to grip a stubby bulbous pistol tucked in there. Norman, on the other hand, was a ball of nerves but he kept his own hand steady on his gun, ready to shoot.

"Never hurt one another," Richard said. "May her spirit live on forever."

Norman held on tight to his gun. Richard was sweating profusely, blabbering nonsensically through tears.

"You too can live with us Norman. Norman—the dream. I can't escape it. The figure of eight going round and round like a merry go round. Sound. Bound. It's a mirror Norman. Everything's a...mirror. In the end, *we* are the angels and brutes. You scorned Father and I, but *you* and *I* are no different! Just look around you. We exploit destruction and chaos to fulfil our needs."

"Richard." The choice was becoming clear to Norman now—this was the end.

"Norman, that day you shot the hare. Guess what? We went into the room. We went in."

Norman felt the tip of his finger touch the trigger. Feebly, his body drenched in hot sweat, Richard pulled his gun out.

"We went to Nemes..." Richard aimed the gun at Norman, his hand trembling.

"No, you didn't," Norman said. Either brother could shoot. "And I'm going to prove it. I'm going to blow the lid on the whole fucking thing."

"Nemes *is* real."

Norman dropped his gun, letting it fall to the ground with a clatter, his body was ready for Richard to take his shot, claim his victory and live another day.

"No Rich, it's not. Grandpa knew it. Mum knew it. And I know it."

Richard bit his bottom lip, tightening his hand. "I *went* to...NEMES."

Squealing as he squeezed the trigger, he shut his eyes and exhaled. A gunshot rang out, the bang reverberated through the space all around them. The bullet struck Norman's protective vest with enough force to shove him back a step. Norman pulled his Zlock free. He stood with his arm outstretched. It was a good choice as a backup. His forearm gripping the gun tight once more. And with the last shot he would hear for a long time he shot Richard through the head.

He stared at his brother's open eyes, stunned. Richard had forced his hand. He hadn't wanted to do it…had he? But it didn't matter. Norman had broken the promise he'd made to his mother; the rules she'd sworn them to live by. He had tried to be so good. But how could he be good when someone so bad roamed free?

Norman's shoulders sagged and he whispered over his brother's dead body, "enough."

He took the gun from Richard's hand—a wicked-looking thing, the barrel long and thin, the front sight shaped like a barbed fishhook, deciding that he would make sure it was melted down. Richard's fingers contracted as Norman leaned in to take the gun, and he caught a glimpse of four letters tattooed in black ink on Richard's palm:

I WIN

Norman unlocked the chamber. Half the cylinder was loaded with bullets, except for one chamber. The other half held something else—something that wasn't a bullet. He carefully removed them: pawns, pieces from the chessboard they used to play on as kids.

*

The summit of Silbak Hill felt like the bleakest place in the world. The wind screamed, lashing the treetops. With shoulders hunched against the gale, Norman gave the van door a slam. The dogs were on their best behaviour today. From up here, Silany was laid out, its sky a sepia colour, the trees spindly and gnarled and its land dusty and dry. In the distance, you could just about make out the Fal, and beyond it—who knows. You could never see Nemes. It was one of the things Mum once told Norman she actually liked about the Fal. Sometimes, she'd even say, "it's better not to look."

Arora stood waiting at the cabin door. It had transformed into more of a cottage now. A lot of work had been done to turn A Hunter's Paradise into the kind of place where a family could settle down.

"Come in, quickly, out of the wind," she urged. Norman stepped inside, the cold air still clinging to him as he crossed the threshold. He hadn't talked to anyone. He had no family left. His only connection was actually Rusty Barnfather, his godfather, but he hadn't seen him in years. Besides, he would rather shoot the man than confide in a Nemerian arms dealer. There was no one in Silany he could talk to.

"I thought I'd come and see you in person," Norman said. He realised he was jittering, flitting from side to side. "You're free to return home now."

"I'm not sure I know where home is, anymore," Arora told him.

"It's not here?"

"Well, it's not The Castle."

"Ah, The Castle. It's owned by the banks now."

"You look famished, Norman."

"Richard's gone, Arora."

"I know," she said, softly.

His head dropped; his mouth opened. "He was my brother."

"He made choices."

"We all make choices."

"She asked us not to harm one another." He dropped to the step, suddenly exhausted, and she came to him. She put her arm around him. And though he couldn't yet see the bump of the new Wise child, he imagined it there and how it would make him feel. He wept great, wracking sobs while she held him gently and soothed him.

"There was this moment, Arora, I think I've been trying to explain it my entire life."

"Shh, we all have moments like that. We wouldn't be alive if we didn't."

"Not that sort of moment. The opposite. I was a kid. There was a day. My father took Richard to my uncle's house. They practised shooting on a range, and then they went to "Nemes". You can imagine, Richard came back full of Nemerian ideology and excitement..."

"He was always bursting with excitement at the idea of Nemes."

"He was, wasn't he? He came back and I just didn't care about, well, Nemes. But the shooting range—I wanted to go there, so I did. I snuck in and wandered the corridors, looking for Uncle Rusty. I called and called, but I also didn't want to get caught, like."

"No one wants to get caught."

"Up at the top. This room, there were men, all sitting on sofas around a big glass table. There was stuff on the table, vials, bottles. I didn't know what it was then. Thinking back now, it was probably White Milk. And the men, they were wearing visors, and had electrodes attached to their heads and their necks. When Richard came back from Nemes. He had these markings, on his temples. I remember Mum... noticing them. I don't know what I saw, but I think I've always known it wasn't right what I saw."

"I think I've always known it, too," she said. "I think it has something to do with the other side."

"With Nemes."

"With Nemes."

A hush fell around them. Norman lifted his head and moved back away from her. Then softly he said to her, "I want to look after the baby."

*

Norman watched silently as the earth was shovelled, spade after spade, onto Richard's coffin. He felt nothing but numbness, a chill that spread deep inside. Each load of dirt felt like another layer of dead dreams—dreams his parents once had for him and Richard and their children. It was all so sad. Yet, beneath all the crushed hopes, something stirred. New shoots, tender and fragile, wanted to push their way through the soil and reach for the light of a new dawn. But Norman couldn't let himself accept them. Not yet.

No one came to the funeral apart from Arora. The only friends Richard had who he hadn't alienated, Tom and Ares, were on the run. Rusty had stayed away. He was also on the run now that the force was looking for him. With his life filled with more ghosts than people now, Norman pictured his mum there with him. Otherwise, it was just the gravediggers, the cleric, Win Cater, and Arora. The cemetery crept up the slope of a stunted mound-like hill. The winds refused to abate, not even for the service.

Win Cater looked at him pointedly as if he were waiting for Norman to say something in honour of his brother, but Norman had nothing to say. Besides, he had never had much to say. Richard had been the one with all the words.

The wind lifted up the hem of Arora's black dress. She didn't say anything either. What was there to say about the man who could have had everything, but who'd ended up being nothing. A man who had robbed himself of his humanity to become more of a person. The irony.

After the funeral, Norman walked down the lower footpath, his arm linked with Arora's. He glanced up toward the hilltop and noticed two men, their jackets fluttering gently in the breeze. One of them was Superintendent Shepard. What was he doing here? He didn't even know Richard, or at least he didn't know him beyond a sketch in a case file. Norman gave him a casual wave. Squinting into the sunlight, Norman couldn't see the face of the other man, only that he was wearing a Trilby hat. For a brief moment, a cloud crossed the sun and, as if a sunburst had gone off inside him, Norman thought he was looking at Richard. He blinked and suddenly it wasn't Richard anymore. Trying not to make it too obvious, he glanced again. This time the man's face was half hidden beneath the rim of his hat. Norman could only make out his thin lips and a twitchy smirk. He did not like the man, and he did not like that they were both here now. He'd look into that later, not now. For now, there was only silence to listen to, dogs to walk, Arora to settle, and Silany to tidy. His work here—clearing the streets of junk, dream pills, elixirs, pop potions, vision parties, blood rituals, and false promises—had only just begun. His search for Silany's wellspring would inevitably lead him to the Fal and beyond, to the world that lay on the other side. Nemes, the dream that had cost his family so much—its days were numbered.

EPILOGUE
Tabula Rasa

Extract from the Afterword to The Nemerian Manifesto

We are futurists and progressives—egalitarian and unsentimental. By definition, we are efficient; by nature, we are orderly. In thought, we prioritise function, and in form, we reflect it.

An undisciplined self is a betrayal of the body. Discipline and a lack, thereof, is the most stark distinction between us and those who dwell beyond the divide.

Trust us now, because like your past, your world is ***dead***. You are the beasts of the old world, marooned in our new cyber-digital age. Your suffering is the inevitability that we warned you of long ago. You did not listen then.

But you will listen now.

You too can live with us ...

NOTES AND ACKNOWLEDGEMENTS

This book is the result of many hearts and hands. I've been fortunate to be surrounded by friends, mentors, and family whose encouragement gave me the courage to write across boundaries—with ambition, authenticity, and openness.

First and foremost, my heartfelt thanks go to Felicite Mbenga, my editor and writing coach. Her insight was instrumental in shaping not just the tone of the book, but also its clarity and reach. Felicite guided the editorial process with care and precision, and I'm deeply grateful for her steady hand and thoughtful support.

Many others contributed along the way, starting with Isobel Lans, who read every chapter with care and helped me strengthen both the message and the rhythm of the prose.

Throughout the writing of this book, I found myself continually drawing on the conversations, memories, and experiences I've shared with those around me. Friends and peers like Stephen Ingledew OBE, Amirah Jiwa, Matt Helt, Irma Alashe, Louise Beaumont, Victor Baumann, Toyin Peters, Tom O'Brien, Shalom Ayidu, Tom Laing-Baker, Ghela Boskovich, the Kuku family, Yinka Akomolafe, Junior Ifayemi, Elizabeth Vega OBE, Robin Knowles, James Gamble, Sunmisade Ademola, Holly Miller, Ben Liao, Bibi Awoloto, Clive Crawford—and many others—your presence in my life has quietly shaped this story from the very beginning. The worlds and characters on these pages carry echoes of your influence. Whether through the ideas we've debated, the laughter we've shared, or the challenges we've faced together, you've helped shape both the philosophical heart and emotional grounding of this book. In many ways, the characters and societies you'll meet are reflections not only of my life, but also of the lessons I've learned through knowing you.

I'm also deeply grateful to a friend (who shall remain unnamed) whose encouragement and reflections reminded me of why this work matters:

'The Fallible is an essential read for anyone interested in philosophical themes of belief and nihilism–opposites which often play out in the same psychic arena. Throughout, there is much uncertainty as to what exactly exists beyond the Fal; whether Nemes–the techno-futurist ideal–is real or illusory. Is the promise of human perfectibility being used to manage the consent of the Silanese? Given the epic scope of the novel and the detail of the world that has been created, there is considerable potential to develop The Fallible into an entertaining series of novels that explores some of these questions head on."

Visually, this story owes so much to Attila Vaszka and Justyna Kaźmierska, whose artistic talents brought to life the soul of a world I had only imagined. Through your creativity, patience, and attention to detail, you transformed abstract ideas into vivid, emotionally resonant visuals that now feel inseparable from the story itself. Thank you both for your imagination, your craft, and the care you poured into every illustration.

Finally, to my family—my mother, Dolapo Olusoga, my stepfather Henry Foluso, and my siblings, Daniel, Stephanie, and Joshua—thank you for being my constant source of support. You gave me the space to create, challenged my thinking, and believed in the story even before it was fully written. I dedicate this book—and so much more beyond it—to you.

SAGE ABIOLA

In the ancient Japanese tradition of Zen calligraphy, there is a symbol called the *Enso*—a single, imperfect circle, drawn in one unbroken brushstroke. It represents many things: the beauty of imperfection and even mistakes, the acceptance of transience, and the quiet power of completion that comes not from perfection, but from presence. That symbol has stayed with me for years.

The Fallible is, in many ways, my *Enso*.

I did not write this book to offer answers. I wrote it to explore a tension that shapes much of modern life. The pull between our relentless pursuit of perfection—in our systems, our technology, even ourselves—and the messier, more human truths we often try to escape. That we are flawed. Emotional. Contradictory. That we are, and always have been, fallible beings searching for meaning in an increasingly automated world.

At 32, I've been fortunate to move through several worlds. Formerly the founder of a tech company working with large institutional clients, I now work at the intersection of government, technology, industry, and academia—spaces where the future is being built at breakneck speed. As a student of neuroscience, artificial intelligence, economics, and psychology, I've wrestled with what all this means—for our minds, our relationships, and our societies. And as a sculptor, artist, and writer, I've searched for beauty in the incomplete.

Born in Surrey to Nigerian parents, my identity has always been marked by duality—African and British, scientific and artistic, analytical and intuitive.

That duality lies at the heart of *The Falliblle*: a philosophical sci-fi novel about a world that tries to eliminate failure, only to discover that without it, nothing real can grow.

This story is not just fiction. It is a mirror. A way of asking: *What do we lose when we chase perfection? What do we become when we forget how to fall?*

In a world that rewards optimisation, *The Falliblle* is a love letter to the imperfect—a call to reclaim the vulnerability that makes us human.

For more information visit sageabiola.com